# *Water Management Organization in the People's Republic of China*

# THE CHINA BOOK PROJECT Translation and Commentary

*A wide-ranging series of carefully prepared translations of books published in China since 1949, each with an extended introduction by a Western scholar.*

**The People of Taihang: An Anthology of Family Histories**
*Edited with an introduction by Sidney L. Greenblatt*

**Fundamentals of the Chinese Communist Party**
*Edited with an introduction by Pierre M. Perrolle*

**Shang Yang's Reforms and State Control in China**
*Edited with an introduction by Li Yu-ning*

Li Jui
**The Early Revolutionary Activities of Comrade Mao Tse-tung**
*Edited by James C. Hsiung. Introduction by Stuart R. Schram*

**The Rustication of Urban Youth in China: A Social Experiment**
*Edited by Peter J. Seybolt. Introduction by Thomas P. Bernstein*

**Workers and Workplaces in Revolutionary China**
*Edited with an introduction by Stephen Andors*

**Fundamentals of Political Economy**
*Edited with an introduction by George C. Wang*

**Chinese Approaches to Family Planning**
*Edited with an introduction by Leo A. Orleans*

**Water Management Organization in the People's Republic of China**
*Edited with an introduction by James E. Nickum*

Xu Liangying and Fan Dianian
**Science and Socialist Construction in China**
*Edited with an introduction by Pierre M. Perrolle*

EDITED WITH AN
INTRODUCTION BY
JAMES E. NICKUM

# Water Management Organization in the People's Republic of China

Routledge
Taylor & Francis Group
LONDON AND NEW YORK

First published 1977 by M.E. Sharpe

Reissued 2018 by Routledge
2 Park Square, Milton Park, Abingdon, Oxon OX14 4RN
711 Third Avenue, New York, NY 10017, USA

*Routledge is an imprint of the Taylor & Francis Group, an informa business*



Reading 3 first appeared in *Chinese Economic Studies* X:4 (Summer 1977). Readings 5 and 6 first appeared in *Chinese Sociology and Anthropology* XII:2 (Winter 1979-80).



A Library of Congress record exists under LC control number: 80005458

ISBN 13: 978-1-138-89651-2 (hbk)
ISBN 13: 978-1-315-17912-4 (ebk)

*TO MY PARENTS*

*Whether there is a harvest depends on water; how big it is depends on fertilizer.*

PEASANT SAYING

*Water conservancy is the lifeline of agriculture.*

MAO ZEDONG

*. . . the maddening nature of water. . . , with its tendency to flow, seep, evaporate, condense and transpire.*

ROBERT CHAMBERS

# Contents

# Preface

The development and use of water resources traditionally has been the exclusive domain of engineers and politicians, with occasional advice from economists and, more recently, ecologists. One consequence has been an emphasis on project construction — usually the larger and more magnificent the better — rather than improved management of existing resources. This "builder's bias" has pervaded both capitalist and socialist economies, developed nations as well as the Third World, with the economic and administrative institutions involved in water use merely serving to reinforce this bias. In recent years, however, the importance of improving the management of existing hydraulic structures has become increasingly evident. Indeed, such "water reform" may now be more important than land reform for improving both the amount and the distribution of agricultural output and rural incomes in most of Asia.

The concept of water management includes a number of different components. Bromely, Taylor, and Parker note that improved water management (here, in irrigation) means at least five things: "(1) rehabilitation of existing projects in terms of modifying the distribution network; (2) more intensive operation and maintenance of this infrastructure; (3) more careful planning of cropping patterns and schedules; (4) greater care in the allocation and scheduling of water both among and within systems; and (5) greater enforcement of, or changes in, the rules and regulations governing access to irrigation water by individual farmers."[1] The first four characteristics of water management depend crucially upon the rules and regulations and the degree of compliance with them. The major concern of this volume is to examine these "institutional parameters" of water management within the People's Republic of China (PRC) and to look at the operation of some of the most effective individual project managements.

The organization and operation of water management in the secondary and tertiary systems below the main structures has only very recently been studied systematically for Third World countries. Most of this research has been done by Asia specialists outside the PRC.[2] One purpose of this collection of readings is to help fill in the gap by offering a representative sample of the Chinese literature on water management organization to those interested in rural development but without a reading knowledge of the original language. Another goal is to bring together materials for China specialists and students on a vital but often neglected component of agricultural development in the PRC.

A final point: the political line has changed considerably in recent years, rendering obsolete much of the rhetoric of the translated texts. The organizational descriptions remain substantively valid, however.

It has been a number of years since this collection was suggested to me by Douglas Merwin, China Publications Editor at M. E. Sharpe, Inc. In the interim, this work has benefited from a number of helping hands. The Center for Chinese Studies at the University of California, Berkeley, and the Center for East Asian Studies and the Department of East Asian Languages and Cultures at the University of Kansas have provided valuable harbor and resources. I would also like to express my gratitude to Robert Dunn, Annie K. Chang, C. P. Chen, Grace Wan, and most especially to Lois Hager, for their help on the translations. Thanks are also due to friends, colleagues, and consultants at Lillian Li's summer 1980 Workshop on Food and Famine at Harvard for their comments on my introduction;

and to Doug Merwin, for his patience, encouragement, and nipperkins.

## Notes

1) In "Water Reform and Economic Development: Institutional Aspects of Water Management in Developing Countries," Economic Development and Cultural Change, 28(2), January 1980, p. 366.

2) An excellent collection of these works is E. Walter Coward, Jr., editor, Irrigation and Agricultural Development in Asia (Ithaca and London: Cornell University Press, 1980).

J. E. N.

Berkeley, California
February 1981

# Note to the Translations

A canal-fed irrigation system which is separated from its headworks is linked to the latter by a feeder canal (zong qu 总渠).[1] Within a system, water is carried from the headworks or feeder canal to the field (tertiary) distribution system by a conveyance network consisting of main canals (gan qu 干渠), branch (or lateral) canals (zhi qu 支渠) and subbranch (or sublateral) canals (dou qu 斗渠). These are all permanent structures. In small irrigation districts within the commune sector, there are sometimes only one or two of the above levels of conveyance canals.

Within the area controlled by a branch or subbranch canal is the distribution system, consisting of farm ditches (nong qu 农渠), field ditches (mao qu 毛渠) and, when appropriate, supplementary field ditches. There is no standard Chinese term for the latter. The farm ditches are usually permanent, but most field ditches and supplementary field ditches are semipermanent or temporary.

As in the conveyance network, there may only be one or two levels within the distribution system. This is due not to the size of the system but to the field layout and irrigation method employed. The Chinese divide surface irrigation methods into three kinds: basin irrigation (yan guan 淹灌) for paddy rice, furrow irrigation (gou guan 沟灌) for row crops, and border or border-strip irrigation (qi guan 畦灌) for densely planted dry crops. In the latter, water is applied in a sheet to narrow bordered rectangular plots called strip checks or border strips (qi 畦).

At the various levels of water supply there are usually counterpart drains (pai shui gou 排水沟, or simply gou). Sometimes the same channel is used for both irrigation and drainage.

Because of the uniqueness of topographical and hydrological conditions, there is much variation in project characteristics. In general, a Chinese gan qu controls about 20,000–30,000 mou (1,300–2,000 ha.), a zhi qu about 10,000 mou (600–700 ha.), a dou qu either 1,000–2,000 mou (60–130 ha.) or 3,000–5,000 mou (200–330 ha.), a nong qu 300–500 mou (20-33 ha.), and a mao qu 40–80 mou (2.6–5.3 ha.). In southern paddy rice areas, where there are no mao qu, a nong qu controls 100–200 mou (6.6–13.3 ha.).

## Note

1) Terminology, especially in English, is not completely standard or systematically employed. The concepts used here are those adopted by the International Commission on Irrigation and Drainage. The levels of canals and methods of irrigation in Chinese generally appear to be equivalent to the English counterparts. It is not clear, however, whether the Chinese have a separate term for a feeder canal. Often it too is called a gan qu. Shaoshan has a level of canal higher than gan qu, called zong qu. This is tentatively assumed to refer to a feeder canal.

# Water Management Organization in the People's Republic of China

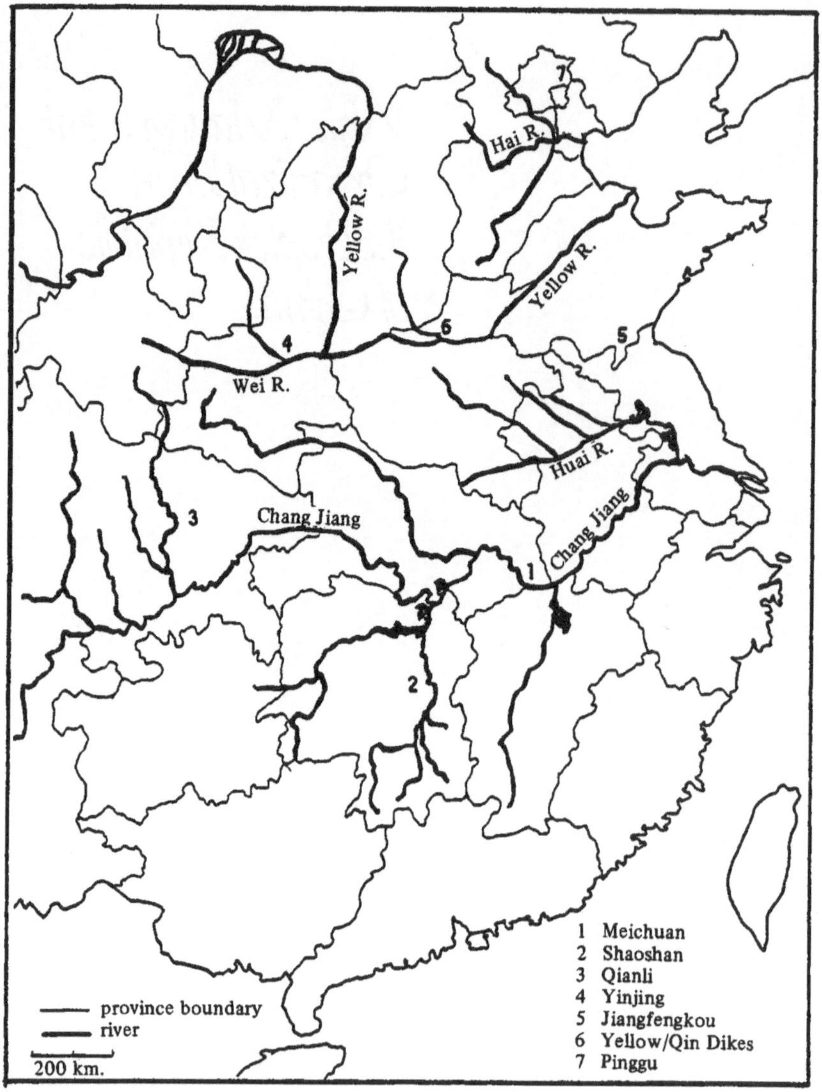


Location of Case Studies.

# Introduction

James E. Nickum

Water is the elixir of life. Space probes have scanned earth's sister spheres in vain for traces of that simple but maddening liquid which covers our globe, rainbows our skies, and courses in our veins.

Water is essential to us. But it can also cause great harm. Ever since we traded gills for lungs, water has been able to drown us. It can inundate our lower-lying habitations. And it can tear away at hills and mountains in torrents of rain, rivulets, and groundwater.

This duality extends to the crops whose agri-culture sparked civilization. Water makes deserts bloom. In surfeit, however, it does not allow plants to breathe or hold to the soil; or it buries them under layers of silt.

In some countries, such as Egypt before the Aswan Dam, the supply of water has been modulated by nature in such a way that human agriculture could easily adapt to it. Other places have not been so fortunate. The control of water – the construction and maintenance of works to divert and direct it from its natural course – has played a significant role in the history of these areas. This is particularly true of China, where the natural water regimen has been unusually perverse, especially in the north.[1]

With a few notable exceptions, however, the historical Chinese state concerned itself primarily with manipulating water for purposes other than irrigation, especially flood control and navigation, the latter to transport tribute grain to the capital.[2] Dynasties, and political careers within dynasties, rose and fell with the dikes girding the Yellow River.[3]

On-farm application and removal of water was left in the hands of local village or intervillage organizations. These bodies varied in form from place to place and from time to time. Sometimes they were built and run by families separate from landholdings. At other times, especially in recent centuries, they were operated by landlord or other farmer associations, usually with full-time managers.[4] This was one of the few instances of professional, task-oriented management independent of direct village administration in traditional Chinese society.

In present-day China, as illustrated in the case studies and regulations translated for this volume, economic and political functions at the local level have been integrated to a large degree. This type of consolidation underlies the original rationale of the rural people's commune system. The construction of water works, a central activity in the countryside over the past quarter century, has been carried out under the regular state or collective (commune, brigade, or team) apparatus, which has had the exclusive right to mobilize the labor of the peasantry.[5] The operation of irrigation, drainage, and flood control facilities affecting more than one production team is commonly placed in the hands of an entity with a full-time staff which, as in times past, is separate from the regular state and village administration. This entity, usually termed an "irrigation district management office" when irrigation is its primary concern and it affects more than one brigade, is ordinarily based on a key installation, such as a reservoir, a canal system, or an embankment. Its geographical extent is determined largely by the commanded area of that installation.

Projects and their management bodies vary according to different hydrological, cropping, and topographical conditions and the objectives of development. In line with the categorization for "water management" used by the Chinese, the focus in this work is on irrigation districts and to a lesser degree on flood control management. Projects for hydroelectric power generation and urban and industrial water supply are not covered. A basic typology of irrigation and flood control works and their principal management problems is as follows.[6]

## Irrigation

### A. Water Source

1. Flow diversion. This is the earliest source of irrigation water used, with the possible exception of hand-dug wells. Water is simply diverted from an existing flow into natural or artificial channels, or directly into the fields. In the most rudimentary systems, which Reading 1 indicates were all too common in old China, the flow is not regulated, and management consists of keeping the diversion and field channels repaired and dredged. The principal problem with this type of system is that water supply conditions rarely coincide with crop requirements.

More complex systems include diversion control structures such as sluice gates. The water supply, if adequate, can be regulated to match crop needs during the growing seasons. If water is short, one major management task is to determine how the available supply is to be distributed among users.

Examples of projects relying on flow diversion are the Zhengguo Canal and the Dujiangyan system mentioned in note 2 above, the famous Red Flag Canal and, for the most part, the Qianli and Yinjing Canals (Readings 6 and 7).

2. Surface storage. The use of reservoirs and ponds allows water to be stored in bountiful times and released when the natural supply falls behind crop requirements. Management, now involving decisions to store and release, is considerably more complex than with flow diversions. This is especially so when the stored water serves purposes other than irrigation, such as power generation, fishery, or drinking water, that may conflict with agricultural demands. Moreover, siltation, reducing a project's life expectancy, is a major headache in many places.

Large-scale water storage has become significant in China only in the past thirty years. There were fewer than 10 large reservoirs (with storage capacities exceeding 100 million cubic meters) in 1949; now there are about 300. In addition, over 1,500 medium-sized reservoirs (between 10 and 100 million cubic meters) and tens of thousands of smaller impoundments have been created. Recent detailed maps and satellite imagery show landscapes dotted with countless water surfaces.

The centerpiece in this volume, the Meichuan Reservoir Irrigation Project (Reading 3), relies on water storage based on a medium-sized reservoir. The headwork of the Shaoshan Irrigation Project (Readings 4 and 5) is a river diversion dam, but this is just downstream from the Shuifumiao Reservoir, which regulates the flow of water into the Shaoshan system. (The Shaoshan project management does not seem to directly govern the reservoir, however.) Most irrigation projects have incorporated some water storage components into them.

3. Subsurface storage. This is a relatively new type of project which has been publicized recently in China. It depends on the existence and identification of an appropriate geological structure which allows the formation of an underground reservoir.

4. Groundwater. Natural subsurface (groundwater) reservoirs and flows have been tapped for centuries through the use of hand-dug wells. Over the past decade, machine-dug deep tube wells ("mechanized wells" — jijing in Chinese), outfitted with electrical or diesel pumps, have become quite common, especially on the north China plain. Since a tube well irrigates at most a few dozen hectares, it can be operated by a single village or production brigade. A principal management task at the local level is the maintenance of the machinery. A larger problem which may arise, however, owing to inadequate information and improper overall planning and coordination, is that of mining the water strata. When this happens, administrative intervention is required.

An example of mechanized well development in a suburban

xian of Beijing is given in Reading 10.

5. Integrated ("conjunctive") use. A common type of irrigation system in China is one called "melons on a vine," which incorporates field ponds into an overall network of reservoirs and canals. For example, the Meichuan Irrigation District includes one main reservoir, 21 smaller reservoirs and 5,983 ponds, linked together by over 600 kilometers of canals. The use of ponds allows greater total storage and more flexibility in field application. To be successful, a "melons on a vine" system requires detailed planning and a good working relationship between the project management and water using units.

Besides the Meichuan Project (Reading 3), the Qianli Canal (Reading 6) governs a "melons on a vine" style irrigation network.

In some areas of the world, such as the Punjab, private tube wells have provided greater security of water supply to the farmer than exclusive reliance on a larger public canal. Presumably, collectively owned tube wells often serve the same purpose in China. As in the case of ponds, however, the interests of individual units may not coincide with those of the overall project. In particular, water users in the upper reaches of a district usually have an ample and relatively secure supply of water from the main project and thus have little direct incentive to build or maintain ponds, which consume valuable land, or to dig tube wells, which are expensive.

In the Yinjing Canal Irrigation District (Reading 7) a relatively complex conjunctive use system is being set up. Communes and brigades in the upper reaches have taken to relying more on well water, while those in the lower reaches have built a number of "melon"-like ponds and reservoirs.

## B. Energy Source

The traditional method of letting gravity move water is less demanding on technical maintenance and considerably less expensive than the use of electric or diesel pumps to lift water. Sometimes there is no reasonable alternative to pumping, however. In 1978, electromechanical irrigation and drainage facilities in China had a total capacity of 64 million horsepower and governed just under 30 million hectares, over half the total irrigated acreage.[7]

C. Size

A project may vary in size and complexity from a single tube well operated by a production brigade to a complex, multi-xian system such as the Dujiangyan, which irrigates nearly half a million hectares, or even the cross-provincial Bishihang Irrigation District, which covers over 500,000 hectares. The general rule, described in Reading 2, is that an irrigation district should be established under the lowest administrative level whose boundaries encompass the area benefited. An irrigation district which serves more than one commune is usually operated by the state, while one which lies within a single commune or production brigade is normally operated by a collective. A reservoir used primarily for irrigation, with a storage capacity of over 10 million cubic meters (80,000 acre-feet), may have separate management bodies for the reservoir and its irrigation district (e.g., Meichuan, Reading 3). As indicated in the staffing guidelines in Reading 2, larger districts and those using electromechanical equipment are likely to have more complex and more technically oriented staffs.

In all cases, the basic water using unit is a production brigade, production team, or state farm. These are the smallest units of the regular administrative-economic system as well. A small irrigation district may allocate water directly to these users. A larger district has one or more intermediate levels, such as management stations and basic-level management organizations (Reading 11, Articles 6, 7, and 19).

D. Age

An older irrigation district usually has both the advantages and the liabilities of age. The "learning process" which every new project management and user has to undergo has already occurred. Experience has been gathered in how the project functions, how the water is supplied, and how to adapt cultivation practices to that supply. The peasants understand irrigation practices, and principles of allocation and maintenance have usually been worked out.

On the other hand, the project design may be outdated and the customary practices inadequate for contemporary cropping technologies, agronomic practices, and considerations of equity. A typical pre-1949 irrigation project was built to supply water to fragmented private landholdings, often by flood irrigation (covering the fields with a deep layer of water) and without any watering at night. It was also likely to be in a state of some deterioration after a prolonged period of political instability. Now there are larger collective fields, which can be reshaped to facilitate water application. Irrigation techniques are frequently much more refined, and night watering is common.

As part of the continual adaptation of irrigation water supply to changes in water sources, cropping and the like, a management organization must be able to change the rules of water allocation to individual users. This is probably easier in a newer project where customary rights are less crystallized.

## Flood Control

Most Chinese live on flood plains. The floods which brought the soil down from the highlands in geological times have continued, possibly at an accelerated pace, into the historical era, plaguing populations and their governments. Most prone to disaster has been the north China plain, crossed from west to east by the Yellow, Huai, and Hai rivers.[8]

Flood prevention works were high priority items of new dynasties and were the main focus of water control by the central government in the early years of the People's Republic of China (PRC). Now they are commonly constructed and supervised under relatively high levels of the state, usually the provinces or Beijing itself. Management functions, however, are often decentralized to a much smaller project-specific body. In addition, local beneficiary collectives are sometimes relied on for maintenance. In these regards, flood control management organization has a number of features in common with irrigation management organization and thus merits inclusion here.

Methods which have been adopted to prevent floods or minimize their damage include the following:

## A. Dikes

The most famous method of flood control in China has been the use of dikes on one or both sides of unruly rivers. The most extensive diking has been along the downstream stretch of the Yellow River, whose heavy silt load precludes other options, such as dredging. In some places, the riverbed now flows more than 10 meters above the surrounding farmland and continues to rise by about 10 centimeters per year. The dikes have to be raised accordingly. A long-term method to end the race between riverbed and embankment is to eliminate the heavy erosion of loess along the middle reaches. That solution, however, is not yet in sight.

The story of an important maintenance section of dikes at the confluence of the Yellow and Qin rivers is presented in Reading 9. In addition, the Shandong rivers mentioned in Reading 8 are extensively diked.

## B. Diversion

Flood waters may be led off into detention basins or into other drainage systems, either natural (rivers) or artificial (canals). Detention basins may be lowland areas which have been especially prepared for emergency use, or they may be existing lakes. Examples of both may be found along the middle Yangtze, especially in Hubei. The Yangtze itself, in its lower reaches, is used as a diversion channel for the Huai River system, via the Jiangdu Pumping Stations near Yang-zhou.[9] The areas reserved for flood diversion, if not already under water, are often good farmland, which is then sacrificed in times of high water danger.

An example of a diversion gate which also provides irrigation water in ordinary times along its flood diversion channel is given in Reading 8.

## C. Dams

Aside from providing water for irrigation and electricity generation, a large dam may control floods by impounding or moderating excess waters. An advantage of such impoundment in China, where there is a definite monsoon, or rainy season, is that it allows water use to be regulated seasonally, more in keeping with human needs. Thus it helps prevent drought as well as flood. The trouble-ridden Sanmen Gorge Dam on the Yellow River, often cited as an example of careless planning because of the rapid siltation of its reservoir, has played a major role in the past two decades in preventing downstream floods.

A major dam is usually run by a management organ under a high state administrative level, and there is little direct linkage to the units benefited by its flood prevention. Perhaps the chief management problem is the regulation of the supply of water in the reservoir to serve the multiple and often conflicting purposes it is put to. For example, electricity generation (and, sometimes, silt control) requires a continual release of water, while irrigation necessitates storage in the off-season and release in the watering periods, and flood control often involves a lowering of the water level before the commencement of the rainy season.

## D. Drainage

In some places, the threat of flood may be diminished through increasing the discharge capacity of the water system. Beginning in 1964, the central government directed a major reconstruction of the Hai River system, more than sextupling its discharge capacity.[10] Other large channels have been dug or widened for flood and field drainage throughout the north China plain.

## The Readings

As indicated in the above discussion, this volume brings together seven model experiences, concentrating on those of the project types which require continuous professional-mass interaction. These examples are representative of the dozens published in China. To provide additional background to the reader, I have preceded these studies with a translated introduction and a brief review of staffing and management tasks, both taken from a 1965 manual on irrigation management.[11] Appended, as Readings 11, 12 and 13, are most of the available rules and regulations governing water management.

### Introduction to "Irrigation Management" (Reading 1)

The first section of the initial reading, a brief historical introduction, notes that irrigation management, like other forms of water management and the economy in general, was in a parlous state in 1949. This was especially true along the vital but labile Yellow River system. Other Chinese sources indicate that neglect of major water works began as early as the nineteenth century when the Qing dynasty entered its final decline. A number of rehabilitation plans, not mentioned in the text, were drawn up by Chinese and foreign engineers during the Republican period (1911-1949), but these could rarely be carried out amidst the political and military turmoil which dominated that era.[12]

Hence, after the founding of the PRC, the new government had to perform two sequential tasks in water management: first rehabilitation, and then reform. The latter became particularly important, and feasible, with the collectivization of agriculture in 1956.

The traditional forms of village-level water management, while varied, were all grounded in private or clan ownership of water rights or land. The land reform of the late 1940s and early 1950s broke this up but at the same time fragmented the landholdings and did little toward consolidating the water systems. Collectives, incorporating villages (now usually production brigades) or subvillage units (production teams), provided new basic-level water user organizations which could be integrated as the "mass" component into a multilevel water management system. These systems developed rapidly in the late 1950s and early 1960s. The form and functions of water management organization have remained essentially the same since that time.

The second section of Reading 1 provides a standard Chinese taxonomy of management functions. There are three basic categories: water use management ("the core"), project management ("the base"), and organizational management ("the guarantee").[13] These correspond roughly to the hydro-agronomic, engineering, and organizational functions, respectively.

<u>Organizational Management</u> (Reading 2)

Under organizational management, the Chinese include organizational structure, the maintenance of auxiliary facilities (e.g., communications equipment and access roads), and financial management. Reading 2 discusses these in some detail. Most of the translations in this volume focus on the structural and financial aspects of organizational management, for it is in this area that one might most expect China to be unique.

The guidelines presented in the text are reasonably specific, yet flexible. For example, the decision as to whether an irrigation district should be managed by the state or within the collective sector is usually determined by its geographical extent; yet loopholes are written into the rules for situations where "convenience" or "custom" may override geography.

The distinction drawn between the state and collective sectors is important, although sometimes blurred in practice (e.g., the collective is subject to state cropping and procurement plans, and commune-level administrators are state employees). The lowest level of the state, aside from a relatively small number of state farms, is the county, or xian. Each xian contains an average of approximately twenty-five rural people's communes, which are the highest level of the three-tiered collective sector.

The communes, and to some degree their subdivisions, combine administrative and economic functions (zhengshe heyi) – a unity which has come under fire during the past two years for being excessively bureaucratic. In particular, the political leadership which has directed the local economy has had weak entrepreneurial incentives.

A commune is subdivided into a number of "production brigades," which are comprised of "production teams." The latter are the basic "accounting unit" in the countryside, and peasants receive the bulk of their income from their production team.

Financially, enterprises which are state operated normally have their revenues and expenditures included in a unified state budget. Profits go to the state; losses are made up by the state. This does not always encourage management to operate in an economically efficient way. A state enterprise is supposed to engage in detailed "economic accounting" (jingji hesuan), however, and many, such as irrigation districts, are enjoined to be "self-sufficient with a surplus" (zigei youyu). Also, water fees are kept separate from general revenue and are targeted for irrigation district operations. This gives an irrigation district a collective as well as a state character.

Income from collectively owned enterprises goes to the commune or brigade which owns them. The specific financial arrangements are less standardized than for state enterprises. For example, a collectively operated irrigation district is not required to levy water fees to help defray operating costs.

A unique feature of Reading 2 is its specification of guidelines for staffing the full-time management structure of an irrigation district office.[14] The presentation of these set formulae may obscure the practical difficulty of finding an appropriate staffing level. If a mangement office has too few employees, it may of necessity take an excessively narrow view of its responsibilities and remain isolated from its water-using constituents. One solution to this problem, touted in many of the studies herein, is to rely on semiprofessional, part-time "mass" personnel who are remunerated by their production teams.

If a mangement office is overstaffed, its operating costs may be excessive, leading either to high water charges or to deficits which must be made up by an allocation from the external state or collective budget. One acceptable approach to this problem, at least in certain political periods, appears to be to discharge excess staff (see Reading 6, where the number of employees was reduced from 180 to 44). Another method is to put supernumeraries to work in other activities, usually agricultural, which bring in extra food and revenue to the management unit.

In most countries, the release of water to the fields and the construction and maintenance of works below the watercourse (tertiary, subbranch, or farm) level is left to farmers' organizations. In China, the conceptual divide between state and farmer is at the commune level. Even in the state-operated irrigation systems, on-farm operations are usually carried out under "mass" or "democratic" organizations within the collective sector. Because of the three-tiered structure and the size of the commune (equivalent to a township, or xiang, with an average population of 14,000), the mass organizations may be quite complex and adopt a variety of forms. The basic water-using unit is usually the production brigade, which more often than not is a natural village, or cun. Some brigades further allocate water among their individual production teams, which have their own distinct fields.

## The Case Studies (Readings 3 through 10)

The core of this collection is a set of readings on specific projects. These are all model units. That is, they have successfully overcome a number of serious problems of water supply, organization, funding, meeting different crop water requirements, settling conflicts between villages, and the like which may not have — presumably, have not — been solved as well by a modal water management administration.

At our present state of knowledge, we can say very little about how well a run-of-the-mill project works. We do know that from time to time the Chinese government expresses concern about water management inadequacies. That is one of the reasons materials on exemplary organizations are available, for they usually accompany a campaign to upgrade management.[15] Projects frequently operate below their designed capacities, and it is common for the amount of water fees collected to fall below that needed to cover operating expenses.[16] Such inefficiencies are hardly unique in the Third World, however — or entirely absent from economically more developed countries, for that matter.[17]

What can we learn from case studies which are official, model not modal? Quite a lot. If a campaign is to yield productive results, it has to provide models which are truly didactic, which deal with real and commonplace problems. An exemplary unit must also use methods which are proper within the Chinese organizational framework to solve these problems, and indicate which methods are improper. All of this yields quite a bit of information.

## Meichuan Reservoir Irrigation District (Reading 3)

Many models are chosen not because of beneficent endowments by either nature or the state, but precisely because they have succeeded despite serious hydraulic, financial, and staffing deficiencies. A prime example of this is the Meichuan Reservoir Irrigation District, a model among models since 1973. Reading 3 is by far the longest and most detailed description presented in this volume, and it constitutes an entire pamphlet in the original.

In Meichuan, a medium-sized reservoir, the principal obstacle is a serious "contradiction between supply and demand"[18]: the water in the main reservoir falls far short of meeting the needs of the district's double-crop rice. The "empty belly" reservoir was full in only two of its first fifteen years and, in one particularly parched year, water was even pumped out of its dead storage.

A myriad of organizational and economic problems arose from the operation of the Meichuan District under conditions of extreme scarcity. These include the development of new water sources and their coordination when owned by different units; the sequencing of water use and the handling of conflicts, real and potential, among water users; the levying of water fees; the financing of irrigation district operating expenses; and the accountability of management to the final users and to higher authorities. Reading 3, by providing what by Chinese standards is an extraordinary amount of technical, organizational and behavioral detail, yields much information on how these problems are handled. These methods may be summarized as follows:

1. Expansion of supply through new construction. The main reservoir alone can provide only 30 percent of the water requirements for double crop rice when it relies on the runoff from its own catchment basin. The irrigation district has therefore sought out alternative sources of water both for storage elsewhere and as a supplement to the Meichuan Reservoir's inflow. This has involved the construction of twenty-one smaller reservoirs with a total beneficial capacity of 17.689 million cubic meters, nearly two-thirds that of the Meichuan. In addition, nearly 6,000 ponds owned by the user organizations can provide a supplemental 12 million cubic meters of water each year.

2. Coordination of works. The problem of exploitation of supplemental water sources is more organizational than technical. Impoundment works other than the Meichuan are usually owned by one of the three levels of collective, and all labor mobilized for construction purposes is from the commune sector. In the early years of the irrigation district, the ponds of

teams in the upper and middle reaches were often neglected and even filled in to create fields. The reservoir irrigation district has had to include the management of its users' works as part of its agenda. Meichuan has set up a "melons on a vine" system, linking reservoirs, canals, and ponds in a coordinated manner. The management office has assisted the collectives in the survey, design, construction, and overall management of their ponds and reservoirs. It has also trained "water technicians" for user organizations. This extension work even includes fish raising classes, so as to make the ponds a more attractive investment.

One organizational problem involves the original division between the "reservoir district" above the reservoir, which had to rely on pumping and hauling for irrigation, and the "irrigation district" below the reservoir, which relies on less expensive gravity irrigation. The conflict between reservoir and irrigation districts became particularly acute when the water level was low in the reservoir. The solution adopted was to build a smaller reservoir (the Baiyuan) on higher ground and lead its water to the reservoir district via a tunnel, and then to build a still smaller, more upland reservoir (the Fengkou) above the Baiyuan to provide water to <u>its</u> reservoir district.

3. <u>Promotion of more efficient water application</u>. The management office had first of all to bring its objectives into line with those of its clients (and the state). At first, it viewed its role in the most narrow of senses, as the management of water release. Then the objective was expanded to the needs of irrigation, and later to the requirements of increasing crop output. In other words, the organization "learned" to bring its objectives into line with those of its putative beneficiaries.

After 1960, the irrigation district management office ran irrigation stations to determine the patterns of water inflow and crop requirements. This information provides a basis for seasonal variation in release of reservoir and pond water and for the day-to-day application of moisture to the rice crop at different stages of its growth. Shallow irrigation techniques were developed which use the water sparingly, although with greater weed growth.

The problem once again was only partly one of technology, which appears to have been acquired or developed relatively painlessly; it was more one of organization, of implementation of acquired knowledge and techniques at the basic, mass level. The experimental stations, run by specialists, remained separate from the production teams in essence if not in form until an effort was made in 1964 to bring the masses in. The support of team leaders and peasant technicians was then solicited, and the latter were provided with the skills requisite to the implementation of a more precise watering regimen. In addition, a "backbone squad" was organized to help serve as a transmission belt of policy and information to the masses.

4. Land improvement. Efficient water application requires level land, a water table which is neither too high nor too low, and proper drainage. In addition, erosion control improves both water and soil conditions. This sort of "farmland capital construction" requires massive amounts of peasant labor to be mobilized by the regular administrative apparatus.

The ability of an irrigation district management office to successfully promote land improvement activity depends critically on its relationship with the local Party and revolutionary committees. In Meichuan, farmland capital construction campaigns were carried out under the *qu* (a sub-*xian* level of the state found in Hubei) Party committee, with which the irrigation district management has established and maintained good ties.

5. Establishment of adequate water allocation procedures. Water fees may be set either to generate revenue or to provide a means of allocation, or both. At Meichuan, charges are made to help cover current costs, but they are not used for market-style allocation according to price-based demand. Fees are lowered or waived in the times of shortage when supply and demand would mandate their increase. Further, the "I pay you the money, you release the water" attitude which was present when Meichuan used a volumetric charge is considered quite improper. The irrigation district switched to an acreage

charge, less efficient in encouraging frugality in water use, precisely because of its more attenuated effect on motivation.

In practice, therefore, Meichuan has adopted nonmarket water allocation procedures. Irrigation sequencing principles which are adequate to the varying needs of different parts of the district were worked out in the course of Meichuan's experiences.

The task proved a complex one. At first, the district used the principle of "first near, then far" (i.e., nonintervention), which drowned the upper reaches and left the lower reaches without water. "First far, then near" fared little better, as it was extremely difficult to implement and was still too simplistic for the concrete conditions of varying parts of the district. Finally, the principle of "three firsts, three laters" was evolved. This principle is considerably more complex but appears to be more adequate to the realities of water needs and implementability.

6. Development of multiple operations. Partly to make full use of the resources at hand and partly to help meet administrative costs and maintain an adequate standard of living for district management staff, the Meichuan District has "used the reservoir to sustain the reservoir." Multiple operations centering on fishery but including crops, trees, and hog raising have been developed by the staff and its dependents, providing self-sufficiency in grain, cotton, and oilseeds and a sizable net income to the management office and its employees. This was done without any increase in full-time personnel by mobilizing dependents and some temporary labor, and by making everyone into a "jack of all trades."

Shaoshan Irrigation District (Readings 4 and 5)

The Shaoshan Irrigation District is a multipurpose showcase project in Hunan. Its main structures were built in a few months just before the Cultural Revolution under the direction of Hua Guofeng, then a provincial Party secretary.

In April 1976, when Hua succeeded Zhou Enlai as premier, he was not very well known, even in China. Consequently, when

Chairman Mao bestowed his famous imprimatur on Hua ("With you in charge, I'm at ease."), he also directed that "we must give publicity to Comrade Hua Guofeng so that the nation's people will gradually get to know him." Within five months Hua succeeded Mao as well, and it became increasingly important to get to know him.

Reading 4, a description of the building of the Shaoshan project, is drawn from a 1977 collection publicizing Hua's accomplishments, entitled (in translation) Chairman Hua in Hunan. This selection has been included in the present collection to provide some background on Hua and on the subsequent management of the district, described in Reading 5. It also illustrates the continuing political significance of water control in China.

From 1949 until his transfer to Peking in 1971, Hua worked in Hunan Province. Among his many other posts, he has been identified as the director-general of the Shaoshan project construction and as the one who suggested that its design, originally more modest, be expanded to include the village of Shaoshan, Chairman Mao's hometown.

Hua's accomplishments at Shaoshan and in water control are given prominence in Chairman Hua in Hunan, even though these are brief (and late) episodes in his provincial career.[19] The analogy is not drawn explicitly, but the association of the new leader with his predecessor by means of the construction of hydraulic works brings to mind the legendary Yu the Great. In thirteen years of diligent work as Minister of Public Works, Yu tamed the Great Flood and as a reward was named by the virtuous ruler Shun to be his successor.[20]

Hua's deeds at Shaoshan and the later Ouyang Hai Project are more modest, even in the ex-post panegyrics, than those of the ancients who directed corvée labor to wrestle with the Yellow River or drain the swamps along the Yangtze. Although one of the 150 large irrigation districts in China, Shaoshan is far from being the largest. Even after a decade of expansion, it only provides water to two percent of one province's farmland.[21] Nonetheless, it is the first single large water project in Hunan, and it remains the largest in irrigated area. Its main components were built under Secretary Hua's few months of direction with Great Leap speed and mass mobilization (100,000 laborers out of a total population of 800,000), but post-Leap attention to quality. Hua himself emerges from the narrative of Reading 4 as a busy but competent administrator with an unassuming yet precise sense of politics.

The Shaoshan Irrigation Project diverts up to 46 cubic meters of water per second from the Lian River downstream from the Shuifumiao Reservoir to irrigate approximately 60,000 hectares of farmland. Unlike Meichuan, which irrigates 8,000 hectares within a single xian, the Shaoshan project brings water to fields in several xian. Because of its location, it affects portions of three prefectures and one prefecture-level municipality as well. This overlap of prefectural boundaries, and possibly its political significance, have led to Shaoshan being built and managed under the province.[22]

One of the consequences, shown in Reading 5, is that the irrigation district management is very closely tied to the administrative apparatus. The management committee is headed by cadres from the provincial and prefectural bureaus of Water Conservancy and Electric Power. Maintenance and repair responsibilities are subdivided along xian and commune boundaries rather than according to project components such as branch and subbranch canals. A commune's maintenance costs are therefore usually not proportional to the benefits it derives from the project. Those with relatively greater maintenance burdens, such as Nanzhushan Commune, are not subsidized.

Countering the unequal distribution of burdens are said to be the greater responsiveness of the local political administrative units to maintenance problems and the ability to decentralize many professional tasks to the commune level. The functions of the irrigation district bureau itself are quite specialized and engineering-oriented, centering on irrigation and the formulation of regulations and designs, inspections, technical outreach, and personnel matters. Water fees and grain levies are collected and held separately by the xian finance and grain departments. While this sort of division of labor may lead to departmentalism, it allows broader multilevel participation in the affairs of the irrigation districts and therefore perhaps greater commitment to making it work well.

Qianli Canals Irrigation District (Reading 6)

The combination of a professionalized management and decentralization to administrative units did not work quite so well for the Qianli Canals project in Szechuan. Even though it had over three times as many professional personnel as the maximum stipulated in the guidelines of Reading 2, Qianli's management office could not complete its annual maintenance and repair tasks on the main canals, much less ride herd on the communes in the upper reaches who kept taking more than their share of the water.

The problem appears partly to have been one of communication. Few information channels seem to have been open between the project office and the beneficiary teams. To tackle this, a district conference of representatives was set up to meet twice a year to let both top and bottom know what is going on. Over 70 canal-based but elected temporary water management officers were installed as middle level personnel. Finally, over 140 joint "professional-mass" management committees were set up, apparently based on branch canals.

One of these joint committees is described in Reading 6. With the reorganization along branch canal lines, an upstream production brigade which had been prone to blocking off the water in times of drought was put on the same committee as two downstream brigades. Thereafter, more attention was paid to "unified planning and overall arrangement" and "strengthening revolutionary unity."

Another problem leading to the waste of water by upstream units during a drought was the use of an acreage charge for water use. Extra water cost them nothing, so upstream collectives had no financial incentive to be sparing in its use.

Since the levies appear to have been based on the designed or normal irrigated area, downstream collectives were sometimes dunned for water they never received and were understandably reluctant to pay up. Qianli therefore instituted a partially volumetric charge. This is the opposite direction from Meichuan, which abandoned volumetric charges. Meichuan appears to have much greater direct control over the total water supply then does Qianli, however.

The "thousand li canal managed by 10,000 people" is actually less massive — and less mass — than the headline indicates. The three main canals have a total length of but 400-odd li (200 km.). The total canal system, down to the field ditches, is 1,200 li (600 km.) long, slightly less than that of Meichuan. Although its irrigated area is a bit larger, Qianli has far fewer mass components than Meichuan (e.g., 300 ponds compared to 6,000). The narrative does not provide a specific figure, but it is clear that the total number of people involved in the system's management, including at the user level, is in the hundreds, not thousands. The "10,000" is clearly meant figuratively — a hyperbole for "many."

Two observations should be made here. First, despite the rhetoric, water management at Qianli remains a specialized function engaged in professionally or semiprofessionally by designated personnel and administrative organs. The difference between before and after lies not in despecialization but in the linkage forged between system management and the existing water personnel in the user units via interbrigade canal-based committees. The resultant decentralization of most maintenance and allocation functions allowed the district management office to cut its staff by three-quarters.

Second, the system which Qianli developed is not much different from that of other models and is in line with the guidelines of Readings 2 and 12. This raises the question of why Qianli was publicized. Are hill-dwelling Sichuanese not normally amenable to the cooperative use of water? (Unlike Chinese peasants elsewhere, Sichuanese do not live in nucleated villages.)[23] Or is the modal medium-sized irrigation district management in China still like Qianli's "before" — overstaffed, excessively burdened with maintenance and repair, and isolated from "beneficiary" units which are themselves riven by conflicts over water allocation?

People's Yinjing Canal Irrigation District (Reading 7)

Simple economics tells us that investment is a two-edged sword. It requires present sacrifice, for the labor and other resources diverted to the construction of fixed capital cannot be used to provide consumption goods for daily living — or military goods and personnel for defense or conquest. On the other hand, productive investment expands economic (and, if desired, military) possibilities in the future.

Some 2,200 years ago, toward the end of the Warring States period, the state of Han (韩) concentrated on making the first edge of the investment sword (present sacrifice) work against its contentious western neighbor, the Napoleonic state of Qin. Soon thereafter, Qin made use of the military might provided by the other edge to conquer Han and all the other feudal states.

Sima Qian tells the story as follows:

> The Han heard that the Qin liked to build things. They wanted to tire out the Qin and prevent them from attacking to the east, so they sent the hydraulic engineer Zheng Guo as a secret agent to the Qin to persuade them to order the digging of a canal from the Jing River.... During the course of the work, he was found out and the Qin wanted to kill him. Zheng Guo said, "Although I came as an agent, this canal, when complete, will benefit the Qin." The Qin felt that that made sense and completed the canal.... Guanzhong [central Shaanxi] became fertile without years of famine. The Qin became wealthy and strong and in the end annexed all the feudal lords. They named the canal the Zheng Guo Canal.[24]

The People's Yinjing Canal is a descendant of Zheng Guo's "ruse," although it is many times removed from its precursor. It waters much the same latitude and longitude, and therefore may be considered the "ancient irrigation district" in the title of Reading 7. Nearly all of the area lacked irrigation in recent historical times, however, and periodic famine had returned to the land. By the time of the early Qing dynasty three centuries ago, the successors of the Zheng Guo Canal had one by one been made virtually useless by silting and the continual deepening of the bed of the Jing River below the level of the canal intake structures.

The project inherited by the PRC in the late 1940s was actually built in the early 1930s, under the auspices of the China International Famine Relief Commission and the Nationalist Shaanxi provincial authorities. Most of the funding, $634,000 out of $799,000, was provided by U.S. philanthropists, including the overseas Chinese community.

What was then called the Wei Bei (north of the Wei River) Irrigation Project was begun in December 1930. It was built with the design and direction of Major O. J. Todd. The principal project components consisted of a 215-foot (66 meter) -long masonry overflow diversion dam, a 1,300-foot (396 meter)-long tunnel, a mile (1.6 km.) section of canal cut out of rock on the hillside designed to carry the normal flow of 16 cubic meters per second, and an open-cut canal 3.85 miles (6.2 km.) long below that. With some extension of the distribution system, the project irrigated 600,000 mou (40,000 ha., or 100,000 acres) in the mid-1930s.[25]

Later, the Wei Bei became the "Jinghui Canal." During the Cultural Revolution, it was again renamed, to the present "People's Yinjing (Jing diversion) Canal."[26]

The Yinjing has the largest benefited area of the cases presented here, over 80,000 hectares. The irrigation district includes an additional 60,000 hectares watered by mechanized pump wells. Like Shaoshan, it is a province-run project, one of at least four in Shaanxi, although provincial leaders do not appear to participate on the irrigation district committee.

With a canal commanded area twice the original 40,000 hectares, Yinjing, like Meichuan, has faced a serious water deficiency in its main projects. Its solution has also been to "open up new sources and economize on the flow" (kaiyuan, jieliu).

Because it is basically a river diversion from a variable flow and not keyed to reservoir storage, Yinjing has not set up a Meichuan-style "melons on a vine" system, although ponds and reservoirs in the lower reaches have permitted some seasonal regulation of water availability. In the upper reaches, Yinjing's equivalent of "melons" are subterranean. As in other plains areas of northern China, deep tube wells were dug here during the late 1960s and early 1970s to provide considerable supplemental irrigation from groundwater supplies. Tube wells, like ponds, are built and owned by production brigades or teams, but their use is coordinated in the overall "chessboard" arrangements of the irrigation district as a whole, much as in a surface "melon on a vine" system.

The sources of water have been expanded with improvements in the headworks and the canal system as well as the digging of wells and tail-ender ponds and reservoirs. Nonetheless, water supply conditions remain tight on occasions, especially in the face of drought and at certain critical growing periods. An interesting feature of Yinjing is its automatic change of allocation principles in keeping with the degree of water sufficiency. When the supply is adequate, water is distributed according to "need," presumably on demand. When the water available falls below requirements, it is still distributed continuously in the main and branch canals, but proportionally among the turnouts. When the water flow is reduced further (in 1958 the standard was set at 40 percent of normal), it is rotated in the main and branch canals.[27]

Yinjing has developed a well-articulated, hierarchical, four-level water distribution structure based on the canal system. The levels are the irrigation district management bureau, stations,[28] subbranch canals, and production teams. Water "rights" (shuiquan) are "centralized" at the next highest level over those who actually allocate the water. The precise nature of these "rights" is unclear, but they seem to include the authority to make ad hoc changes in the distribution among subordinate units as long as the total planned allocation is unchanged.[29]

Jiangfengkou Flood Gate (Reading 8)

The next two brief readings are on flood control facilities which have some ongoing interaction with mass beneficiaries. In the case of flood gates association with the rural collectives appears to be especially unusual. Gates besides Jiangfengkou are usually cited rather for their activism in carrying out technical measures, such as the installation of fish ladders and doing anticorrosion painting.[30]

This relatively isolated professionalism is due in part to the passive nature of flood control. Floods are rare events, and even when they occur there is usually no necessity for the beneficiaries to be involved in the operation of a flood gate if it works well. Maintenance is relatively technical and requires little unskilled labor (dikes are different – see Reading 9). If necessary, a handful of part-time workers may be hired from nearby production teams.

Organizationally, a flood gate is usually subordinated to a larger river management organization. In the case of Jiangfengkou, this is the Yi and Wu River Management Office. This unit, presumably under Linyi Prefecture in southern Shandong, is also responsible for the dikes along the two rivers.

Jiangfengkou is known for its linking up with the masses because it has branched out to include water release for irrigation among its functions. The gate is located at the most flood-prone site along the flat middle reaches of the once unruly Yi River in southern Shandong. To prevent flooding in the more extensive downstream areas of the Yi, it diverts the water into the smaller Wu River, which serves as a flood channel.

The Chinese are loathe to allow cultivable land to go idle,

especially fertile riverine land, so the local peasants grow crops on 100,000 mou (66 sq. km.) along the banks of the Wu. In time of emergency, these crops are sacrificed to the greater good. The management of the flood gate is lauded in Reading 8 for considerately sparing the land along the Wu by waiting out a flood crest, even though authorization had been given to release water if necessary.

Jiangfengkou Gate, which releases water at flood time, can also release water during the growing season. In 1964 the gate was changed to serve irrigation as well as drainage.[31] The actual management of the water after release, however, is handled separately by four irrigation districts under two downstream xian. This has not been added on to the burdens of the gate staff.

One factor making irrigation attractive in the Wu River channel was the reduced probability of flood owing to the building of reservoirs in the upper reaches of the Yi, in the mountains of central Shandong. With their fields more secure from being sacrificed, farming units along the Wu found it more attractive to build fixed structures for systematic irrigation. The management personnel of the flood gate also played an important role in technical outreach. They helped the collectives survey canals, repair culverts and build electrical pumping stations. This points to the scarcity of technical survey and design talent within the rural villages. This is surprising in Linyi, an area which has been extremely active in "farmland capital construction."[32]

Jiangfengkou is also a model of financial self-reliance in management expenses. The gate management takes in no revenue from water fees, for it does not control the irrigation districts. Funds have rather been generated through other productive operations — by reclaiming the nearby wasteland and developing some of the chief money-making operations in China's countryside: fruit trees, medicinal herbs, and hogs.[33]

It is not clear what "management expenses" cover; nor is it obvious what incentives, positive or negative, are brought into play to make the staff do the extra work which is necessary to bring in income. The gate belongs to the state, and ultimately its accounts are, presumably, included in a larger state budget. We know very little about the wage structure of water management employees, but they are probably on fixed salary much as other state workers. Perhaps here, unlike in state factories until recently, the organization is allowed to retain a significant portion of its revenue.

Yellow/Qin Rivers Dike Maintenance Section (Reading 9)

Zhengzhou, the present capital of Henan Province, lies near the Yellow River shortly after its debouchment onto the plain. The city incorporates a portion of the southern bank in its greater municipal boundaries. Visitors are often taken to the site of Huayuankou, where in 1938 the Nationalists breached the dikes and flooded the plain in a last ditch effort to stem the advance of the Japanese army. The breach was closed in 1947 under a joint Nationalist-Communist agreement. Since then, the dikes have been enlarged and strengthened considerably, with grouting and stone masonry revetments.[34]

When one stands at Huayuankou, the northern dike of the Yellow River is a thin line on the horizon 10 km. away. This dike includes the eastern end of the portion of the northern embankment which is the responsibility of Wuzhi xian and its Yellow/Qin Rivers Dike Maintenance Section.

Although there is a Yellow River Commission directly under the national Ministry of Water Conservancy, it is responsible only for planning and surveying the river and managing the hydrological stations. The provinces are in charge of other aspects of river management.

In Henan at least, dike maintenance is divided along xian and municipal boundaries. That this can lead to wide variations in performance is indicated in Reading 9, where it is said that the Wuzhi section was once "a backward unit in dike maintenance in Xinxiang [Prefecture]."[35]

The symptoms of Wuzhi's former backwardness are implied in the description of the cure. Administrative neglect appears to have been pandemic. The dike management committees in the commune sector had ceased to function. The fulltime mass dike maintenance personnel (apparently, a contingent residing in the villages and paid locally but under the direction of the dike section) appear to have had a poor work attitude. Dike facilities were damaged through carelessness or selfish disregard, seemingly without sanctions being imposed, owing, perhaps, to a lack of formal regulations.

There were three aspects to the treatment of this problem, as described in Reading 9. The first was organizational strengthening, with direct Party involvement at the mass level and a blend of centralized and decentralized maintenance responsibilities. Second, some financial incentives were provided to the collectives and their member peasants. Third, detailed regulations were promulgated and enforced.

The six commune Party committees and the fifty-four brigade Party branches along the dike sections have designated a member, sometimes a deputy secretary, to be in charge of dike maintenance work. This person also directs the revived commune and brigade management committees, which meet at irregular intervals. Curiously, the section's Party branch has also assigned a deputy secretary to the specific task of dike management. This is a curious move, since dike management is already the stated function of the section.

Centralized control has been exerted by sending eleven out of about ninety section staff members out to the collectives to take charge of day-to-day dike management. Also, the fulltime mass maintenance contingent of thirty-nine people was restaffed with members who have good "political ideology," who are healthy, and who "warmly love dike maintenance work."

At the same time, the dikes are subdivided to the production team for ordinary maintenance tasks. Included are the maintenance of the dike, the gates, the telephone lines, and the materials kept for repair.

Trees have been planted to help protect the dike. They also provide lumber, which is a scarce building material, and fruit, an economic crop. A sharecropping, or proportional, tax principle of "state owned, brigade operated, with the benefits shared" is adopted.

The state (xian) receives 60 percent of the income from lumber and 30 percent from the fruit.[36] Income from the sale of tree branches and tops and mown grass all goes to the dike maintenance team. Presumably, this helps reduce or perhaps even eliminate the burden on the collectives of paying maintenance team members.

Individual peasants are given bounties for capturing animals whose burrowing weakens the dike structures. Historically, this tunneling was the principal cause of dike failure. Honan Province as a whole has mobilized nearly 100,000 peasants to capture 315,000 animals.[37]

Finally, the xian revolutionary committee promulgated a set of prohibitions. These include bans on fishing with explosives near the dangerous sections, farming or gathering soil on the dike body, driving caterpillar tractors on the dike top, and chopping down trees or using flood contingency materials without permission. These rules give some insight into the sort of deviant behavior which occurred when leadership and discipline were lax – and which may still go on.

Now, those who "accidentally" violate the regulations are "patiently criticized and educated." Repeat offenders or those whose actions have had serious consequences are dealt with "strictly."

Pinggu Xian Mechanized Wells (Reading 10)

"Mechanized" tube wells were encountered in the reading on Yinjing, where they have been incorporated into a canal-based "chessboard." After the mid-1960s, grain output on the north China plain, which had lagged behind the southern rice areas, increased considerably. A major cause of this improvement was the drilling of myriad pump-operated wells to tap the deeper aquifers. The number of these wells increased from about 100,000 in 1965 to over 2.3 million in 1979. They are generally 30 to 40 meters deep, but they may reach depths of over 200 meters. Most are lined with 100-300 mm. diameter tubes made of wood, brick, plastic, glass, or cement.[38]

Pinggu xian, in the far eastern corner of Beijing Municipality, lies in the foothills just above the northern limit of the plain. The Great Wall winds through its northeast corner. Tube wells have played an important part in bringing water to this historically drought-ridden area.

Pinggu, which began digging tube wells earlier than most areas, is a model xian in their development. The 447 deep wells irrigate an average of just under 20 hectares each. This is considerably above the national average of 5.6 hectares. Even Yinjing's average tube well waters but 6 hectares.[39]

Low operating efficiency can be due to faulty design, inadequate or even absent management, poor coordination of use with other wells or surface flows, a lack of land leveling, inefficient electric power transmission, or overexploitation of the groundwater aquifers. Given the speed of tube well development, it is not surprising that all these factors are present to one degree or another in large parts of the north China Plain.

Tube wells are often dug by professional teams organized by the xian or commune, which levels are also supposed to assume responsibility for planning and regulating their placement and operation. The wells are owned and managed, however, by the production brigades or, on occasion, jointly by a production team and its brigade.

Brigade management is preferred. As one manual puts it,

> The advantages of brigade management are that it unifies the management of specialists, the deployment of machinery and pumps, and the arrangement of water use. This allows the thorough development of the potential of mechanized wells and their pumping equipment. It avoids contention between production teams for water and electricity which affects the watering of the land.[40]

Often, however, brigades are slow to set up management systems and to do the necessary ancillary projects, including land leveling, that would allow the full use of the wells.[41] The reasons for this are not too obvious from the narrative of Reading 10, but some speculation is possible.

First, there is a pervasive bias in the PRC toward project construction, not management. The number of works completed, or the amount of earth and stone moved, are easy to measure and report. Good management is more elusive. This leads to a relative neglect of follow-up operations.

Similarly, the bandwagon effect of the campaign style used to stimulate farmland and water conservancy construction may lead to brigades building works which are improper for local conditions, which do not have the necessary supply of electricity or other inputs, or whose operation is technically too demanding for local laborers. A "more is better" mentality at all levels may override rational planning of well placement and depth.

In addition, the xian and commune often push tube well construction and provide the drilling crews (although at a fee). Administratively, tube well oversight involves a number of different departments which may lead to uncoordinated development.

As a result, there has often been a wave of tidying up and "overall planning" after a high tide of construction. (This applies of course to other aspects of the Chinese economy and polity besides well construction.) Some wells have to be closed, new ones have to be dug, and pumping depths changed. A striking example of a rearrangement of tube wells and power lines is shown for a Hebei brigade in Figure 1.

Pinggu is successful because its Party and administration have emphasized management, technical training, and planning and have done a good job of tidying up the problems of the initial stage of development. The departments of agricultural machinery, water conservancy, and electric power have formed a joint "electrical irrigation project planning group," which assumes joint responsibility for the construction and inspection of tube wells and other electrical irrigation projects such as pumping stations. It trains mechanics to run them. It regu-

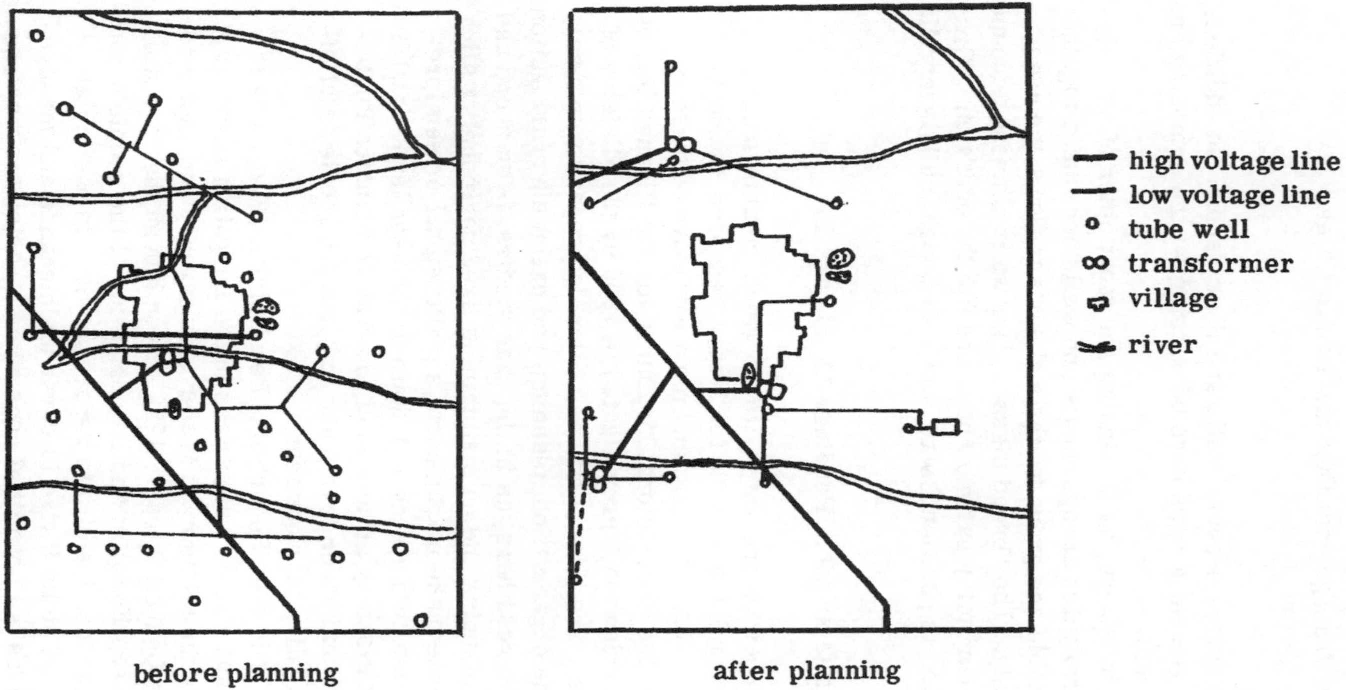


Figure 1. Houtuo Brigade, Wangdu Xian, Hebei, tube well and power line layout.
Source: Pingyuan jing guanqu dixia shui kaifa liyong, pp. 44-45.

lates the distance between wells and their depths. In addition, fixed management groups have been set up at the commune and brigade levels.

Finally, in Pinggu, as in Yinqing and most other effectively run well-irrigation areas, canals and wells are linked together where possible and groundwater and surface flows are used conjunctively. The "broad masses," known in Chinese accounts for their many pithy sayings, have one for the occasion: "Gravity irrigation is positional war, and well irrigation is guerrilla war."[42]

Regulations (Appendix: Readings 11, 12, and 13)

In the Appendix are three items which contain most of the known legal framework for water resource management in the PRC. The first and most extensive of these is Reading 11, the "Provisional Measures for the Planned Use of Water for Irrigation," promulgated in 1965 by the Ministry of Agriculture. The thirty articles of this document cover many facets of the organization, planning, and execution of irrigation. One major stress here, as in the case studies, is on sound and multilevel planning and on maintaining fixed personnel at all levels. These make management a professional or semiprofessional operation all the way down to the user level. Stabilized expectations by all and good two-way communication between upper and lower levels are important ingredients of effective irrigation management.

Reading 12 is the "Report of a Few Opinions Regarding the Collection and Use of Water Fees in the Irrigation Districts," prepared by the Ministry of Water Conservancy and approved by the State Council in early 1958. Even though they predate the Great Leap Forward and the formation of the people's communes, the principles of this report persist. In particular, water fees are to be levied to cover maintenance and management expenses but not initial construction costs; and they should not be used for local general revenue.

This would appear to provide an irrigation district with some degree of autonomy from the unified budgetary system. It also safeguards the production teams against the use of water fees as an instrument of extraction by the government.

In practice, excess extraction does not appear to be a major problem, although charges may be rather high when electricity or diesel oil are required. The financial problem appears to be quite the opposite. As in 1958, many irrigation districts continue to run in the red.

Reading 13 is the nine-article "Regulations Concerning Water Project Management in Zhejiang Province (Trial Draft)," issued in May 1972. For the most part, these regulations corroborate in a concise form the continuity of the principles of the two prior readings. In keeping with the growing complexity of water development, some additional concern is given to rural uses of water other than irrigation. The increasing urban and industrial water requirements do not come into the purview of the Zhejiang regulations, however.[43] Reading 13 also provides new specifics on some financial matters, notably on staff remuneration and the use of income from nonirrigation activities such as fisheries.

## Conclusion and a Noninvidious Comparison

The readings in this volume are a small but reasonably representative sample of the literature in the PRC on water management organization. It is apparent that while there are general rules, there is much variety in practice. For example, fees may be set on the basis of either volume or area benefited, or a combination of the two; and management tasks may be subdivided along either administrative lines or according to project components.

This lack of uniformity allows a great deal of flexibility of operations at the project level. That is a good thing, for water and other conditions vary widely from project to project and require different responses. Irrigation and flood control can rarely be produced by standardized assembly-line techniques. On the other hand, too much flexibility can lead to passivity or distortions based, among other things, on particularistic relationships.

There are two very important aspects of water control, especially irrigation, which may present organizational difficulties. First of all, except for the smallest and most isolated of projects, farm water management involves an agency, usually state operated, outside the village. State bureaucracies and village communities do not always operate on the same wavelength.

In the past, the Chinese bureaucracy, oriented toward a "revenue economy," rarely intervened directly in the production process. Yet this is mandatory in modern irrigation management. The involvement of official agencies is multifaceted, including not only the regulation of at least a portion of the water supply but the provision of high yield inputs, such as seeds, fertilizer and pumps, the popularization of new cultivation practices, and the planning and execution of land improvement.

Obviously, such intervention can be cooperative and beneficial to total farm output and income, but it can meet with some resistance as well. Water is a classical case in economics of an input with pervasive "externalities." When individuals (including people, production teams, villages, or entire provinces) are allowed to do what best serves their own interests ("maximize their utility"), the interests of the greater whole are usually ill-served. This is especially the case when water is scarce.

Thus some sort of externally imposed discipline is necessary. This usually includes a set of rules and fixed procedures, together with means for punishing their violation and rewarding compliance. It also tends to require responsibilities to be specified and fixed in certain individuals.

Such discipline is not always present. In much of Asia, farmers have considerable freedom of choice in operations with relatively loose supervision by state agencies. The latter may compound difficulties, however, in issuing water from the headworks and major turnouts without much sensitivity to actual crop requirements.

Such projects tend to suffer from common headaches:

> Headreach farmers exceeding their water quotas, using water wastefully and leaving tail-enders short . . . ; illegal piping of water, obstruction of channels, etc., together with ineffective penalty mechanisms . . . ; low overall water use efficiencies . . . ; neglect of O & M [operations and maintenance] in favor of new construction elsewhere . . . ; low water rates . . . ; weak agricultural extension and poor liaison between agricultural and engineering staff.[44]

These symptoms are not entirely absent in the PRC. Although model units have overcome most of them, many problems, such as a bias toward new construction and low use efficiencies in existing projects, are quite common in PRC water management.

The second important aspect of water control is that it requires a blend of professional expertise and grass-roots implementation by producers who have less formal know-how but a greater economic interest. Good irrigation management requires both engineering and agricultural expertise at the district level. It usually necessitates an administrative structure which is subordinate to the political and state apparatus but clearly separate from it. If it is too separate, however, the operators of an irrigation district find it difficult to get anything done. One theme which comes through loud and clear in these readings is the necessity of Party and state involvement. If the Party and revolutionary committees do not take water management seriously, no one else will.

Similarly, no irrigation district management can remain isolated from its water using constituents. It has to bring its objectives into line with those of the producers it serves. Channels of communication have to be opened and maintained.

One sign of a successful integration between the professionals and the "masses" is that the latter are willing to maintain the project. Another is the presence of "melons on a vine" or "chessboard" conjunctive use schemes, which require coordination between major and minor works.

When I have presented the model experiences of the PRC to international irrigation experts, they have consistently compared them to Taiwan's irrigation associations. The comparison is flattering, as Taiwan's decentralized public agencies are renowned as among the success stories of the Third World.

There is not enough space here to go into the many similarities and differences of irrigation management under the two Chinese administrations. Yet a brief description of the principal ingredients of Taiwan's success may shed some light on what the "outside experts" have seen in the PRC studies.

Abel lists four interrelated factors in Taiwan's approach. These are the recognition of water as a scarce factor which must be developed and managed intensively; a legal and administrative system which allows decentralized management of irrigation systems; an active and effective exchange of agronomic and engineering information between the users of water and the managers of a system; and efficiency-oriented incentive structures for both managers and users.[45]

Bottrall also notes that Taiwan's management system is the outcome of a long evolutionary process, independent of the Chinese mainland. This process has depended, among other things, on a strong and enduring government commitment to agricultural development, a well-trained technical management, and educated, disciplined farmers. He suggests, quite properly, that it is the dynamic aspects of Taiwan's experience, not its operation at any given time, that should be studied by those proposing that it be emulated.[46]

Not all of the static elements are present in the PRC. In particular, there are relatively few formally well-trained engineers and technicians, or even mechanics, as evidenced in the technical and mechanical outreach services of many management offices. Yet most of the ingredients that are in Taiwan are also in the PRC, albeit often cloaked in different rhetoric, e.g., "join professional organizations and mass management," "mobilize the masses," or "sum up experiences."

Most important, perhaps, is this continual "summing up of

experiences." This provides a dynamic, evolutionary feedback process that, when tied to a commitment to make things work, is a key to the success of the studies that follow.

## Notes

1. The key works by the two scholars most renowned for their (quite different) deterministic views of the role of water control in Chinese history and society are Chi Ch'ao-ting, Key Economic Areas in Chinese History (London: Allen & Unwin, 1936) and Karl A. Wittfogel, Oriental Despotism (New Haven: Yale University Press, 1957).

2. The most notable exceptions involving state construction are the Zheng Guo Canal (246 B.C.), which provided the Qin dynasty with the economic muscle to unify China for the first time (see Reading 7 and commentary); and the Dujiangyan Project (ca. 250 B.C.) in Sichuan, still in operation. The latter was built primarily for transportation but was vital in turning the Chengdu Plain into one of China's "rice bowls." Even on these projects, however, the actual management of irrigation water below a certain administrative level was probably left to local organizations. See Chi, passim, and Ru Fa douzheng yu woguo shuili fazhan shi gaikuang (The Struggle between Confucianists and Legalists and the History of China's Water Development) (Beijing: Shuili dianli Press, July 1975).

3. Klaus Flessel, in Der Huang-Ho und die historische Hydrotechnik in China (Tübingen: Klaus Flessel, 1974), provides a fascinating account of how the question of Yellow River "control" directly involved the political lives of many famous personages of the Northern Song dynasty, including Wang Anshi, Su Dongpo, and Sima Guang. For a longer historical view of the debate between "Confucians" and "Daoists" over dike emplacement, see Charles Greer, Water Management in the Yellow River Basin of China (Austin and London: University of Texas Press, 1979), Chapter 2.

4. See, for example, Wang Sung-hsing, "Pa Pao Chün: An 18th Century Irrigation System in Central Taiwan," The Bulle-

tin of the Institute of Ethnology, Academia Sinica, Taiwan, No. 33, Spring 1972 (issued April 1973), p. 175; Ramon H. Myers, "Economic Organization and Cooperation in Modern China: Irrigation Management in Xing-Tai County, Ho-bei Province," in The Policy and Economy of China: The Late Professor Yuji Muramatsu Commemoration Volume (Tokyo: Toyo Keizai Press, 1975), pp. 189-212; and Reading 1.

5. James E. Nickum, "The Organisation of Water Resource Development in the People's Republic of China," Agricultural Administration, Vol. 6, July 1979, pp. 169-186; and James E. Nickum, "Labour Accumulation in Rural China and Its Role Since the Cultural Revolution," Cambridge Journal of Economics, Vol. 2, September 1978, pp. 273-286.

6. Different methods of applying water to crops – surface, subsurface, and sprinkler – are also not included here. The examples in this work all rely on surface application. Subsurface and sprinkler methods, though relatively rare, are becoming more common. They save land, and subsurface application saves water, but both techniques require more capital investment.

7. Interview with Li Boning, vice-minister of Water Conservancy, reported in Foreign Broadcast Information Service (FBIS), Daily Report, Vol. 1, August 6, 1979, p. L 14.

In the past, water was often moved by human or animal labor as well. This arduous task has in general been taken over by pumps and gravity flow structures.

8. In the past 2,000 years, 1,500 dike breaches and 26 major changes in course have been recorded for the Yellow River. Chen Rinong, "Survey of the Huanghe River," China Reconstructs, March 1980, p. 5.

In the 580 years after 1368, there were 387 floods in the Hai River system, over 70 of them inundating the city of Tianjin. Hai he qu bian (Major Transformation of the Hai River) (Beijing: Renmin Press, November 1973), p. 2.

Over 350 major floods occurred in the Huai River system between 1400 and 1900, and millions of people died in the floods of 1921 and 1931. Huai he xin pian (A New Chapter in the Huai

River) (Beijing: Renmin Press, June 1975), p. 6.

Even the Yangtze (Chang jiang) has had an average of one major flood each decade for the past two millenia in its middle and lower reaches. Wan li Chang jiang qi hong tu (Great Prospects for the 5,000 Kilometer Yangtze River) (Beijing: Renmin Press, March 1976), p. 9.

9. James E. Nickum, Hydraulic Engineering and Water Resources in the People's Republic of China (Report of the U.S. Water Resources Delegation), United States-China Relations Report #2 (Stanford: United States-China Relations Program, 1977), pp. 74-77.

10. Nickum, Hydraulic Engineering, pp. 15-17. See also Hai he qu bian.

11. Guan'gai guanli (Irrigation management) (Beijing: Zhongguo gongye Press, 1965), pp. 1-13.

12. Greer, Water Management, p. 42. An interesting collection of contemporary observations by an eminent U.S. engineer working in China is O. J. Todd, Two Decades in China (Beijing: The Association of Chinese and American Engineers, 1938) (reprinted — Taipei: Ch'eng-wen Publishing Co., 1971).

13. Scientific experiment and multiple operations are sometimes separated out, although they can be subsumed under water use and organizational management as well. The Chinese literature also stresses that the "ultimate goal" of water management is to increase farm output — a matter which is sometimes lost sight of in China as elsewhere when the linkages are weak between professional project management and end users.

14. The guidelines appear to provide fewer personnel per unit area served than in Taiwan, widely known for its successful water management. In 1966, Taiwan's 26 irrigation associations employed 4,126 persons, about 60 percent of them technical and 40 percent administrative, to serve 505,000 hectares (7.5 million mou). This works out to 5.6 employees per 10,000 mou, a density recommended in the PRC guidelines only for the smallest irrigation districts. In addition, the PRC guidelines call for a much smaller technical component, 30 to

40 percent, with the goal being to reduce even this proportion.

For Taiwan, see L. T. Chin, "Irrigation Associations," in Food and Agriculture Organization, Farm Water Management Seminar, Manila, Irrigation and Drainage Paper #12 (Rome: FAO, 1972), pp. 243-253.

15. Two such campaign periods of particular interest were 1963-65, under the first "readjustment" policy (the second "readjustment of the national economy" began in 1979), and in 1973-74. All of the case studies here, except for the relatively political tract on Chairman Hua in Shaoshan (Reading 4), were published in the latter period. Many of the other materials are from the earlier period (Readings 1, 2, and 11).

More recently, there has been renewed concern with improving economic management in general, and as before, this is occasionally applied to water management in particular. For example, Renmin ribao (People's Daily), March 20, 1977, p. 1, presented the example of a Shandong xian which "joins professional organs and mass management, scientifically manages water, rationally uses it, and thoroughly develops the effectiveness of existing water control." The newspaper notes that "their experience merits serious attention."

16. In 1963, it was claimed that as much as 100 million mou (ca. 7 million ha.) could be brought under irrigation through improved management of existing facilities. Renmin ribao, December 13, 1963, p. 2. The same article called on irrigation districts and irrigation and drainage stations to become self-sufficient in funds within one or two years.

17. Joe S. Bain, Richard E. Caves, and Julius Margolis, in Northern California's Water Industry (Baltimore: Johns Hopkins, 1966), deal in great extent with the inefficiencies of water development and use in a highly developed part of the world.

18. This term was used in an article on Meichuan in Kexue shiyan (Scientific Experiment), April 1976, pp. 23-25. Another article on Meichuan appeared in Renmin ribao, March 23, 1973, p. 3.

19. After Shaoshan, Hua directed the construction of the Ouyang Hai Irrigation Project in southern Hunan. Although

slightly smaller in irrigated area than Shaoshan, Ouyang Hai was technically and administratively more demanding than its predecessor. Its key installation is China's first double curvature, thin arch concrete dam. This was an advanced, state-of-the-art design pioneered by the Italians and the French. While it saves on labor and materials, it requires the use of a computer for stress analysis. Nickum, *Hydraulic Engineering*, p. 40.

Ouyang Hai was built in late 1966 and 1967, a political whipsaw period involving succeeding waves of "economism" and economic nihilism, but Hua kept the project going on schedule. See *Hua zhuxi zai Hunan* (Chairman Hua in Hunan) (Beijing: Renmin Press, May 1977), pp. 36-46.

In contrast to the primacy given to Hua's direction of water works construction in domestic publicity, Michel Oksenberg and Sai-cheung Yeung devote but a single paragraph of their extensive article, "Hua Kuo-feng's Pre-Cultural Revolution Hunan Years, 1949-66: The Making of a Political Generalist," *The China Quarterly* (*CQ*), No. 69, March 1977, pp. 3-53, to Hua's direction of the Shaoshan Project (p. 49). They do not mention the Ouyang Hai Project at all.

20. Yu is said to have founded the first prehistoric dynasty, the Xia, in 2205 B.C. According to Sima Qian, Yu "was active, obliging, capable, diligent... (and) he restricted his clothing and his food, while he displayed an extreme piety towards the divine powers." Cited in Marcel Granet, *Chinese Civilization* (New York: Meridian Books, 1958), p. 16.

While the analogy should not be pressed too far, similar virtues are claimed for Hua Guofeng.

The political significance of water in the past may be seen etymologically in the presence of the water radical ( 氵 ) in the character 治 (*zhi*), which means "to control, manage, or bring order to." *Zhi* appears in the term for politics, 政治 (*zhengzhi*).

21. Hunan has 50 to 60 million *mou* under cultivation, with a total irrigated area of approximately 40 million *mou*. After a decade of expansion, the Shaoshan Irrigation District appears

to have reached its designed irrigated area of 1 million mou (67,000 ha.).

As late as the summer of 1976, the irrigated area claimed for Shaoshan was 800,000 to 830,000 mou (e.g., Reading 5). Soon thereafter, however, 1 million mou became the standard reporting figure, as in Reading 4. This upgrading may have been partly political, to help boost the new Chairman Hua. Reading 2 indicates that districts serving 1 million mou and above are in a separate category from smaller units.

On the other hand, the difference does not seem to be one of "large" versus "medium." Minister of Water Conservancy Qian Zhengying indicated in 1979 that a "large" irrigation system serves over 20,000 hectares (300,000 mou). By her standard, Shaoshan easily qualifies as a large district and is probably one of the largest two or three dozen in China.

22. To some degree, the overlap of prefectural boundaries may be due to Shaoshan's construction under provincial aegis. The core of the project appears to lie wholly within Xiangtan Prefecture, with extensions into other regions tacked on. For example, the headworks lie just inside Xiangtan, but an upstream "reservoir district" in adjoining Shaoyang Prefecture has been appended to the irrigation district.

23. Benedict Stavis, People's Communes and Rural Development in China, RLG No. 2 (Ithaca, N.Y.: Rural Development Committee, Cornell University, November 1974), p. 47.

24. Shi Ji, Vol. 29, Book on Rivers and Canals. This passage is cited in Chi Ch'ao-ting, pp. 75-76, although here I have abridged and retranslated it (with the generous help of Grace Wan).

25. O. J. Todd, Two Decades in China, pp. 131-136 et passim.

26. The 1958 winter water use plan of the Jinghui Canal is presented in Guan'gai jihua yongshui shili (Examples of Planned Water Use in Irrigation) (Beijing: Shuili dianli Press, June 1958), pp. 33-55. Its experiences in irrigating cotton are in Nongtian shuili yu shuitu baochi (Farmland Water Conservancy and Erosion Control), 1964, No. 1, pp. 19-21.

27. A more elaborate description of the allocation principles of Yinjing (Jinghui) is in Guan'gai jihua yongshui shili, pp. 46-52. Schematics are included for determining the supply to each main and branch canal during each watering based on the amount diverted at the canal head.

28. The stations, also called "distribution stations" (peishui zhan), are based on the physical layout of the canal and distribution gate systems, but they are not coterminous with the main or branch canals. In 1958 there were seven major and two minor stations (the latter including a pumping station on the feeder canal), but five main and ten branch canals. Each station and larger canal is listed in Guan'gai jihua yongshui shili, pp. 35-36.

29. This is indicated in Guan'gai jihua yongshui shili, p. 52: "If unusual conditions are encountered, in order to guarantee an increase in crop output, a cooperative has the power [quan] flexibly to distribute water already given it. Under special conditions, a collective makes suggestions about the distribution between turnouts lying within its area, and the water management station may make alterations as long as it does not exceed the total water diverted. But it definitely cannot affect the irrigation of other collectives."

30. E.g., Doulonggang and Sanhe in Jiangsu, both described in Shuili guanli gongzuo jingyan huibian (Compilation of Experiences in Water Management Work) (Beijing: Shuili dianli Press, December 1973), pp. 100-105, 115-120.

31. A similar dual-purpose gate, governing 320,000 mou of farmland and with a staff of four, is the Zhujia Station Gate in Pingyang xian, Zhejiang, described in Shuili guanli gongzuo jingyan huibian, pp. 106-114.

32. Agro-Economic Unit of Shandong Provincial Economic Research Unit, "Yikao laodong jilei jinxing nongtian shuili deng jiben jianshe" (Rely on Labor Accumulation to Carry Out Capital Construction of Farmland, Water Conservancy, etc.), Jingji yanjiu (Economic Studies), September 1965.

33. Jiangfengkou raises and sells piglets to individual households. Although pig raising is predominantly a private

activity, breeding is frequently done by the collective or state. The provision of shoats is sometimes tied to a commitment on the part of the purchasing household to sell the grown animal in the state marketing channels.

34. The breach is mentioned, not surprisingly, in nearly every Communist piece on the Yellow River and independently in O. Edmund Clubb, 20th Century China (New York and London: Columbia University Press, 1964), pp. 224-225. The closure is discussed in E. B. Vermeer, Water Conservancy and Irrigation in China (Leiden: Leiden University Press, 1977), pp. 16-19. The closure was done under the direction of O. J. Todd and the UNRRA (personal communication from Grace Wan).

For a brief description of the present dikes at Huayuankou, see Nickum, Hydraulic Engineering, pp. 82-83.

For overall discussions of water management in the Yellow River basin see Greer, Water Management, and Cheng Xuemin, "Water Resources Planning of the Yellow River," paper presented to the Workshop on Water Resources Planning: Experiences in a Regional and National Context, Rome, 1979 (mimeo).

35. This implies that the prefectural level is also involved. Almost all the northern dikes lie within Xinxiang, except for a few kilometers in eastern Henan which are in Anyang Prefecture. The southern dikes lie in Zhengzhou and Kaifeng Municipalities and Kaifeng Prefecture.

Wuzhi's poor performance may have been tolerated because, at least along the Yellow River, the northern dikes are set back farther from the river and are less likely to be tested by the stream than are the southern ones.

36. This sort of sharing by different administrative levels of the proceeds from new agricultural ventures is not often reported, but may be a quite common method which higher levels have used to accumulate funds via de facto taxation. Twenty percent of the crop grown on a reclaimed riverbed in Lin xian, Henan, was to go to the commune level, which "operated it jointly" with its production teams. Nickum, Hydraulic Engineering, p. 88.

37. Nickum, Hydraulic Engineering, p. 83.

38. Nickum, Hydraulic Engineering, p. 28, and FBIS, July 10, 1979, p. L 22.

For grain output estimates, see Kenneth R. Walker, "Grain Self-sufficiency in North China, 1953-75," CQ, No. 71, September 1977, pp. 555-590; and James E. Nickum, "Provincial Patterns of Grain Output in China, 1957-1975" (mimeo.).

39. The area each well irrigates depends on a number of factors, including the number of wells in a given area. See, for example, Pingyuan jing guanqu dixia shui kaifa liyong (The Exploitation and Utilization of Groundwater in Plains Well Irrigation Districts) (Beijing: Kexue Press, 1977), p. 27 et passim.

Pinggu's wells, usually 80 to 120 meters, are deeper than the average.

40. Nongyong jijing (Mechanized Wells for Rural Use) (Beijing: Shuili dianli Press, 1974), p. 206.

41. Henan's agricultural scientists are quoted as having said, "If we also add the necessary ancillary projects to the more than 110,000 mechanically operated wells, the province's irrigation area could be increased by 40 million mou (2.6 million ha.). This is a very large figure, equivalent to two-thirds of the province's existing irrigated area." FBIS, March 12, 1979, p. H 1.

42. "Ziliu guan, zhendi zhan, jijing guan, youji zhan." The quote continues: "[wells provide] suitable timing and quantity and are very convenient, and they lower the water table to prevent salinity and alkalinity." Pingyuan jing guanqu, p. 25.

The same source, on pp. 24-25, enumerates why exclusive reliance on canal irrigation, as is the case in the Henan and Shondong Yellow River diversion districts, creates difficulties of timing, saline-alkalinity, insufficiency, and seasonal variation in supply. On the other hand, it notes, exclusive reliance on wells usually provides insufficient water, causes the water table to subside and is expensive.

43. He Zhi, in "Shui ziyuan di heli kaifu liyong jidai jiejue" (What Urgently Needs To Be Resolved in the Rational Exploita-

tion and Use of Water Sources), Guangming ribao (Guangming Daily), September 14, 1979, p. 4, complains about the growing and wasteful use of water for urban and industrial purposes. He criticizes the lack of a (comprehensive) law on water sources and the resultant "anarchistic" scramble for water.

Problems of tight urban water supply are noted in FBIS, November 29, 1979, pp. R 4-5 (Beijing) and pp. T 1-2 (Xian).

44. Anthony Bottrall, "Comparative Study of the Management and Organization of Irrigation Projects," ODI Irrigation Management Workshop, September 1976 (mimeo.), p. 13.

A more extensive treatment of some of the points in this conclusion may be found in James E. Nickum, "Chinese Water Management in Comparative Perspective," paper presented to ASPAC 79, Evergreen State College, Olympia WA, June 16, 1979 (mimeo.).

45. Martin E. Abel, "Irrigation Systems in Taiwan: Management of a Decentralized Public Enterprise," Water Resources Research, Vol. 12, No. 3, June 1976, pp. 341-348.

46. A. F. Bottrall, "Evolution of Irrigation Associations in Taiwan," Agricultural Administration, Vol. 4, No. 4, October 1977, pp. 245-250.

Taiwan's evolutionary process took a new turn in the 1970s, when the irrigation associations faced a fiscal crunch. The government amalgamated the 24 associations into 16; appointed association chairmen and "temporarily" suspended the member-elected representative councils; reduced staff numbers; and dispensed large grants to reduce outstanding debt and to repair and rehabilitate facilities. Fung Chung-Yue, "Water Resources Activities in Taiwan, 1968-1978," Industry of Free China, Vol. 52, No. 1, July 1979, pp. 23-24.

# I Introductory Readings

# Reading 1

# INTRODUCTION TO *IRRIGATION MANAGEMENT**

## Section 1. The General Condition of Farmland Water Management in China

Farmland water conservancy activity in China has had a long history, and the working people of the past have left behind many valuable legacies. The various kinds of gravity-flow irrigation projects diverting water from the rivers and lakes, the dikes and dams in the rice fields of the South, the water wells of the various North China provinces, and the pit-wells and suspended water-conveyors of the Northwest have all played a positive role. The construction of farmland water conservancy projects, however, only lays a good foundation for increases in farm output; irrigation management is required to make them effective. At the same time, in the process of management, it is necessary continually to improve the conditions of irrigation in order continually to upgrade water conservancy standards. In old China, quite a few water conservancy projects were built, but even so, because of the limitations of the social system, not only was the rate of construction slow, but their management was particularly poor. For example, in

*"Gailun." Guan'gai guanli [Irrigation Management], Beijing, 1965, pp. 1-6.

some irrigation districts along the Yellow River, management merely consisted of diverting water into the fields, and ordinarily no control works were set up at the canal headworks. The amount of water intake merely followed the changes in the water level of the river. At the canal headworks of some of the large-scale irrigation districts, water intake gates were subsequently added, but the main and lateral canals still lacked control facilities. Moreover there were no water utilization plans. The loss of irrigation water was serious, the groundwater table rose, and the salinization area increased from year to year.

During the period of reactionary Guomindang rule before liberation a small number of farmland water conservancy projects were built, such as the Jinghui Canal and the Weihui Canal in Shaanxi Province. On the whole, however, there was more damage than construction. Even the original projects were often gradually abandoned. In individual districts, there sometimes existed a management system and a set of regulations, but under the reactionary regime, these basically could not be implemented. In management organization, water rights were entirely controlled by the bureaucrats, landlords, and local despots, and the distribution of water was very unfair and unreasonable. In water allocation the contradictions between the upper and lower reaches during periods of water shortage were always very acute, and armed fights often broke out. There was also no scientific irrigation system for calculating water usage, and figures for irrigation water could only be approximated. Irrigation techniques were even less well studied. In the great majority of cases, flood irrigation was used. The large applications of water, with extensive cultivation and poorly leveled land, resulted in great water losses. In some irrigation districts, the water table gradually rose and even reached the critical water level or higher. In farmland water conservancy projects, the collapse of canal banks, the silting up of canals, and the destruction of structures were quite widespread. Thus, even though historically quite a few projects were built, few were actually passed on to later generations, and even when they were preserved, the areas they served became smaller and smaller.

After liberation, under the leadership of the Party and Chairman Mao, water conservancy, like other construction, developed with great speed. During the period of national economic recovery from 1950 to 1952, on the one hand, there was rapid restoration of the irrigation projects which had not been repaired for years and of those which were damaged during the war, thus eliminating the monopoly which the landlord class had on water conservancy and doing away with the bad feudal management customs. On the other hand, a series of new water conservancy projects was built. Moreover, in 1952, following the great victory in land reform, the first upsurge in water conservancy construction occurred. Between 1953 and 1957, China carried out its First Five-Year Plan for the development of the national economy. During this period, construction began on many large-scale, modern irrigation projects, as well as on several tens of thousands of small-scale canals, wells, and ponds. Large quantities of irrigation machinery and other water-lifting implements were developed. Old canal systems were also repaired, expanded and reconstructed. In addition, a large number of on-field projects and management measures were added and fixed up. Planned irrigation water utilization was progressively extended along the main and branch canals of the Luohui Canal Irrigation District, Shaanxi Province, the three main canals of the Erling Irrigation District, Jiangsu Province, and the key subbranch canals of the Huangyang Canal, Gansu Province. During this period, the water utilization plans of the various irrigation districts generally covered only water diversion and water allocation. Moreover, they distributed water to the feeder canals according to the sown crop acreage and the general water requirements for different periods. They could not, however, formulate a comparatively comprehensive water utilization plan according to the use of water by the basic levels. Beginning in 1956, some irrigation districts began selecting key branch and subbranch canals for carrying out a two-level water allocation plan for those branch and subbranch canals and for the entire system.

The progressive extension of planned water utilization preliminarily overcame such backward irrigation techniques as flood irrigation with large amounts of water and irrigating only in the daytime. By the end of the First Five-Year Plan (1957), some areas were already carrying out furrow irrigation for row crops, most areas were carrying out border irrigation for densely planted crops, and a portion of the rice-growing area was using frequent, shallow irrigation. All of these constituted a material base for good irrigation management. Furthermore, beginning in 1952, individual localities (such as Linfen xian, Shanxi Province) began to establish irrigation experimentation stations in order to ascertain the laws of water requirements for crops and the proper irrigation systems and irrigating techniques, so as to achieve scientific water utilization and soil improvement and thereby obtain high and stable yields. These stations not only experimented on such major crops as rice, wheat and cotton, but also huma, rape, tobacco and sugar beets. The number of experimental items gradually increased, and the results of these experiments were promoted as models, thereby increasing output to varying degrees.

In organizational management, the water conservancy departments [ting] or bureaus [ju] of the provinces throughout the country generally set up specialized organs for irrigation management. Some areas improved management organization. At the same time, all localities successively set up and strengthened basic-level watering organizations.

Concurrently, areas throughout the country accumulated practical experience in the management of the canals and the canal system structures, from the observation of the principal farmland water conservancy projects to their regular maintenance and repair and the control of operations all the way to emergency repairs.

Beginning in 1958, China entered its Second Five-Year Plan construction period. Under the brilliant radiance of the General Line, large-scale water conservancy construction was carried out in the two successive years of 1958 and 1959. During this period the irrigated area grew markedly, the area with planned water utilization expanded a great deal, and many mass experimentation stations were combined with these to form a set of station networks. After 1960 some comprehensive water conservancy and soil improvement experimentation stations were set up. During this period there were new developments in water irrigation techniques and irrigations systems, resulting in the accumulation of many new experiences.

After 1959, China experienced three successive years of severe drought and natural disaster, and the existing water conservancy and irrigation projects played a tremendous role in combating them and reducing the degree of damage. During this period, the Party Central Committee adopted a series of measures to restore and increase agricultural production. Work was also carried out on farmland water conservancy projects under the direction of the eight character guideline, "tiaozheng, gonggu, chongshi, tigao" [readjustment, consolidation, filling out and raising standards]. After 1962, agricultural output climbed steadily and farmland water activity developed accordingly. The irrigated area rose gradually. With respect to the scientific and technological aspects of irrigation projects, the work of scientific analysis and summing up to raise standards was continually carried out through practice. Management was also strengthened greatly after being reorganized. Henceforth, with the continual increase in the degree of water conservancy, electrification, and mechanization in agriculture, agricultural output and farmland water conservancy will certainly move forward at a faster pace. The demands on canal system management will also increase gradually. This is the glorious but difficult task of farmland water management workers.

## Section 2. The Tasks and Content of Farmland Water Management Work

The construction of farmland water conservancy projects provides the material conditions for resisting drought and natural disaster. In order fully to utilize water resources and project facilities so as to improve the soil and achieve the goal of increased agricultural output, our management work should be done properly on the basis of existing projects. Thus it has always been considered an important principle in the development of China's water conservancy since liberation that "construction and management are of equal importance," and it has been strongly advocated that after any single site is built, it should be managed and utilized well, and continually consolidated to yield good results.

Farmland water conservancy management work includes three main aspects: water use management, project management, and organizational management.

Water use management is the core of management. Its main tasks are: to coordinate arrangements for agricultural production with technical measures for crops so as to obtain a rational allocation of water in accordance with the laws governing the water requirements for agricultural crops and the demands of water conservancy and soil improvement, together with conditions such as irrigation water sources and projects; to organize in a timely manner on-field irrigation and drainage work; to provide favorable soil moisture conditions for crop growth and soil improvement; and at the same time to raise the rate of water utilization and conserve on the amount of water, so as to expand the irrigated area and also to control changes in the water table in order to prevent soil deterioration as well as to improve saline-alkali soil and soil which has become marshy.

The importance of water use management can be seen from the above tasks. In general, the contents of water use management are as follows:

1. Planned water utilization. "Planned water utilization" means to formulate and implement water use plans in accordance with irrigation water sources, project conditions, arrangements for agricultural production, and agricultural technology. The water use plans involve the rational arrangement of water diversion from the canal headworks, water conveyance, water allocation, the timing of water diversion, the se-

quence of water allocation, and the timing of irrigating. The formulation of water use plans must be linked to the actual conditions. The documents, tables and charts which are drawn up must be simple and easy to understand so the broad masses can easily grasp them.

2. Canal system water measurement. The aim here is to guarantee accurate implementation of the water use plans and to provide reliable data for their formulation. Through water measurement, it is possible to regulate and control the quantity of water in accordance with the stipulations of the water use plans and the directives of the water allocating organizations, to accurately divert and convey water from its sources to the fields according to fixed quotas, and to check the quality of irrigation water and the efficiency of irrigation, guiding and improving water utilization work. In addition, water measurement provides data for design and scientific research.

3. Reduction of water loss in the canals to increase the utilization rate of irrigation water. A portion of the water which is diverted from the source to the field is consumed in field irrigation for crop growth, while another portion is lost. Often the latter is proportionally very great. Thus it is very important to reduce water losses in the canals in order to increase the utilization rate of irrigation water. The chief measures to implement this include rotational irrigation, improvement of irrigating techniques, strict control of water quantity, and adopting additional measures to prevent canal seepage.

4. Irrigation experimentation. To provide scientific data for the accurate formulation and implementation of planned water utilization and other management work, experimental research work should be carried out according to the individual characteristics of the irrigation districts on irrigation, drainage, the improvement of saline-alkali soil, and so on. The larger irrigation districts may also set up special organs for experimentation.

The main tasks of project management are: to guarantee the completion and rational operation of projects, to extend the operational lifetime of projects, and to promote and expand the effectiveness of projects. At the same time, through project management, it is possible to check out the correctness and quality of the original project program, design, and construction operations. Moreover, it provides reliable data for subsequent improvement and new construction of projects. The main contents of management are:

1. The rational operation of the projects. This includes the formulation and implementation of the annual control and operations plans for the projects. When formulating the operations plan for a project, each year it is necessary to formulate an annual operations plan according to concrete conditions, and on the basis of the original plan and a summing-up of the operations of the previous year. In addition, it is also necessary to draw up operations standards for the management of the projects and to set up a card file system on the structures.

2. The observation of hydraulic structures. The purpose is to guarantee rational operation of the projects. Through the observation of its structures, it is possible to stay informed of a project's condition and its laws of change so that it can be operated rationally, scientifically and economically. At the same time, reliable data can be provided for design and construction.

3. Project maintenance. The purpose is mainly to maintain the projects in good condition, to restore their functions, and to prevent them from being subject to damage or allowing damaged conditions to worsen. This involves inspection, maintenance [yanghu] and repairs at fixed intervals. The purpose of inspecting the projects is to understand their operation and their damaged conditions in order to provide the basis for their repair. Maintenance on the damaged parts of projects is a regular activity. Such repairs prevent the occurrence of accidents. The repairs at fixed intervals and the silt-removal work are carried on in an overall fashion, mostly during the intervals between irrigations and between farming operations.

4. The improvement and rebuilding of projects. With the continuous rise in production levels, existing project facilities may not be able to satisfy the needs of production, or the original projects may have contained defects in their planning,

design or construction. Thus improvement and rebuilding must be undertaken during the management stage.

The main tasks of organizational management are to rely on the poor and lower-middle peasant masses under the leadership of the Party and thoroughly carry out the Party's policies; to organize the masses and develop their activism and creativity; to utilize fully and rationally the various facilities of the irrigation districts to carry out water utilization management and project management effectively; and in addition, to raise continually the quality of management in order to expand continuously the irrigated area and thus cause agricultural crops to attain high and stable yields. The main features of this are:

1. The building of a strong management structure at every level. According to the size of the irrigation district and the Party's policies with regard to "being industrial as well as agricultural," a strong management structure must be established at every level. The management structure should rely on the broad masses and, in accordance with the concrete conditions of the irrigation districts, set up various management rules and regulations and formulate plans for production and finance. It should be responsible for carrying out related Party and government policies and technical measures and, using water scientifically, maintain project facilities. In order to facilitate management and make it relate closely to the masses served, it is necessary to rely on the poor and lower-middle peasant masses benefited to build up a mass democratic management organization representing water using units in the irrigation districts. This organization is to study and discuss the major problems of the work of the irrigation districts, and to supervise the personnel of the management organs in the execution of their duties. As for the small-scale projects operated by the masses themselves, a management organization from among the poor and lower-middle peasant masses served should be created.

2. Management of facilities. The purpose is to facilitate the implementation of water utilization management and proj-

ect management. The main facilities include: communications facilities, water measurement equipment, groundwater survey equipment, management roads, management buildings, experimentation stations, and other auxiliary equipment. This equipment must be subject to continual improvement.

3. The management of enterprises. Mass irrigation districts must become self-reliant and use the canal to sustain the canal. State-operated irrigation districts must become both industrial and agricultural. They must be economical in all expenditures, exercise diligence and thrift in water conservancy operations, and carry out economic accounting. They must reduce the amount of water-fee payments and accumulate capital for the state. In addition, they must carry out investigative and statistical work for the irrigation districts and fully understand the conditions of the irrigation districts in order to provide the basis for good management of the irrigation districts. The management organization must strengthen ideological work and carry on class education and socialist education among their personnel to elevate their consciousness. It must develop evaluative competitions and encourage the management personnel and irrigation personnel to be enthusiastic about labor so that management can be done well.

*Reading 2*

# ORGANIZATIONAL MANAGEMENT AND MANAGEMENT OF FACILITIES*

After a large number of farmland water conservancy projects have been built, they should be well utilized and managed. As proven by experiences already gained in the various areas, the key to effective management lies first in setting up a professional management structure, a strong management organization, and a clearly defined management system, and in implementing management by different levels under unified leadership. At the same time, the management of farmland water conservancy projects is directly related to the production and livelihood of the peasants. It also involves a great deal of work. Thus, in accordance with the principle of the coordination of professional organizations with mass organizations, project management committees should be set up, as well as such mass organizations as conferences of delegates of the irrigation districts, in order to help the professional management structure develop the various aspects of its work.

## Section 1. The Management System

Before setting up and strengthening the management struc-

*"Zuzhi guanli yu guanli sheshi." Chapter 2 of Guan'gai guanli [Irrigation Management], Beijing, 1965, pp. 7-13.

ture, it is necessary to clearly define the management system. At present, China's management system is roughly as follows:

In an irrigation district, there is unified leadership and management by different levels according to the area benefited, the scale of the project, and its degree of importance. In accordance with the size of the area benefited and convenience of management, it is decided whether newly built irrigation districts are managed by the state or by the commune sector. The decision about whether an irrigation district which has been handed down through history should be managed by the commune sector or by the state is generally made in accordance with the size of the area benefited and its historical customs.

For state-managed irrigation districts which service areas within a single hsien, district, or province, the respective hsien, district, or province will set up a separate management organization. When the areas benefited cross hsien, district, or provincial boundaries, when the area served is within one region but the irrigation district is comparatively large and the relationships involved are comparatively important, then the next higher level sets up a structure responsible for management, or the various units served, under the direct leadership of the next higher level, organize a joint structure responsible for management. When the area benefited by an irrigation district which is managed by the commune sector crosses commune lines, the relevant communes organize a joint management structure subject to the leadership of the xian. When the area benefited is within one commune, the commune sets up a special structure to be responsible for management. When the area served crosses brigade lines, then under the leadership of the commune, the relevant brigades [dui] organize a joint management structure to carry out management.

The irrigation district sets up a management structure with unified leadership and unified management for the entire project system. Thus, reservoirs of under 10 million cubic meters which are used mainly for irrigation generally can have unified management by a special management structure of the irrigation district. Large- and medium-sized reservoirs of over 10 million cubic meters may be managed separately from their irrigation districts, but under the right conditions, a unified management structure may also be set up. The management of sluice gates and culverts in dikes is generally unified under the management structure where the dike is located. The management of hydraulic engineering works and systems, such as dikes, canals, sluice gates and dams, is the responsibility of the water conservancy departments. No department is allowed to build projects on the canals or to damage or obstruct the normal operation of the projects without the approval of the water conservancy department in charge.

With respect to the organizational leadership of the state-managed irrigation districts, the administrative functions of their professional management structure (including personnel management, financial management, project inspections and observation, maintenance management, keeping informed of water conditions, the control of operations, production management, and so on) should be under the leadership of a higher-level department. Their political thought work and the organizational relationship with the Party and Youth League is under the leadership of the local Party committee. The functional leadership departments help the Party committee strengthen ideological education work.

## Section 2. Management Organization and Staffing

### 1. The Professional Management Structure

The professional management structure is the administrative unit which concretely carries out the management operations and implements the Party's policies, as well as the directives from higher-level organizations. In the past several years, China has gained a certain amount of experience in building a sound organizational structure for irrigation-district management. In general, irrigation-district management staffing is roughly as follows:

Irrigation districts with effectively irrigated areas of more than a million mou [67,000 ha.] establish a management bureau. The total number of personnel (not including professional maintenance crews, as below) is from one to three persons for every 10,000 mou.

For irrigation districts with effectively irrigated areas of between 100,000 and a million mou, a management bureau or station [chu] is set up. The total number of personnel is from two to four persons for every 10,000 mou.

For irrigation districts with effectively irrigated areas of between 10,000 and 100,000 mou, a management station or office [suo] is established. The total number of personnel is from three to eight persons for every 10,000 mou.

In the above staffing, the technical cadres should constitute 30-40 percent of the total number of cadres, and engineers should be allotted for 200,000 mou or more.

Irrigation districts of less than 10,000 mou should also establish a professional management structure, or else have professional personnel for year-round management.

The personnel of the irrigation experimentation stations and the professional project maintenance crews in the irrigation districts are not included in the staffing mentioned above, but may be allotted additionally in accordance with actual requirements.

The management personnel needed for the electromechanical equipment in electrified and mechanized irrigation districts are similarly not included in the above staffing.

The staffing of the professional management structure in the irrigation districts must be appropriately adjusted in accordance with concrete situations and the complexity of the tasks, the level of management personnel, and the water utilization experience of the peasants. In addition, one must carry out the guidelines of "being industrial as well as agricultural" and effect a gradual reduction of full-time personnel.

The irrigation district hydrologic stations are responsible for regular testing and the development of information and forecasts which directly serve management. If an irrigation district hydrologic station has already been incorporated into the state network of basic stations, then it is regulated by the hydrologic departments. The hydrologic stations used exclusively in the irrigation districts are regulated by the management departments, with the hydrologic departments responsible for technical guidance. Their staffing is separate from that mentioned above.

The powers and functions of the professional management structure of the irrigation districts are: Under the leadership of higher-level Party committees, to implement the Party and state policies and strive in every way to effectively manage and utilize water conservancy facilities; to unify water quantity regulation and control the operation of project facilities; to unify the formulation of programs for the repair, improvement, and expansion of the projects; and to carry out the resolutions of the conferences of delegates of the irrigation districts. Its tasks are: inspection and survey to ascertain the conditions of the project work; maintenance, to preserve the good condition of the projects and continually improve project facilities; controlling operations to continually raise the water utilization rate and fully develop the effectiveness of the projects; implementing rational methods of irrigation and coordinating them with other agricultural measures to improve the soil and increase output; and conducting experimentation, research, and summarization of experience in order continually to raise the level of management.

In accordance with the tasks of the professional management structure of the irrigation districts, the actual content of the work is as follows:

1) To take over project management and related data files from the construction departments and also to collect relevant data from the survey and design departments;

2) To formulate and carry out management plans and systems of regulations;

3) To carry out the necessary inspection, survey, and experimental research;

4) To carry out regular maintenance and renovation and reinforcement of the projects at fixed intervals, and continually improve the projects to broaden their effectiveness;

5) To formulate and implement the plans for the control and operation of the projects;

6) To formulate and implement the irrigation water use plans, to organize and lead the units benefited by benefited by the irrigation districts to level the land and arrange their strip checks,* to make rational use of water, to promote advanced irrigating techniques and engage in soil improvement, and to prevent the soil in the irrigation districts from becoming saline or marshy;

7) To carry out the work of flood prevention, drainage, and the removal of excess surface water;

8) To organize and carry out the work of spreading greenery and erosion prevention in the areas surrounding the reservoirs and adjacent to the canal embankments and structures;

9) To organize production management;

10) To levy water fees;

11) To carry out protection and security work to guarantee the safety of the projects;

12) To set up and maintain custody over files and compile records of major events; and

13) To train basic-level cadres and workers and to carry on publicity and educational work among the masses.

The professional management structure of an irrigation district should be planned and set up during the construction period of the project. During the planning and establishment period, this body should acquaint itself with the conditions of the projects and participate in the work of inspection and survey of project quality and in the installation and survey of the

---

*Qi, bordered rectangular plots used for densely planted dry crops. Irrigation using strip checks is called border irrigation (qi guan). — J. E. N.

equipment. Furthermore, in coordination with the design and construction departments, standards for the management of the projects should be formulated in order to have good production management.

## 2. The Democratic Management Organizations and Basic Water Use Organizations of the Irrigation Districts

The management of the irrigation districts should implement the principle of coordination between the professional management structure and the mass organizations. Thus the irrigation district, in addition to the professional management structure, should set up democratic management organizations of the beneficiary poor and lower-middle peasants, such as irrigation district conferences of delegates, irrigation management committees, and basic level organizations such as branch and subbranch canal committees. The irrigation district management committees should include representatives of the agricultural departments.

At present, the democratic management organizations in the various parts of China do not have the same organizational forms, even within the same province. This is due to the differences and lack of uniformity in the actual conditions of these areas. Nevertheless the differences are not great. Take, for example, the democratic management organizations of the various irrigation districts in Hanzhong Prefecture, Shaanxi Province. Before 1963, the irrigation management committees were for the most part divided into the following three levels: the canal system irrigation committee, the committees of the management stations (that is, the management stations set up under the state-operated canal management bureau), and the subbranch canal (or weir) affairs committees. The management below the subbranch canal was the direct responsibility of the production brigade. On the other hand, in Fanglaizhuo Irrigation District of Baoding Prefecture and Baiquan Irrigation District of Xingtai Prefecture in Hebei Province the democratic management or-

organizations before 1963 for the most part were the irrigation district management committee (also called the conference of delegates), the main and branch canal committees, and the production brigade water conservancy committees or water conservancy sections [gu].

The main tasks of the mass democratic management organizations, on the whole, are: convening meetings at fixed intervals to study and discuss relevant matters of importance such as project repairs, water utilization plans, canal system rebuilding, the levy of water fees, and the formulation of relevant contractual systems. The matters discussed and decided upon by the conferences of delegates and management committees are reported to higher-level leadership departments for approval and then implemented.

The professional irrigation crews, also called the professional watering crews, are the basic-level water utilization organizations of the mass management organizations. They play a very important role in management because they are the direct implementers of the water utilization plans, directly affecting the quality of watering. During the early period after liberation, the water utilization organizations of most of the irrigation districts in China were scattered and organized on a temporary basis. Subsequently, they were gradually developed into seasonal and even year-round irrigating organizations. Due to the development of agricultural cooperatives and the changes in production relations, the watering organizations also developed and changed. After the introduction of the communes, the water use organizations developed further and their organization improved, thus providing a good foundation for raising the quality of watering and the productivity of irrigation labor.

The watering organizations of the commune sector may basically be divided into two kinds:

1. The year-round professional irrigation crews.

During the irrigation season, the year-round professional irrigation crews are responsible for the irrigation of the farmland, and during the nonirrigation season, they take care of maintenance and, under certain conditions, can also develop sideline production. Most of these organizations are based on the production brigade and draw their personnel on a unified basis in accordance with the area benefited in each production team (generally one labor power for each 100-250 mou of land). The crews have a unified organization under the leadership of the brigade.

2. The seasonal professional irrigation crews.

The seasonal professional irrigation crews are under the leadership of the production brigades in some places, but others are under the direct leadership of the production teams. In addition to providing fixed personnel responsible for watering the farmland during the irrigation season, they immediately participate in agricultural production once the watering is concluded. That is, when the water comes, they water, and when it goes, they work on the farmland, being responsible for the watering but not canal repairs. This organizational form is now more common in irrigation districts.

The experience of the past few years proves that the year-round professional irrigation crews' tasks and responsibilities are clear and their professional thinking is stable. This helps raise the technical level of irrigation and facilitates effective maintenance work on the projects. Their watering efficiency is generally high. However, because the year-round professional irrigation crews are divorced from agricultural production for long periods, they gradually become estranged from the conditions of agriculture and cannot closely coordinate irrigation and agriculture, thus adversely affecting the quality of their watering. In addition, the fact that a portion of the labor force participates for a long time in the professional irrigation crews adversely affects the labor force needed for agricultural production. Therefore, this form has not yet been widely adopted.

The seasonal professional irrigation crews are not separated from agricultural production over long periods, so the quality of their watering is high. Because the jobs of their personnel change, however, their professional thinking is not stable, and generally their watering efficiency is lower. From the viewpoint of agricultural production and the results of the watering, the latter [group] is better. In order to overcome their defects, however, it is necessary before irrigation to do good work on their ideology and their organization.

## Section 3. Management of Facilities

The management of facilities in the irrigation districts generally includes communications facilities, water measurement equipment, groundwater survey equipment, management roads, administration buildings, experimentation stations, and other auxiliary equipment.

1. Communications equipment. The communications equipment of a canal system is indispensable for guaranteeing that all the work of the canal system will be smoothly implemented. Generally, the most common equipment is the telephone system. The management structure must have direct telephone connections within the irrigation district with the head canal section, every water allocation key point, the management stations, and the experimentation stations. It is best to employ the circuit arrangement for the telephone system to avoid interruptions and interference in making normal calls. In the state-operated irrigation districts of Shaanxi Province, an extension is usually set up for every 100,000-200,000 mou, the length of the telephone lines averaging 2-4 kilometers per 10,000 mou. In addition to the telephone, wireless radio communications may be installed when the irrigation district extends more than 100-150 kilometers. Such means of transport as the bicycle, the mule, and the automobile may also be considered part of the communications facilities.

2. Water measurement facilities. In order to ensure the correct implementation of the water utilization plans, there should be sufficient water measurement equipment along the canal system. China, in its main and branch canals, generally uses holes in sluice gates or other structures along the canal line (such as a culvert drop) to measure the flow. Special-

ized water measurement equipment is often installed in the subbranch, farm [nong], and field [mao] canals. Of these, the ladder-type measuring weirs, triangular weirs, and nozzles are the most extensively used. Except in certain individual canals, automatic water measurement equipment is not widely used.

3. Groundwater observation wells. In irrigation districts where the depth of the groundwater is less than 5-10 meters, it is necessary to carry out systematic observation. This is especially important in dry-crop irrigation districts. Groundwater observation wells are divided into baseline observation wells and ordinary observation wells. The baseline wells are used to study the movement of groundwater, the relationship between groundwater and surface water, the nature and direction of flow of subsurface runoff, and so on. The wells are distributed over representative sections of the ground. In general the distance between the baselines is 5-6 kilometers and the distance between wells along the baseline is 1-1.5 kilometers. The baseline should have between eight and fifteen observation wells. The ordinary wells are used to study the effect on groundwater of the irrigation and drainage of sections of land. Generally there may be one well for every 5,000 mou.

4. Management roads. To guarantee that communications will reach out in all directions within the irrigation district is a prerequisite for effective management. The management organization and all the production centers, communes, and residential centers in the irrigation district should have direct access roads. Ordinarily, the tops of main and branch canals are utilized to build a road for carts or automobiles, while on top of the subbranch canals pedestrian paths are built with widths of about 0.5-1.0 meter. In China's experience, the internal road system of the irrigation districts should usually occupy approximately 1-1.5 percent of the total area. The responsibility for road management and maintenance should be by sections to ensure that vehicles will have through passage all year long.

5. Administration buildings and other auxiliary facilities.

The majority of the buildings used by the management are gate buildings, storehouses, offices, dormitories, and so on. In accordance with how long they are utilized, they may be divided into two kinds: permanent and temporary. Management auxiliary facilities and equipment generally includes machine maintenance shops, mining sites for construction materials, carpentry shops, and various kinds of machinery for silt removal, weeding, and transport. These should be gradually strengthened in accordance with the management requirements and the scope of the irrigation districts.

6. Irrigation experimentation stations. In accordance with the needs and objective conditions of large and medium-sized irrigation districts, irrigation experimentation farms (stations) should be set up either individually or jointly with the agricultural scientific research organizations. Aiming at the main scientific and technical problems of present irrigation work, these irrigation experimentation farms (stations) should carry out experimental studies on the water requirements of crops, irrigation systems, irrigating techniques, soil improvement, and so on, in order to seek a scientific basis for increased production through irrigation, thus guiding production and accumulating scientific data.

# II Case Studies

NASA LANDSAT image, July 26, 1978 (band 7).

*Reading 3*

# MANAGEMENT OF THE MEICHUAN RESERVOIR IRRIGATION PROJECT

**Edited by the Bureau of Water Conservancy and Electric Power, Huanggang Prefecture, Hubei, and the Water Conservancy Planning Teaching and Research Section, Wuhan Water Conservancy and Electric Power Institute***

## Foreword

Meichuan Reservoir is situated on the Meichuan River approximately two kilometers north of the town of Meichuan in Guangji xian, Hubei. The Meichuan River has two main branches, one originating between the Henggang Mountains and Bali Cliff and the other in the southern foothills of the Henggang Mountains. The upper reaches encircle the perilous mountain peaks and ridges. The catchment area above the dam, in a hilly and mountainous region, totals 25 square kilometers.

The reservoir was begun in August 1957 and finished in January 1959. Key projects include the main dam, two auxiliary dams, a spillway, and water transport pipes. The main dam is an earth-fill type with a central clay core; it is 22 meters high and 910 meters long at the crest, with a total dam volume of 1.03 million cubic meters. The auxiliary dams have a total length of 290 meters; the larger is 12.5 meters high and has a volume of 98,000 cubic meters. The spillway is an open broad-top embankment 14 meters wide, with a maximum discharge capacity of 37.3 cubic meters per second [cms]. The

*Hubei sheng Huanggang diqu shuili dianli ju, Wuhan shuili dianli xueyuan shuili guihua jiaoyan shi, Meichuan shuiku guanqu di guanli (Beijing: Shuili dianli chubanshe, 1974).

pipes are round reinforced concrete with a diameter of 1.55 meters and a maximum discharge of 10 cms. The total capacity of the reservoir is 35 million cubic meters, with a beneficial capacity of 27 million cubic meters. The planned irrigated area is 70,000 mou [4,700 hectares].

Meichuan is a medium-sized reservoir. For the first several years after construction, due to the inadequacy of water sources, inadequate linkage and rounding out of the projects, and improper management, the reservoir only irrigated 30,000 to 40,000 mou of farmland, about 50 percent of the designed area. With a dozen or so years of continuously summing up experiences under the leadership of Party committees at various levels; conscientiously studying Chairman Mao's teachings on the general policy for the development of the national economy, "Take agriculture as the foundation and industry as the leading sector" and "Water conservancy is the lifeline of agriculture"; and thoroughly implementing the water conservancy policy of "Stress small-scale, ancillaries, and the commune sector doing it themselves," with arduous struggle and self-reliance, the revolutionary activism of the personnel of the reservoir and the broad masses of the irrigation district has been thoroughly aroused, and the irrigated area has been expanded continuously. By 1973, the irrigated area had reached 120,000 mou, 71 percent above the planned capacity. The grain yield throughout the district had surpassed the "Program" for four years in a row. In 1971, when there was a 70- to 80-day drought, the district's grain yield was 1,017 jin per mou [7.62 tons per hectare (t./ha.)]. In 1972, with rather little water in the reservoir, there was an 80-day drought, which was followed after the autumn by a continuous rain of 300 millimeters and an attack of insect pests on the late rice. In spite of this, the grain yield still reached 910 jin per mou [6.82 t./ha.].

The Reservoir Management Office has persisted in developing multiple operations while taking water as its main task, making great efforts to promote fish raising in the reservoirs and the ponds. The catch from the reservoir's 2,500 mou fish-breeding area was 107 jin per mou in 1971 and 108 jin per mou in 1972. On the 3,100 mou breeding area of ponds in the irrigation district, the catch averaged 337 jin per mou in 1971 and reached 419 jin per mou in 1973. The total yield of fresh fish from the reservoirs and ponds throughout the district in 1971 and 1972 alone was 2,396,000 jin [1,198 t.]. The personnel of the reservoir, with the precondition of persisting in using water to serve increases in farm output, have done a good job in running reservoir enterprises; they have emphasized fish raising and combined agriculture, forestry, animal husbandry, and fishery. They have attained self-sufficiency with a surplus in grain, cotton, oilseeds, and meat, thereby using the reservoir to support the reservoir in a self-reliant manner.

Chairman Mao teaches us: "Water conservancy is the lifeline of agriculture." The purpose of constructing waterworks is primarily to guarantee an increase in farm output. The Meichuan Reservoir project is not large in scale and its conditions are ordinary, but it has played an extremely large role in increasing farm output. In the past dozen or so years, they [Meichuan] have sought to sum up a set of beneficial experiences in good management and utilization of the project. Important among these are: by correctly and consistently adhering to the Party's "three-main" water conservancy policy and mobilizing the masses and relying on them, they have constructed an irrigation network with the Meichuan Reservoir at its core; by clearly establishing the thinking of serving increases in farm output, they allocate water rationally and use it scientifically; they pay serious attention to combining the control of water with the control of soil and mountains and combining farm water projects with farmland capital construction in order to create farmland capable of stable yields despite drought or flooding; they have developed a diversified economy while persisting in placing emphasis on water; and they have strengthened the Party's leadership and persisted in the mass line to construct, manage, and use the project well.

Heeding Chairman Mao's teaching that "we must conscientiously sum up our experiences," we stress summing up the water management experience of the Meichuan Reservoir Irrigation District. In the process of writing this book, comrades of the Water Conservancy Office of the Hubei Province Bureau of Water Conservancy and Electric Power, the Bureau of Water Conservancy and Electric Power of Guangji xian, Hubei, and the Meichuan Reservoir Management Office helped us examine [the manuscript] and gave us a number of valuable comments. For this we express our heartfelt thanks.

Bureau of Water Conservancy and Electric Power, Huanggang Prefecture, Hubei, and the Water Conservancy Planning Teaching and Research Section, Wuhan Water Conservancy and Electric Power Institute

December 1973

## I. ESTABLISHING AN IRRIGATION NETWORK

The Meichuan District lies entirely within a hilly and mountainous area. In the north there is the Henggang Mountain Range, with its majestic, uninterrupted row of peaks, bordering on Qichun xian. The eastern border is a low mountain area, including the Ling and Yue mountains, thrusting up among the hills in a line extending from north to south. The western and central portions of the district consist primarily of belts of rolling hills. The cultivated land there is fragmented and only in a long, narrow river valley strip 100-200 meters wide along both banks of the Meichuan River is the land relatively level. The southern border abuts the xian's Siwang qu.

The land throughout the entire district slopes generally from north to south. Aside from the Meichuan and Songyang rivers, there are many small brooks of a mountain-stream nature scattered among the hills and mountain slopes, resulting in a short, rapid flow from the water sources. [Formerly,] whenever there was a heavy rain, the mountain floods would come down in sheets, overflowing the field crops. Whenever it was clear for a number of days, the brooks would dry up and cease flowing.

Before liberation there were no water conservancy works in the district. Irrigation depended in the main on a series of isolated ponds which had been handed down through history and which had a low resistance to drought. A

Table 1

Meichuan Reservoir Irrigated Area and Output Increases

| Item / Amount / Year | 1959 | 1960 | 1961 | 1962 | 1963 | 1966 |
|---|---|---|---|---|---|---|
| Irrigated area (10,000 mou) | 4.5 | 5.0 | 8.5 | 9.3 | 9.3 | 9.6 |
| Grain yield (jin) | 503.1 | 591.6 | 547.7 | 687.1 | 753.7 | 811.4 |
| **Item / Amount / Year** | **1967** | **1970** | **1971** | **1972** | **1973** | |
| Irrigated area (10,000 mou) | 8.0 | 10.7 | 11.5 | 11.5 | 12.0 | |
| Grain yield (jin) | 769.4 | 871.0 | 1,017.0 | 910.0 | 1,026 | |

normal grain yield was only about 400 jin per mou [3.0 t./ha.].

The construction of the Meichuan Reservoir fundamentally changed the appearance of agricultural production in the irrigation district. Grain output has increased from year to year and has surpassed the "Program" for four years in a row (see Table 1). The area under irrigation has continually expanded from the originally designed 70,000 mou [4,700 ha.] to 120,000 mou [8,000 ha.].

Meichuan Reservoir is of medium scale with a beneficial capacity of only 27 million cubic meters, and in most years the amount of water averages only 16 million cubic meters. How have they [Meichuan] been able to produce such great benefits? One of their important experiences is that while managing and utilizing the Meichuan Reservoir, they have mobilized and relied on the masses to undertake in a big way small-scale farmland water conservancy; step-by-step they have constructed a melons-on-a-vine-style irrigation network of integrated large, medium, and small projects centered around Meichuan Reservoir and based on small reservoirs and ponds.

## 1. Analyze the Contradictions, Unify Knowledge

Meichuan Reservoir is situated on the upper reaches of the Meichuan River. The Meichuan is a mountain-stream-type river originating in the southern foothills of the Henggang Mountains. The Henggang Mountains are tall and steep, with surfaces composed mostly of wind-eroded sandstone. Before liberation, trees were sparse and the ground cover thin. This, plus uncontrolled tree felling, led to serious soil erosion. In consequence, the main flow in the Meichuan River in normal years was very small, and in years of drought, it was basically dry. The water flowing into the reservoir relies mainly on trapping the rainfall runoff in a catchment area of twenty-five square kilometers within the reservoir district. For many years, the average rainfall in the reservoir district has been 1,290 millimeters, and the average water inflow has been about 16 million cubic meters. The capacity of the reservoir is large relative to the inflow. In the fifteen years since 1958, the reservoir has been full in only two years (1971 and 1973). For four years, at the end of the irrigating season, the water remaining in the reservoir approached, or even fell below, the dead storage level, with water being pumped out of the reservoir for irrigation (see Table 2). Because of this, the masses called it the "empty belly" reservoir which was "not full for two years, and was used until it was dry in one."

The Meichuan Irrigation District has two main canals, the

Table 2

Meichuan Reservoir Water Use in the Past

| Year | Water released from reservoir (1,000 cu. m.) | Water remaining at end of irrigating season (1,000 cu. m.) | Days of continuous drought |
|---|---|---|---|
| 1959 | 16,400 | 3,870 | |
| 1960 | 9,910 | 9,860 | |
| 1961 | 17,420 | 3,000 (equals dead storage) | 80 |
| 1962 | 9,530 | 7,580 | |
| 1963 | 14,120 | 3,000 | 90 |
| 1964 | 14,510 | 3,760 | |
| 1965 | 7,690 | 6,550 | |
| 1966 | 16,400 | 500 (dead storage pumped) | 100 |
| 1967 | 16,500 | 4,420 | |
| 1968 | 13,100 | 1,900 | 90 |
| 1969 | 5,200 | 22,140 | |
| 1970 | 15,310 | 19,800 | |
| 1971 | 22,130 | 7,870 | 80 |
| 1972 | 10,470 | 5,200 (to July 31) | 80 |

East and West canals, which lead water directly from the reservoir for irrigation (see Figure 2). These canals meander from north to south and control the entire Meichuan River valley along with a portion of the hilly district in the west. The East Canal, thirty-one kilometers long, is located basically along the foothills. A large stretch of hilly land above the canal line cannot be irrigated by gravity. The West Canal, thirty kilometers long, circles the mountains in the region of Hongxing Commune, where the highlands must have water lifted to them for irrigation. After the canal reaches Nanchuan Commune, the canal line lies mostly along the top of the ridge and controls the land on both sides through gravity flow. Based on the flow of water into the reservoir, the two canals have a total designed irrigated acreage of 70,000 mou.

After the reservoir was constructed, the problem of irrigation was basically solved within the irrigation district, and grain output grew steadily. But there was still a large amount of hilly and mountain area both within and outside the irrigation district and within the reservoir district which was not irrigated and was vulnerable to drought, so the development of agricultural production over the entire district was very unbalanced. The Meichuan District has a total of 126,000 mou [8,400 ha.] of farmland, of which 106,000 mou [7,100 ha.] is irrigated paddy, entirely planted in double-crop rice. The dry land is mainly used to plant cotton and requires irrigation. Thus, the problem before the Meichuan Reservoir Management Office was to extend the irrigated acreage to solve the problem of irrigation throughout the entire district in order to make the agricultural output of the district exceed the "Program."*

According to many years of experimental data relating to paddy rice irrigation, a double rice crop requires about 500 cubic meters of water per mou per annum. If we drew up a balance based on the average of 16 million cubic meters of water contained by the reservoir, the 106,000 mou of paddy fields in the district could only receive an average of 150 cubic meters of water per mou. It is clear that there is no way to rely on a single Meichuan Reservoir to satisfy the water demands for irrigation throughout the entire district. Even if we limited ourselves to irrigating the reservoir's 70,000 mou, the use of water would be extremely strained. If the irrigated area were to be further enlarged, not only would the water be insufficient, but at the same time, the limitations of the existing projects and topographical conditions would be felt.

Having made clear the principal contradiction, how does one go about resolving it? The Party branch of the Meichuan Reservoir Management Office, heeding Chairman Mao's teaching that "to investigate is to solve problems," went out both within the irrigation district and beyond to carry out investigation and

*The "National Program for Agricultural Development" set grain yield targets of 400,500 and 800 jin/mou for different parts of the country. These targets were in use from 1960 to late 1980. — J. E. N.

study. They discovered that in the lower reaches of the West Canal, the masses had constructed on their own a small reservoir which stored 500,000 cubic meters of water, a small project with extensive water sources and high effectiveness. In 1961 there were eighty days of continuous drought, yet this reservoir enabled over 2,000 mou of farmland to yield a bumper harvest. The Party branch was greatly enlightened by this. It showed them that one could use the favorable topography of the hilly and mountainous areas to build small reservoirs, enlarge the water sources, and increase the amount of water stored. Small-scale projects could be built everywhere, were amenable to large mass movements, and could be undertaken by relying on the strength of the commune sector. From this small reservoir, they came to deeply appreciate the boundless vigor of the Party's "three-main" water control policy of "primarily small-scale, primarily ancillary works, and primarily undertaken by the commune sector themselves." In order to resolve the contradiction between the insufficiency of water in the Meichuan Reservoir and the need to enlarge the irrigated area, one had on the one hand to properly manage and use the Meichuan Reservoir and strengthen ancillary works in order daily to improve the project; on the other hand, one had to seriously and thoroughly implement the Party's "three-main" water control policy, go outside of the management office into the commune sector to mobilize the masses, rely on the economic power of the collective, and carry out small-scale farmland water conservancy construction in a big way. The entire district had to "draw up an appropriate water control plan." It had to fully utilize the local conditions of favorable topography of the mountainous and hilly areas to build dams across the rivers, construct small reservoirs, dig canals to direct the flood waters, and expand the sources of water for irrigation. At the same time, the old ponds had to be rebuilt to increase the amount of water stored.

Having uncovered the principal contradiction and discovered the approach to its resolution, the tasks of the management office became heavier. Not only did it have to manage and utilize the Meichuan Reservoir, it also had to assist the commune sector to survey, design, and construct a series of small reservoirs, while managing the nearly 6,000 ponds throughout the district. As a result, some people said: "Let the upper levels manage the construction; we manage irrigation," or "We are a reservoir management office, not a pond management office." The Party branch of the management office took the view that the debate over whether or not to grasp small-scale farmland water conservancy was a struggle between the two lines in water management. Thus, they organized the personnel to seriously study Chairman Mao's directives, "Water conservancy is the lifeline of agriculture" and "Building waterworks is a major task in guaranteeing an increase in agricultural output," and the Party's "three-main" water conservancy construction policy. They thoroughly repudiated the revisionist water conservancy policy carried out by swindlers like Liu Shaoqi of "stressing the large and neglecting the small" and "stressing the foreign and neglecting the indigenous," as well as the line that "experts should control water." Everyone came to realize that the only way to achieve greater, faster, better and more economical results in farmland water conservancy was to go outside the management office to mobilize the masses in the commune sector to construct small-scale waterworks and to persist in emphasizing the masses doing it themselves and integrating the large, the medium, and the small. The management office had to manage properly not only the reservoir, but also the irrigation district's ponds. The ponds were the basis, the reservoir was the backbone. The two had to be coordinated in order to achieve greater results.

The reservoir district and the irrigation district are interdependent, relying on each other for their existence and supporting each other. If there were no reservoir district, there would be no irrigation district. If the reservoir district is inundated, it is with a mind to the overall situation. Thus, while agriculture must be improved in the irrigation district, production in the reservoir district must also be done well. But the revisionist line places the two in diametrical opposition so that the contradictions between the two districts become salient and disputes over the stored water become frequent, preventing the reservoir from fully realizing its effectiveness. The project design book only includes the inundated area in the reservoir district and the number of citizens moved. One does not see concrete measures for improving water conservancy conditions in the reservoir district. The management office only takes care of the irrigation district, not the reservoir district. It only looks after what is within the boundaries of the irrigation district, nothing outside. The personnel of Meichuan Reservoir studied Chairman Mao's teaching, "We must wholeheartedly serve the people" and criticized the incorrect thinking of "Put away things of no personal concern." Everyone came to see that they should embrace the thinking of managing water for the revolution and of serving agriculture, that they had to break through the boundaries separating inside from outside in the irrigation district and the reservoir district, and that they ought to go out into the commune sector to mobilize the masses to carry out small-scale farmland water conservancy construction in a big way. Although they had to develop agricultural production in the irrigation district, they also had to pay serious attention to the movement to study Dazhai in the reservoir district and help the commune sector there to construct small-scale water conservancy projects, create "Dazhai fields," plant trees, and engage in erosion control. To sum up, not only did agriculture throughout the irrigation district have to surpass the "Program," but agriculture in the entire Meichuan district had to be stimulated to exceed the "Program."

## 2. Mobilize the Masses to Build Small-Scale Waterworks

Beginning in 1962, the reservoir management office organized survey and project initiation teams for small reservoirs and pond inspection groups to go out both inside and outside the irrigation district to work with the cadres and masses in the commune sector, helping them train water conservancy technicians and whipping up a large mass movement throughout the district to construct small farmland water conservancy works. Each year thereafter, they built a number of small reservoirs and ponds. Some projects produced results in the same year, while those which were a bit larger took another year. When a project was built, it was properly managed and used, closely combining management and construction. The reservoir management office handles water conservancy four seasons a year: in the spring, it handles storage; at flood season, flood prevention; in resisting drought, irrigation; and in winter, construction. This has become a regularized system. This has been greatly welcomed by the masses, who say: "The reservoir management office has become a water management and construction office."

a) Construct Small Reservoirs

Building small reservoirs is an important measure for expanding water sources, sparing the water of the core reservoir while increasing the irrigated area. In working out how to build small reservoirs, the management office has gone through a process of "practice, knowledge, more practice, more knowledge." It began in 1963 by constructing a series of very small reservoirs in the lower reaches of the irrigation district to improve downstream water use and to play a certain role in reducing the water supplied by the core reservoir. But the broad, high mountain fields upstream still did not receive gravity irrigation. For instance, in order to irrigate a dozen or so mou of land, the Wuda Brigade of Zhaozhun Commune actually had to lift the water in four stages from the West Meichuan Canal at high cost with low returns. They deeply felt that they had not taken sufficient responsibility for themselves, so they relied on the masses to construct two small (Type II) reservoirs (Tonggu and Quangou) above the canal line of the West Canal. These reservoirs store 220,000 cubic meters of water and irrigate 630 mou of farmland above the canal. Pumping has been transformed into gravity flow, sparing a large amount of funds and labor power, wiping out a "dead corner" for irrigating, and transforming agricultural production. This has been deeply welcomed by the masses.

With this practical experience, the management office Party branch saw that merely relying on the large reservoir makes it difficult to solve the problems of irrigation in the border mountain areas and that relying on pumping water for irrigation requires a large investment and is not a fundamental approach to developing irrigation in the hilly areas. If they wanted to achieve greater, faster, better and more economical results in solving the problem of irrigating the high mountain fields, they had to build small reservoirs in the high places, make use of the mountain lowlands to build dams to interrupt the flows, dig flood control channels, and construct dams by stages in order to establish control in a tiered fashion. The higher location of the reservoirs not only greatly expands the area under gravity irrigation, but is also beneficial for interreservoir regulation, enlarging the water sources for the core reservoir. In 1965 the Shichuan Reservoir was constructed in the Ling Mountains in the east, holding 1.5 million cubic meters of water, thereby providing gravity flow for over 3,000 mou which had been irrigated by pumping from the East Meichuan Canal and enlarging the high mountain farmland irrigated area by over 1,000 mou. The Shichuan Reservoir is higher than the Meichuan Reservoir, so they linked the North Shichuan Canal with the Meichuan Reservoir in order to lead Shichuan's excess waters into Meichuan. The North Shichuan Canal is 9 kilometers long, most of it circling the mountains. A 3.5-square kilometer catchment area lies above the canal line, but the mountains are high and steep, and the runoff is large. In order to lead this runoff into the Meichuan Reservoir, the North Shichuan Canal was designed to be changed into a flood diversion channel. The canal was divided into four sections in keeping with topographic conditions, with four types of cross-sectional designs. The designed flow increased in stages from 1.0 cms at the canal head to 6.0 cms at the reservoir intake. In this way, one canal serves two purposes: irrigation and flood control. Each year it can provide the Meichuan Reservoir with over a million cubic meters of supplemental water.

"Mankind constantly has to sum up experience and go on discovering, inventing, creating, and advancing." With the construction of the Shichuan Reservoir, they realized that in order to further expand the water sources of the Meichuan Reservoir, they would have to send their forces into the high mountains and cross the boundaries of the drainage basin to search for water sources and construct a reservoir among the lofty summits of the Zong Mountains. In 1966, they also built the Baiyuan Reservoir in the northern branches of the Henggang Mountains. This reservoir is characterized by an even higher elevation and a large catchment area (11.4 sq. km.), with abundant water inflow but a small irrigated area. In order to lead the surplus water of the Baiyuan Reservoir into the Meichuan Reservoir, they dug the 954-meter Baishaling Tunnel and built a 6.7-kilometer diversion canal to lead all the runoff between the districts into the main reservoir. This has increased the amount of water in the Meichuan Reservoir by 3 million cubic meters each year. To solve the problem of irrigating the over 1,000 mou in the district with the highest elevation, they then constructed the Fengkou Reservoir at Fengkou in the Henggang Mountains; it holds 500,000 cubic meters and is over 600 meters above sea level. The masses were full of praise: "Building reservoirs in the high places reduces the dead corners year after year, changes water lifting into gravity flow, and guarantees bumper harvests each year" and "The Meichuan Reservoir's management is broad; they take charge over all the Henggang Mountains."

To date, the entire irrigation district has constructed five Type I [1 to 10 million cubic meters] small reservoirs, and sixteen Type II [100,000 to 1,000,000 cubic meters] small reservoirs, with a total beneficial capacity of 17,689,000 cubic meters (see Table 3), equivalent to 65.5 percent of the beneficial capacity of the Meichuan Reservoir.

In the process of constructing small waterworks, the management office helps the commune sector train their ranks of water technicians in order to create favorable

Table 3

| Type | Number | Catchment basin ($km^2$) | Total capacity ($m^3$) | Active capacity ($m^3$) | Irrigated area (mou) |
|---|---|---|---|---|---|
| I – 1-10 mill. $m^3$ | 5 | 25.85 | 1,897.81 | 1,453.1 | 36,000 |
| II – 100,000-1,000,000 $m^3$ | 10 | 6.4 | 408.63 | 315.8 | 5,910 |

conditions so that they can upgrade their own water management. For instance, the Shihbu Commune's Lishan Brigade is a prominent model in relying on the masses and engaging in water conservancy self-reliantly. The Lishan Brigade has high mountains and numerous gullies with scattered water flows. No matter where they constructed a pond or reservoir, water sources were still insufficient. But they dared to think and act and broke with convention by building a tiny reservoir on a high mountaintop with virtually no catchment area and then digging three flood diversion channels around the mountains with a total length of 2,200 meters (see Figure 1), leading the runoff into the reservoir. By May 1973,

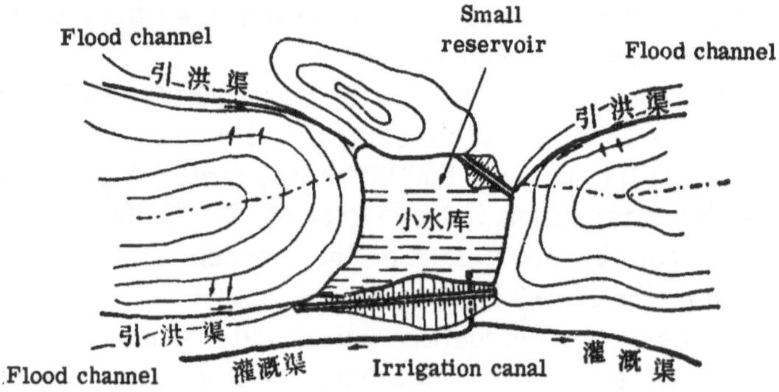


Figure 1

they had already filled it up, and it could irrigate over 200 mou of high mountain farmland. After eight years of arduous struggle, the Lishan Brigade has built thirty ponds and reservoirs of various sizes and dug ten diversion channels totaling 5,200 meters in length. They have a pond on every slope and have rapidly constructed reservoirs so that water no longer flows freely. Seventy-five percent of the cultivated land has gravity irrigation and 88 percent has yields guaranteed in spite of drought or flooding. Tested by nearly two years of drought, these small water projects showed their enormous power by enabling the per mou grain yield in 1972 to reach 1,400 jin [10.5 t./ha.]. At present, the Lishan Brigade, responding to the call "In agriculture, learn from Dazhai," is launching a mass movement for the integrated control of soil, slopes, and water, combining the construction of small waterworks and that of "Dazhai fields" and rearranging the mountain streams in order to make even greater contributions to the cause of socialism.

b) Construct Ponds to Increase Stored Water

Ponds are farmland water conservancy capital construction facilities which have been constructed historically by the laboring masses. Their characteristics are that they are widely distributed, provide timely irrigation, are easy to manage, are shallow, and have a high water temperature. Irrigating with pond water aids the growth of early rice. At present, the district has 5,983 ponds storing 12,880,000 cubic meters of water. Practice has demonstrated that ponds play an important role in the irrigation of early rice and in the prevention of minor droughts and droughts during transplanting.

For a period after the construction of the Meichuan Reservoir, people altogether neglected the role of the small ponds. Some communes in the upper and middle reaches thought that with the Meichuan Reservoir as their mainstay, the small ponds had become unimportant, so they let up on maintenance and repair, and some even filled in their ponds to make fields.

The Party branch of the reservoir management office is just as concerned with the small ponds as it is with the main reservoir. The masses view the reservoir as their mainstay, with the ponds as its foundation. The guiding thought of "We must have both a stable mainstay and a reliable foundation" is extremely correct. Those in the office have taken the management and utilization of the ponds as part of their duty and made it an important task in the irrigation district's management work. They regularly publicize among the masses the importance of storing water in ponds. The masses have been deeply moved when the management cadres have gone into the commune sector and have taken the lead in braving the rain to lead water into the ponds and carrying soil to fill in the gaps. Everywhere in the irrigation district a pond management system has been established, so that leading water into the ponds for storage after a rain has become a mass movement. For instance, on July 31, 1972, just at a critical point in the fight against drought, a widespread rainfall of over 50 millimeters occurred. Right away, the district convened a broadcast mobilization meeting and organized over 10,000 people to seize the opportunity to divert and store the water. They brought out 120 sets of water-lifting machinery, blocked the streams, and pumped the water into the ponds. They brought the direct surface flow under total control and altogether stored several million cubic meters of rainwater, greatly relieving the drought. In order to increase the amount of water stored in the ponds, every winter they combine a mass renovation campaign with regular winter production. This involves dredging out the pond mud, adding earth to the banks, and constructing ditches to fill in gaps, thus deepening the ponds year after year. They have reconstructed the mountain ponds which are located relatively high by raising the dikes and transforming high outlets to low ones, expanding the area irrigated by gravity. In areas lacking water sources, those with appropriate conditions constructed some new ponds.

In order to provide a scientific base for linking the reservoirs and ponds and for rationally using water, the employees of the management office for over a year carried out a general inspection and survey of the ponds throughout the district. They drew up detailed investigative statistics by commune and brigade (she, dui) and by canal on the location of ponds, their water storage capability, irrigated acreage, water sources, and restorage conditions. According to these data, the entire district has 429,000 mou [28,600 ha.] of land, of which the cultivated area is 127,000 mou [8,500 ha.], with a total of 5,983 ponds. The average pond has a surface area of about 1.5 mou [0.1 ha.] (the largest exceed 10 mou), with an average depth about 2.0 meters (some as deep as 5 to 6 meters). The average water stored is 2,151 cubic meters. If we calculate on the basis of half used and half stored, when full, the water which can be supplied for irrigation is 1,075 cubic meters. Calculating that in general there are two restorages in a year, each pond could supply 2,151 cubic meters of irrigation water per annum. Thus, the management and use of these works play an important role in guaranteeing bumper harvests in spite of drought.

In order to further strengthen the ponds and develop their "one water, multiple uses" function, the reservoir management office has also held training classes in pond fish raising and led the commune sector to vigorously promote fish raising in their ponds.

### 3. Establish an Irrigation Network Based on the Meichuan Reservoir

"Often, correct knowledge can be arrived at only after many repetitions of the process leading from matter to consciousness and then back to matter, that is, leading from practice to knowledge and then back to practice." Following the step-by-step improvement of the ancillary works in the irrigation district, the number of small-scale water facilities has increased daily, and the irrigated area of the Meichuan Reservoir has continuously expanded. After many years of practice they came to realize that in order to properly manage and utilize the Meichuan Reservoir and the numerous small reservoirs and ponds, it is necessary to exercise unified management and unified control. Isolated ponds and reservoirs had become no longer consonant with the development of the situation. The reservoirs, canals, ponds and dams of the entire district had to be linked together to form a complete system. After many years of rebuilding and expansion, they gradually formed a "melons-on-a-vine" style irrigation network centered around the Meichuan Reservoir (see Figure 2).

Connect the reservoirs to transfer surpluses and fill in deficits. This is an effective measure for expanding and utilizing water sources. Because of differences in natural conditions and between projects, some reservoirs have a large rainfall catchment area and receive a lot of water but have a small irrigation control area; others have a large capacity but little water inflow and a large area requiring irrigation. In the former, the reservoir water is overabundant, and surplus water frequently leaks away without being effectively utilized; in the latter, the lack of water is often felt, and irrigation demands on water cannot be satisfied. At the same time, it is possible that for another set of reasons some reservoirs during a certain time period must release some water, which is wasted if not utilized. Thus, by linking reservoirs where topographical conditions permit, the surplus water of one reservoir can be led into another, thereby increasing the amount stored which can be utilized as a resource; that is, it enlarges the water sources and thoroughly utilizes them. This is one of the main characteristics of the Meichuan irrigation network. Figure 2 shows the locations of the Baiyuan, Shichuan, Sanba, Tianchong, and Tongshan Type I small reservoirs. The Baiyuan Reservoir has a high elevation, a large rainfall catchment area, abundant water, and a small irrigation control area, while the Meichuan and Tianchong reservoirs are just the opposite, having large capacities, small catchment areas, and insufficient inflow. Thus, linking the

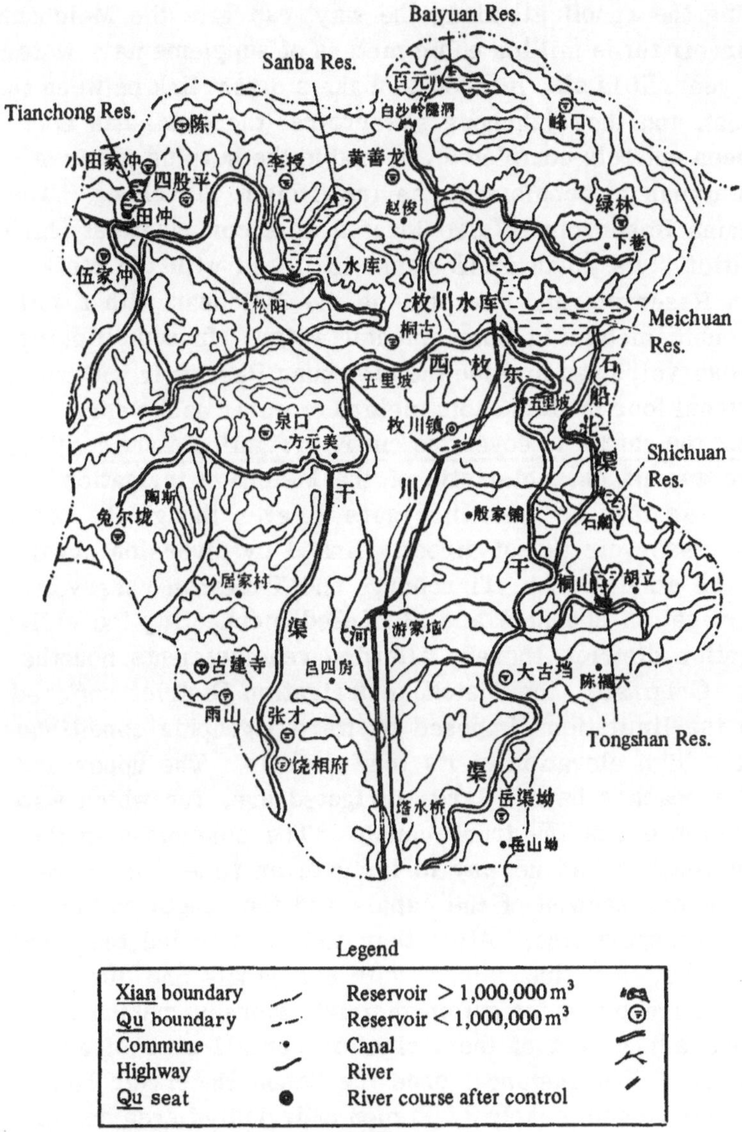


**Figure 2. Schematic of Meichuan Reservoir Irrigation District**

Baiyuan and Meichuan reservoirs by canal, along with intercepting the runoff all along the way, can give the Meichuan Reservoir three million cubic meters of supplementary water each year. It is also planned to make a direct link between the Baiyuan and the Tianchong reservoirs (the canal has not yet been entirely completed), to enable the surplus water of the Baiyuan to supplement the insufficient Tianchong. The Shichuan Reservoir is also located at a comparatively high elevation. Its north trunk canal is linked with the Meichuan Reservoir and can provide the Meichuan with a million cubic meters of supplemental water. In sum, linking the reservoirs can provide the Meichuan Reservoir with an additional four million cubic meters of water each year.

Link the canals to cover the entire irrigation district. This is the second characteristic of the Meichuan irrigation network. As may be seen in Figure 2, even though the Meichuan Reservoir is not directly linked by diversion canal with the small Sanba, Tianchong, and Tongshan reservoirs, the irrigation channels are all linked, connecting the entire irrigation district, thereby allowing readjustments nonetheless. Originally, the Meichuan Irrigation District suffered from the limitations imposed by its topographic conditions and the high elevation of its trunk canals. The upper and middle reaches have a large irrigated area for which water was taken out of the trunk canals. The communes in the lower reaches had no way to irrigate on time due to the small cross section of the canals and the length of the water transport line. After they had constructed the small reservoirs, they linked them with the canals and ditches of the neighboring irrigation district, thereby making a rational adjustment of the irrigation control area of each reservoir. For instance, once the Sanba Reservoir had been constructed, nearly 8,000 mou of irrigated area belonging to the Taosi and Songyang communes in the lower reaches of the West Meichuan Canal was given over by the plan to the East Sanba Reservoir Canal for irrigation. This reduced the burden on the Meichuan Reservoir while thoroughly tapping the effectiveness of the Sanba Reservoir. At the same time, since the water transport line had been shortened, the degree of urgency in water use in these areas was greatly improved. After the Shichuan Reservoir was built, over 4,000 mou of land in the Hongxing and Tuqiao communes which were lifting water from the East Meichuan Canal were transferred in the plan to the Shichuan Reservoir for gravity flow irrigation. This not only saved funds and labor power, but also reduced the burdens on the East Canal in the middle reaches, favoring the collection of water for supply to the Lianglu Commune in the lower reaches. Besides adjusting the irrigated areas, they could also deploy water supplies in an active way, in keeping with the storage conditions of the various reservoirs. For instance, in 1972 the Tongshan Reservoir did not have enough water, so the Meichuan Reservoir supplied the Tongshan Irrigation District with 100,000 cubic meters of water through the irrigation canals. The water was lifted to irrigate Tongshan's farmland. The Sanba Reservoir also transferred over 300,000 cubic meters of water to the Tianchong Irrigation District to reduce the burden on its reservoir.

Link canals and ponds like melons on a vine. In the past, there were mostly isolated ponds having small collection areas, low restorage rates, and low resistance to drought. The management office mobilized the masses to dig channels in the fields to link the canals and ponds like melons on a vine. Once each canal had been linked with the ponds, it could lead water into them after a rainfall, so that the water could be used for irrigation in time of drought. They [Meichuan] expanded the pond collection area and raised the restorage rate, so that now in general the ponds are filled twice a year. In the past, the East Meichuan Canal had a serious problem in that it strung ponds like beads. The canal went directly through more than nine large ponds each with a capacity in excess of 1,000 cubic meters, or a total capacity of 45,000 cubic meters. Each irrigation season, the reservoir water first of all had to fill these ponds. This seriously affected the canal's transport of water. In general it took seven or eight days from the time the water was released at the reservoir to when it reached the tail of the canal in the lower reaches. They mobilized the masses to abandon the ponds and change the canal in order to transform the ponds linked by the canal into "melon ponds" and to allow the canal water to flow through unhindered. Now it only takes a single day for water to be sent to the lower reaches.

The Meichuan Reservoir, 5 Type I small reservoirs, 16 Type II small reservoirs, 5,983 ponds, and 1,735 main, branch, subbranch, farm, and field canals with a total length of 646.5 kilometers have already been connected together. The Meichuan Reservoir controls the entire irrigation district as if it were the principal root of a melon. The canals are like vines, circling the mountains and slopes, connecting reservoirs and ponds. The reservoirs and ponds are like melons, scattered here and there linking the melon roots. This is how they have formed a melons-on-a-vine irrigation system centered on the Meichuan Reservoir. At irrigation time, one place releases water and innumerable places water the fields. The reservoirs, ponds, and canals link the water so that it may be allocated freely. At present, the total amount of stored water which can be dispatched within the Meichuan Irrigation District has reached over 50 million cubic meters, over three times the average water inflow into the Meichuan Reservoir.

"Mankind makes constant progress, and nature undergoes constant change; they never remain at the same level." The Meichuan irrigation network is also being continuously developed and consolidated. In order to further develop water sources, expand the irrigated area, and raise the standards of drought resistance, under the unified planning of the entire xian, they are planning within the next few years to dig a tunnel [or tunnels] totaling 4,800 meters through the Henggang Mountains to lead the tailwaters of the Datong Reservoir hydroelectric plan in Qichun xian into the Meichuan Reservoir. It is calculated that 13 million cubic meters of water may be brought in each year for storage. Beyond this, they intend to link up the medium-sized Meichuan, Jingzhu, Xianrenba, and Dajin reservoirs to provide regulation of the water within all of Guangji xian and form an even broader irrigation network.

Based on the experience of Meichuan, in order to set up a complete irrigation network, the following two problems must be solved:

First, unified leadership and overall planning. For the Meichuan irrigation network, the Meichuan Reservoir Management Office implemented the plans concretely under the unified leadership of the Meichuan qu Party Committee. Because of this, unified arrangements could be made for the water and land resources throughout the qu, overall plans could be made, the boundaries of an irrigation district and between irrigation districts could be broken through, and unified consideration could be given to setting up an irrigation network in order to promote agricultural development in the entire qu. In addition to the Meichuan Reservoir, Guangji xian has three other reservoirs with a total storage capacity of over 10 million cubic meters. In order to bring into full play the key role of these medium-sized reservoirs and create conditions favorable to establishing a qu-level irrigation network, Guangji xian has built on Meichuan's experience to combine the medium-sized Jingzhu and Xianrenba reservoir irrigation districts into the Jingxian Irrigation District, linking 32 small and tiny reservoirs and 5,368 ponds into an irrigation network based on the two larger reservoirs. A unified management organization has been set up for the district. It is also planned to form an irrigation network centered around the Dajin Reservoir with unified leadership over that reservoir plus 19 small and tiny reservoirs and 2,618 ponds.

Second, correctly handle the relationship between management and construction. Construction is the basis; without it, we might as well not talk about management. Management is the key. If it is not done well, the project will not be fully effective; it is equivalent to reducing the amount of construction.

Poor management may even lead to serious consequences. The counterrevolutionary revisionist line promoted by Liu Shaoqi, Lin Biao, and the like of "Emphasize construction over management" and "Only build, don't manage" must be thoroughly repudiated. The experience of the Meichuan Reservoir argues that in order to act as a management department, it is necessary to emphasize management, properly manage and utilize the existing projects, and give full rein to their effectiveness. This is the primary task and cannot be changed. At the same time, one should combine management and construction and construct in the process of managing. Only in this way can projects be improved, their quality raised, and their scope of benefit be continuously expanded. Management and construction are not mutually exclusive, but are interrelated. They are a dialectical unity. If you truly want to manage a reservoir well, you must build on it constantly. On the one hand, you must grasp the ancillary projects and keep on improving the existing projects; on the other hand, you must mobilize the masses to build small waterworks and integrate the large, medium, and small projects. Only then can you give full play to the role of the central reservoir.

## II. SEARCH OUT THE OBJECTIVE LAWS, RATIONALLY ALLOCATE WATER

Once an irrigation network centered on the Meichuan Reservoir had been set up, the water sources were expanded, and the amount of water in storage was increased, creating favorable conditions for an increase in agricultural output. However, in considering the problem of whether or not these conditions could be brought into full play to achieve the aim of increasing production, we need to look at whether or not they could manage and utilize these projects well and whether or not they could allocate that water in a planned manner for timely irrigation and rational water use. The Meichuan Reservoir Management Office came to realize through practice that in order to do this they first had to embrace the guiding thought pattern of serving the needs of increasing agricultural output.

When the Meichuan Reservoir had been constructed and had begun delivering water for irrigation, their thinking concerning serving farm output increases was insufficiently clear: "Just manage the release of water, don't manage on-farm irrigation." Because the canal systems were not combined into networks and the quality of the projects was not good, when water was released, it broke through the embankments in the upper reaches and ruined the fields. In the middle reaches, a large and wasteful amount of water filled the fields. In the lower reaches, the shoots parched and died. Afterward, they firmly grasped the task of combining the canal systems into networks and strengthening the maintenance of projects to enable the water to irrigate the farmland. Nonetheless, at that time, their thinking remained at the level of "just manage the release of water to irrigate the fields, don't ask whether the output is high or low." In consequence, new problems arose during the 1963 drought resistance. The sluice gates were opened wide and, in a day, released nearly a million cubic meters of water. Within a dozen days or so, the reservoir had been emptied. Moreover, they had not properly studied the objective laws of water inflow and water use in order to utilize the limited amount of reservoir water at the most urgent time to fight the drought and guarantee a bumper harvest. The personnel of the management office, conscientiously summing up this experience, came to the deep realization that reservoir management work cannot be restricted to opening up the sluice gates to release water, but that it must also make rational use of the water. They must not only send water to the fields, but must also make a skillful calculation of the high yields.

Thus, one must search out the laws of water inflow and utilization in the irrigation district and establish a set of rational principles and methods for allocating water.

## 1. Analyze the Laws of Water Inflow and Utilization

The average rainfall for many years in the Meichuan Irrigation District has been 1,290 millimeters, which is sufficiently abundant. But it is distributed over the year in a highly irregular pattern. Table 4 shows that the rainfall is concentrated in April through June when there is an average of 530 millimeters, or 41 percent of the year's total. July through September are rather less, with an average 334.8 millimeters, or 25.8 percent. If we look at the relatively dry years of 1959 and 1971, the rainfall from April through June was 543.8 and 548.2 millimeters respectively, or 44 to 54 percent of the annual total, while the July to August rainfall was only 172.2 and 142.3 millimeters respectively, or about 14 percent of the year's total. The most important product of the irrigation district is double-crop rice. Table 5, which is based on many years of

Table 4

Past Rainfall Data for Meichuan Irrigation District

Unit: mm.

| Year \ Month | Jan. | Feb. | Mar. | Apr. | May | June | July | Aug. | Sept. | Oct. | Nov. | Dec. | Total |
|---|---|---|---|---|---|---|---|---|---|---|---|---|---|
| 1958 | 24.8 | 46.0 | 134.3 | 213.8 | 232.4 | 49.0 | 26.6 | 189.5 | 81.9 | 95.0 | 35.3 | 30.9 | 1,159.5 |
| 1959 | 38.6 | 168.0 | 63.8 | 165.1 | 291.9 | 86.8 | 131.7 | 5.5 | 35.0 | 45.0 | 119.9 | 77.2 | 1,229.0 |
| 1960 | 64.2 | 61.4 | 195.2 | 179.0 | 192.9 | 176.0 | 261.0 | 102.1 | 110.8 | 27.3 | 72.1 | 17.3 | 1,459.3 |
| 1961 | 50.2 | 102.0 | 200.2 | 122.8 | 129.5 | 167.9 | 50.2 | 143.0 | 166.4 | 48.6 | 130.1 | 34.3 | 1,345.2 |
| 1962 | 23.3 | 41.4 | 62.0 | 194.8 | 166.3 | 264.4 | 77.8 | 246.6 | 46.8 | 66.4 | 66.4 | 56.1 | 1,312.2 |
| 1963 | 0 | 26.2 | 98.9 | 185.7 | 185.4 | 32.6 | 134.5 | 184.9 | 39.3 | 17.8 | 107.0 | 25.8 | 1,038.1 |
| 1964 | 54.3 | 97.9 | 77.1 | 127.0 | 165.7 | 418.5 | 79.8 | 69.7 | 46.0 | 141.1 | 12.3 | 42.5 | 1,331.9 |
| 1965 | 12.8 | 164.4 | 74.8 | 214.9 | 38.5 | 222.3 | 56.8 | 192.1 | 122.4 | 78.9 | 64.5 | 70.4 | 1,312.7 |
| 1966 | 23.5 | 60.0 | 91.9 | 158.2 | 163.8 | 127.4 | 63.6 | 57.9 | 91.0 | 53.9 | 50.7 | 79.8 | 1,021.7 |
| 1967 | 60.2 | 59.0 | 130.4 | 209.0 | 291.1 | 290.9 | 125.4 | 22.1 | 50.6 | 52.2 | 196.8 | 3.6 | 1,491.3 |
| 1968 | 53.8 | 4.9 | 125.6 | 104.4 | 228.0 | 67.8 | 81.2 | 35.8 | 54.4 | 16.2 | 27.5 | 185.0 | 984.6 |
| 1969 | 91.5 | 41.7 | 108.5 | 152.2 | 48.0 | 322.3 | 567.4 | 233.6 | 107.4 | 12.1 | 44.1 | 14.8 | 1,743.6 |
| 1970 | 30.3 | 111.7 | 152.5 | 153.7 | 186.9 | 334.5 | 179.0 | 97.5 | 139.2 | 27.5 | 60.2 | 41.7 | 1,514.7 |
| 1971 | 28.3 | 97.1 | 64.2 | 122.0 | 158.1 | 268.1 | 19.1 | 101.9 | 21.3 | 70.0 | 20.8 | 41.7 | 1,012.6 |
| 1972 | 13.6 | 152.4 | 112.5 | 79.5 | 163.5 | 104.8 | 89.7 | 125.8 | 165.2 | 247.4 | 114.3 | 47.0 | 1,415.7 |
| Average | 38.0 | 82.0 | 113.0 | 159.0 | 176.0 | 195.0 | 130.0 | 120.0 | 84.8 | 66.5 | 74.8 | 51.2 | 1,290.0 |
| | | | | | 530<br>41.0% | | | 334.8<br>25.8% | | | | | |

Table 5

| Month / Item | Apr. | May | June | July | Aug. | Sep. | Oct. | Total |
|---|---|---|---|---|---|---|---|---|
| Field water consumption | 150 | 126 | 195 | 228 | 183 | 162 | 37.5 | 1,081.5 |
| (mm.) | | 471 | | | 573 | | | |

Note: Field water consumption includes that used to soak the fields, 90 mm. for early rice, 120 mm. for late rice.

experimental data on irrigation within the district, sets out the field water consumption of double-crop rice for each month. Early rice is generally transplanted beginning in April and harvesting begins in the first part of July. During the most important period of growth for early rice, the temperature is relatively low, and it is the rainy season. Agricultural water consumption is relatively low, and the amount of water used for irrigation is not great. During the main growth period for late rice (July to September), however, rainfall is slight, temperature is high, evaporation is great, agricultural water consumption is great, and the amount of water used in irrigation is also great. Particularly at the "double-rush" stage [when the harvesting of early rice coincides with the transplanting of late rice], water becomes critical to take quick advantage of the seasons. This is the peak period of the use of irrigation water. Comparing tables 4 and 5, the amount of water consumption in the fields from July to September is 537 millimeters, but the average rainfall is only 334.8 millimeters, leaving a discrepancy of 238.2 millimeters (which converts to 159 cubic meters per *mou*). In the relatively dry years of 1959 and 1971, this discrepancy reached 400-430 millimeters (267-287 cubic meters per *mou*). Thus there is a rather large contradiction between the distribution of rainfall over the year and the water demands of double-crop rice. In the "double rush" and the main growth period for late rice, water use is heavy, rainfall light. Summer drought occurs regularly. In this period, the timely supply of water determines whether or not there will be a harvest and whether output increases or falls. For this, we must bring into full play the role of the medium and small reservoirs and the ponds, with the reservoirs serving as the backbone and the ponds as the base, allocating [water] in a unified way, and using [water] jointly.

## 2. Skillfully Use Pond Water, Actively Use Reservoir Water

For irrigation districts where the amount of water in the central reservoirs is small and the number of ponds is large, the question of how closely to combine their use, that is, to develop the key role of the reservoir while displaying the base force of the ponds, is at present an important question: in irrigation management work can we further exploit untapped potential to expand the effectiveness of irrigation?

The Meichuan Reservoir Management Office traversed a crooked path on the matter of the joint use of ponds and reservoirs. In the beginning, they did not pay sufficient attention to the water stored in ponds, thinking, "If the peasants have ponds, they can irrigate their land; why do we have to stick our noses in their business?" They were uncertain of the number of ponds within the irrigation district, the amount of water they stored, and their distribution. In reality, each managed its own: the masses managed the ponds and the management office managed the reservoir. With an eye simply to preserving the water in the reservoir, they summed things up by proposing slogans such as "First use the pond water, then the reservoir water" and "It is not permissible to fill ponds with reservoir water." Of course, acting in this way allowed them to save a little water over a given period of time, but it stifled the activism of the masses in using water stored in ponds for irrigation. At the "double-rush" peak water utilization time, the supply of water from the reservoirs was inadequate, and the ponds were also drained dry. This affected agricultural production and pond fish raising. Through repeated practice, the management office came to see that although the ponds were small, there were a goodly number of them, and the total water they stored was well worth noting. If they could combine its utilization with that of reservoir water, it could play a most significant role. With the guiding thought of "use water as on a chessboard," based on the seasonal characteristics of weather and farm activities within the irrigation district and with the precondition of guaranteeing bumper yields in both agriculture and fishery, they summed up a set of experiences to "skillfully use pond water and actively use reservoir water."

a) Skillfully Use Pond Water

In keeping with the concrete conditions of the Meichuan Irrigation District, the pond water is mainly used to irrigate early rice and to fight minor droughts and droughts during transplanting. During the "double-rush" period, pond water alleviates the water use peak. It even irrigates during the final period of late rice.

The growth period of early rice is during the rainy season when precipitation is greatest and irrigation rather low. According to experimental data on irrigation in the Meichuan Irrigation District, the net irrigation norms in past years for early rice are as shown in Table 6.

Table 6 shows that the irrigation norm for early rice varies

Table 6

| Year / Item | 1960 | 1961 | 1962 | 1963 | 1964 | 1972 | Average |
|---|---|---|---|---|---|---|---|
| Net irrigation norms ($m^3$/mou) | 121 | 247 | 104 | 195 | 140 | 198 | 167 |

from 104 to 247 cubic meters per mou, an average of 167 cubic meters per mou. During this period, there are generally numerous minor droughts, or some areas have drought (transplanting drought). But most of the ponds are already full. Pond water is close to the land to be irrigated, so it is more convenient and timely than reservoir water. Moreover, the air temperature at that time is relatively low, and since pond water has a higher temperature than reservoir water, it is beneficial to the growth of early rice.

Every July, the early rice is rush harvested and the late rice is rush transplanted. During this period, the weather is blazing hot, the rainfall low, and precipitation great. This is the key time when water use is greatest, labor is tightest, and the farm season is at its peak. If reservoir water is relied on exclusively to irrigate the farmland, the water supply will never be on time; if only pond water is used, there obviously will be insufficient water. Thus, both reservoir and pond water must be used at the same time and closely coordinated, relying on the reservoir water and using the pond water mainly to alleviate the water use peak.

At the end of September and the beginning of October, after the late rice has finished putting out tillers, irrigation can be reduced, and the fields dried at the appropriate time. But the season of the pond fish catch and mud dredging comes soon thereafter, so as much pond water as possible may be used, reducing reservoir water utilization. This enables the reservoir to store water ahead of time in preparation for the following year's irrigation. For instance, in October 1971, all the saffron suffered from drought. Many in the commune sector demanded that reservoir water be released to fight the drought. The management office analyzed the current condition of the drought and the water stored in ponds and proposed that the pond water could solve the problem of drought. In this way, they saved the reservoir 4.0 million cubic meters of water.

In order to guarantee that pond water is fully utilized for irrigation in the above three periods, it is necessary to do a good job of storing water in the ponds. After all, a pond can store water several times in a year. From January to October 1965, the Meichuan Irrigation Experimental Station carried out a fixed-point survey of a pond. The survey data showed that when there are 5 to 10 millimeters of rain following continuous clear days, no surface runoff is produced; when there is continuous but light rain, there is surface runoff, but the runoff ratio is not large, generally 0.3 to 0.5; if the rainfall is heavy and for a short period of time (around 100 millimeters in a day), the runoff is large, with a ratio of 0.5 to 0.7. During the survey period, there was a total rainfall of 1,032 millimeters, generally concentrated and heavy, with the maximum daily rainfall reaching 130 millimeters. Calculated on the basis of actual measurements, the total runoff flowing into the pond was 12,100 cubic meters. The capacity of the pond surveyed was 7,974 cubic meters, with a catchment area of 17,300 square meters. From this, we can calculate that in an ordinary year a pond can be replenished twice.

In addition, the work of filling the ponds with reservoir water must be done well. Each year in the first part of July when the harvesting has begun on the early-ripening varieties of early rice, the ponds do not normally have much water in storage. We must take advantage of this time to fill the ponds with reservoir water to prepare ahead of time for the middle of July and thereafter when it will be coordinated with the reservoir water to alleviate the "double-rush" water use peak. Every year before the reservoir closes its sluice gates, in keeping with current concrete conditions, reservoir water must be used to fill some ponds. Special attention should be paid to filling the ponds of the marginal districts of the lower reaches to meet their supply needs in later periods.

In order to strengthen the management of ponds, a "four-fixed" system has been instituted, that is, fixing personnel, responsibilities, remunerations, and awards and punishments. In the past two years, they have grasped "combining agriculture and fishery and coordinating them with each other," closely linking the water management personnel and the fish breeders. During the spring rainy season, the fish breeders take the initiative to do a good job of plugging leaks and sealing the water outlets, and they lead water into the ponds. During drought resistance, the water management personnel assist the fish breeders in raising and protecting the fish. Under general drought conditions, the allocation of pond water must be to "use half, leave half, and store water to protect the fish." In a period of great drought they "move the fish when the pond dries up, so the water comes back to the fish" or "catch many and leave few, so that when the water is low, the number of fish is few." Because agriculture and fishery have been combined well, a bumper output in both agriculture and fishing has been guaranteed. The masses report, "We have stored water, irrigated the fields, raised fish and fertilized the fields, increasing the output of both grain and fish."

b) Actively Use Reservoir Water

The Meichuan Reservoir and the five small reservoirs are the backbone water storage projects of the entire irrigation district and the backing for wresting high yields in spite of major droughts, but the total amount of water stored is definitely not abundant. Thus, how properly to utilize the reservoir water in a manner appropriate to local conditions is extremely important. In 1963, the reservoirs began to release water at the end of May and, by the beginning of October, were entirely empty. Through continual summing up of their experiences, they came to realize that to make maximal use of the limited reservoir water they had to use it as on a knife's edge and during the critical periods. Their experience has been: for early rice, basically do not move; at the "double rush," actively enter the battle; for late rice (seedling protection and strengthening periods), irrigate everything.

The early-rice growth period is the rainy season, and the ponds are full. Aside from exceptional circumstances, the irrigation of early rice in general basically does not use reservoir water. Thus, the period when the Meichuan Reservoir releases water each year is rather late. Since 1964, seven years out of eight, the sluices have been opened to release water after the tenth of July.

The "double rush" is the key water use period in the entire irrigation district. The seasonal nature of late rice is particularly strong. If it is not rush transplanted at the right time, its yield can be seriously affected. Thus, the reservoirs must take the initiative in entering the battle, and before the peak water use comes, they must fill the ponds with reservoir water. At the slightest sign of drought, they must prepare to release water. For instance, in the first part of July 1971, although the masses in the commune sector had not yet all begun to demand the release of water, the management office had already detected the beginning traces of drought and, on its own initiative, released water on July 10. The masses felt the reservoir water arrived just in the nick of time. Not only did this guarantee the completion of "double-rush" tasks, but it also greatly improved the water-use sequence, putting an end to the phenomenon of contending for water.

During the growth period of late rice, rainfall is generally sparse, evaporation great, and water needs greatest. After the "double rush," there is no longer much pond water, so the irrigation of the late rice depends on reservoir water. Only after the second weeding is reservoir water used for irrigation. Since 1964, the Meichuan Reservoir has always shut the gates at the end of September or in the first part of October, storing

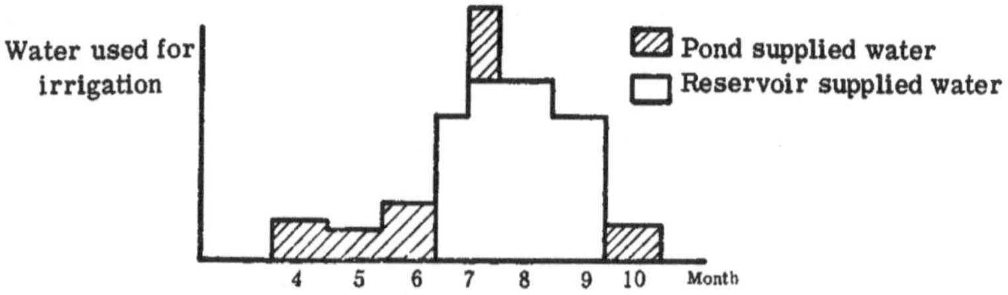


Figure 3. Schematic of joint water supply process for reservoirs and ponds.

water in preparation for antidrought irrigation the following year. For instance, in 1971 after fending off eighty days of continuous drought, the reservoirs throughout the xian had been basically emptied, yet in the end, the Meichuan Reservoir still held 8 million cubic meters of water to provide the conditions for wresting high yields in spite of drought in 1972.

Figure 3 is a schematic representation of the joint water supply and utilization process for reservoirs and ponds.

### 3. Maintain the Water Use Principle of "Three First, Three Later"

The problem of how to rationally allocate water in order to guarantee the timely irrigation which promotes agricultural output and uses water sparingly has great significance in the united struggle against drought. In the beginning, the Meichuan Reservoir Irrigation District lacked experience in allocating water and proposed the principle of "first near, then distant." This resulted in having "the upper reaches drown to death, while the lower reaches parch to death," with a vast amount of water wasted and a number of water-use disputes. In particular, water could not be guaranteed to the border areas in the lower reaches. Later, they switched to the "distant first, then near" principle. Although the water use in the lower reaches was improved somewhat, it was always difficult to hold to this principle because the amount of water was too deficient. Furthermore, not enough ideological work was done. The upper and middle reaches blocked off the water, and the phenomenon of waste was still quite serious. Because the water source conditions and the porosity of the soil are different in various places in the irrigation district and there are gradations in local weather and local drought severity, the "distant first, then near" principle was rather too all-encompassing and could not handle the different specific concrete conditions. As a result, some areas which did not urgently need irrigation were often allocated water first, while water could not be delivered on time to places which urgently needed irrigation, thus affecting agricultural growth. After continually summing up their experience and uniting it with the actual conditions in the Meichuan Irrigation District, they adopted the water allocation principle of "Urgent first, then not urgent, and control the near to send to the distant; high land first, then low land and look out for the borders; and look first then release, grasp the entire situation."

### a) Urgent First, Then Not Urgent; Control the Near to Send to the Distant

Based on the water conditions in each locality in the irrigation district, the porosity of its soil, the urgency with which its crops need water, and the course of the drought there, when water is released it is first allocated to areas urgently requiring irrigation. At the same time, water must be properly supplied to areas in the lower reaches.

Contradictions break out easily between upper and lower reaches within the irrigation district, and these come even more to the fore under severe drought conditions. Because of this, the key is to do ideological work well with the communes in the upper and middle reaches and to adopt effective measures to control the near to send to the distant in order to guarantee water for the use of areas in the lower reaches. The Meichuan Reservoir Management Office analyzed conditions in the upper, middle, and lower reaches and handled their principal contradictions separately. The upper reaches are close to the reservoir and can obtain water easily. They waste a lot of water. We should urgently and seriously demand that they emphasize "using water sparingly." The communes in the middle reaches are favorably situated, and it is convenient for them to block off the water. We should take aim at this thinking of "the water flows through my place, so I should be allowed to use it first," and advocate that these communes take the entire situation into account and send "unity water," "Dragon River water" to the lower reaches. The lower reaches and border areas are faced with a canal line which is too long, a small amount of water transported, and difficulties in sending water. It is important that they grasp the "rational use of water." Communes are organized to think of every means to open up water sources of many types and grasp favorable opportunities to irrigate and store water in ponds.

In carrying out the principle of "urgent first, then not urgent; control the near to send to the distant," they have adopted the tactic of "irrigating the upper and middle reaches in the daytime, gathering the waters together at night to send to the lower reaches." During the day, the water flows are scattered about to allow the upper and middle reaches to obtain some water and promote their irrigation. At night, the areas in the upper and middle reaches are all forbidden to open their gates for irrigation in order to facilitate the gathering of water for transport to the lower reaches. In this way water use in the broader area is heeded in an all-round way, and the guarantee of irrigation in the areas in the lower reaches is highlighted. Thus, the contradiction between upper and lower reaches is resolved comparatively well, and the water utilization sequence is improved considerably.

During the 1971 struggle against drought, responsible personnel of the Meichuan qu Party Committee and the reservoir management office went to the lower level units and divided the responsibility for releasing water. They organized the cadres and masses to study Chairman Mao's directives, "We must take the whole situation into account," and "Unite to win still greater victories," and requested them to release "unity water" and send "friendship water." Moreover they undertook "one, look; two, count up; and three, support." "One, look" means to organize the commune sector cadres in the areas along the upper and middle reaches of the trunk canals to go to the lower reaches to look at the drought conditions there and study the militant spirit of the people arduously struggling against drought. "Two, count up" means to calculate the loss from sending one cubic meter less of water and planting one less mou of late rice, in order to bring home the truth that the only true bumper harvest is an overall bumper harvest. "Three, support" means to adopt various measures in support of sending water to the lower reaches.

Three teams of the Congzheng Brigade of the Nanquan Commune in the middle reaches of the West Canal originally could utilize the canal water for gravity irrigation. In order to support the lower reaches, they built a dam across the river and pumped the return waters to fight drought. Ten teams of the Guanshan Brigade also preferred to arrange for over fifty mou of land along the canal to be irrigated at the very end.

In July 1972, the East and West Canals of the Meichuan Reservoir released water at the same time. Since the policy of "control the near to send to the distant" was carried out, water arrived in only twenty hours at the Huilong Brigade at the tail end of the West Canal, a flow of forty-seven Chinese li [23.5 kilometers]. The commune members said excitedly, "This year '[political] line' water was released; we are using 'Dragon River water.'"

b) High Land First, Then Low Land, and Look out for the Borders

The hilly and mountainous areas are characterized by up and down peaks, slopes separated from each other, and scattered cultivated land of varying elevations. In irrigating with reservoir water, it is first necessary to water the high fields and then the low fields. The high fields are elevated and lack water sources. In general, ponds cannot supply them through gravity flow. The low fields are relatively low, on comparatively level ground, and can in general be supplied by gravity flow irrigation from the ponds. By first irrigating the high fields, they can be irrigated on time, and the seepage from the high fields flows toward the low fields to be used again, reducing the water needed for irrigation. Some elevated fields located along the border regions of the irrigation district are generally difficult to water. Whenever water is released for irrigation, a bit more must be sent to these areas, both to irrigate the fields and to fill the ponds. With the ponds filled, they can ward off common minor droughts and transplanting drought. Thus, this system can reduce the number of times canal water is delivered to the border areas and enables those areas to achieve punctual irrigation.

c) Look First, Then Release, Grasp the Entire Situation

To scrupulously observe the water release system, they persevere in "looking first, then releasing" and "reporting the acreage first, releasing water in a planned way." Each water-using unit must submit a request to the management section before water is released for irrigation. The professional administrators of the management section and the leadership of the commune go together to the water-using unit to investigate, determine the drought condition, confirm the irrigated acreage, and carry out the "four fixes," that is, "fix specific people to administer, fix the acreage to be irrigated, fix the amount of water to be released, and fix the time of release." Only then are the gates opened for rational irrigation.

During drought resistance, the full-time administrators must grasp the situation as a whole and look into the development and transformation of drought conditions at all times. They must persist in putting proletarian politics in command and carry out the "three diligents," that is: diligent feet — go out into the fields to investigate and gather firsthand materials on the drought conditions; diligent mouth — regularly publicize among the masses the management system for water use and advocate taking the entire situation into account and utilizing water sparingly to guarantee a bumper harvest despite the drought; and diligent hands — go out personally and participate with the masses in the practice of irrigation. The full-time administrators and the cadres of the communes usually hurry to the edge of the fields during the day to determine the drought and irrigation conditions, and in the evening, they protect the canal lines and gather the water flows to send to the lower reaches.

## III. THE RATIONAL IRRIGATION OF RICE

The Meichuan Reservoir Management Office has undergone a [feedback] process of practice and knowledge in determining how to manage the irrigation district so that it better serves increases in farm output. In the beginning, they only knew that "whether or not there is a harvest depends on water, and the size of the harvest depends on fertilizer," but they had not mastered exactly how much water rice actually needs to obtain a high, steady yield. Through study and by clarifying their thought of serving agriculture, they afterward realized that the purpose of constructing waterworks is mainly to guarantee increased agricultural production. To assess whether a water project is being properly managed and utilized, it is important to look at its role in increasing agricultural output; only high yields count. Thus those who work in water management must comprehend the laws governing the water requirements of crops, stress practical results in agriculture, and use materialist dialectics to study nature and lead production.

### 1. Experiments in Rice Irrigation

Observing Chairman Mao's teaching, "Subject everything to experimentation," since 1960 the Meichuan Reservoir has established irrigation experiment stations to undertake scientific experimentation, seeking the laws of water utilization in irrigation and rice-irrigating methods which result in high yields and low water consumption. According to experimental data

Table 7

Double-Crop Rice Growing Period Irrigation Water Use

| Year | Early rice ($m^3$/mou) | Late rice ($m^3$/mou) | Two crop rice ($m^3$/mou) |
|---|---|---|---|
| 1960 | 121 | 162 | 283 |
| 1961 | 247 | 223 | 470 |
| 1962 | 104 | 147 | 251 |
| 1963 | 195 | 146 | 341 |
| 1964 | 140 | 292 | 432 |
| Average | 161.4 | 194 | 355.4 |

for 1960 through 1964, the total amount of water used in irrigating double-crop rice was 495.4 cubic meters per mou. This consists of the basic water-use figure (see Table 7) plus the amount of water used to soak the fields twice for early and late rice (calculated at 60 cubic meters per mou for early rice and 80 cubic meters per mou for late rice). During the years of experimentation, the drought in 1961 was the most severe, lasting eighty days. The amount of water used in double-crop rice irrigation was the greatest in that year, reaching 470 cubic meters per mou, which when added to the 140 cubic meters per mou of water used to soak the fields for early and late rice, yields a total irrigation water use of 610 cubic meters per mou.

Before 1964, the irrigation experimentation carried out by the Meichuan Reservoir was mainly specialized and was carried out by a small number of full-time personnel in plots within the large fields. This method of experimentation seemed to involve leaving the experimental station and linking up with production, even though the experimental plots were not in the large fields of the masses. In reality, however, it was divorced from the masses and from production. It just meant that a small number of experimenters made several rounds of the fields each day; the masses did not understand what they were doing. Because the masses did not understand the significance and purpose of irrigation experimentation, it was difficult to popularize the results of the experiments.

The Meichuan Management Office summed up its experiences and lessons in irrigation experimentation from the previous several years, studied Chairman Mao's teaching that "all work must involve a mass movement, without a mass movement it won't work," raised their consciousness, clarified their orientation, and changed their closed-door method of carrying out experimentation. In 1964, they adopted the methods of "combine small-acreage experiments with large-acreage experiments" and "combine specialized experiments with mass experiments." They carried out rice irrigation water-use experiments on a large area of 2,400 mou in three brigades (Baishi, Wuli, and Wangsheng) in Hongxing Commune, linking this with the station's plot experiments and the experimental fields of the management sections. The concrete steps were, first, to call a meeting of production team leaders and peasant technicians to raise their consciousness and solve the Three Fears (the fear of expending labor, the fear of trouble, and the fear of reduction in output), to clarify the significance of scientific farming and of carrying out irrigation experiments, and to teach simple survey methods and the requirements for experiments in irrigation water use. In addition, they organized a twenty-five member backbone squad and required each member to personally grasp 1 to 8 mou of experimental fields and use this to promote the mass experimental fields of the production teams. They had them measure the water depth every two to three days and also whenever there was a rainfall or irrigation was being carried out, and they had them calculate the cumulative water consumption. Since the Meichuan Irrigation District has little water and a large irrigated area, the large-acreage experiments adopted the method of storage with shallow irrigation. Ordinarily, they carried out shallow irrigation, and when it rained, they increased the depth of the water appropriately, to make better use of the increased rainfall. From the large-acreage experiments, the masses saw the advantages of the shallow irrigation of rice: it saves water and increases the yield. For instance, the 1.1 mou of early rice planted in Chen Xiaoqing's experimental fields in Baishi Brigade had a yield of 660 jin per mou [4.95 t./ha.] and, during the growth period, consumed 357 cubic meters of water per mou. The 1.1 mou of late rice planted in Gao Youru's experimental fields in Wuli Brigade yielded 483 jin per mou [3.62 t./ha.] with a water consumption of 430 cubic meters per mou over the entire growth period. The masses said in praise, "This kind of experiment is really good; the water used is less, and the output is high."

Irrigation experimentation is professional scientific research and is the responsibility of specified professionals. They select experimental plots of a representative nature, and they procure relatively comprehensive sets of surveying tools and equipment in order to carry out more systematic and accurate surveys. This is entirely necessary. At the same time, however, such experimentation also has a mass nature. The masses must be broadly mobilized to carry out experiments over large areas. Only then can experimental work and the realities of production be closely combined. The former is the point, the latter the area. Only by combining the point and the area can the point guide the area and the area promote the point. Only when this kind of plot experiment has a broad base can its results be propagated more rapidly. Moreover, the experimental results in the larger acreage can supplement the insufficiencies of plot experimentation, improve the precision of plot experiments, and enable them to be more representative. In the past several years, the Meichuan Irrigation District has already universally popularized the method of shallow irrigation and sun-dried fields for rice. This is inseparable from the development of irrigation experimentation on the larger acreages.

## 2. Rational Irrigation of Paddy Rice

"Paddy rice, paddy rice, raise rice with water." In the past in the Meichuan District, the masses were accustomed to deep-water irrigation because it enabled them to raise the rice, store water, and reduce weeds. They only looked at the affinity of rice for water, not its aversion to it. For paddy rice, "Water is the life force of the seedlings, but it is also their sickness." Without water, they cannot grow normally, but if there is too much water, it can hinder growth and affect yields. Therefore, rational irrigation of rice not only can use water sparingly, but it is also an important measure in wresting high rice yields. In the past, the Hongxing Commune used deep-water irrigation, and its rice yields were generally only 300 to 400 jin per mou [2.25 to 3.0 t./ha.], with high-yield fields having no more than 600 to 700 jin per mou [4.5 to 5.25 t./ha.]. Before 1965, the commune's total grain output was only about 7 million jin [3,500 t.]. Since then, they have carried out scientific experiments and introduced the rational irrigation of rice, linking it with other production measures to cause a marked increase in the double-crop rice yield. For instance, in 1971 the experimental plot of Commune Secretary Wang Derong had an early-rice yield of 1,024 jin per mou [7.68 t./ha.] and a late-rice yield of 1,203.5 jin per mou [9.03 t./ha.]. The commune's total grain output reached 11.79 million jin [5,895 t.], 59 percent greater than in 1965.

The results of experiments in rice irrigation over the past several years in the Meichuan Irrigation District, along with their study of the Xishuishiyue Brigade and summing up of the rice irrigation experiences of the masses in the irrigation district, prove that the frugal irrigation of rice with shallow water, combined with the sun drying the fields at the appropriate time, can achieve the goals of saving water while attaining high yields. In concrete terms, their experience is to rationally control the water depth in the fields according to the different growth stages of rice. For early rice, this is expressed as: "Transplanting, mud-skin water; revival of green, shoot-nourishing water; tillering, mud-moistening water; sprout promotion, letting the water out; ear formation and flowering, root submerging water; and milky ripening stage, field-crossing water."

a) Transplanting, Mud-skin Water

The quality of transplanting directly affects the growth of rice. Following the introduction of new farming techniques, the method adopted for early rice has been mainly one of storing the seedlings and transplanting the sprouts when they are small. In the main field, a machine is commonly used to mark out the crisscross rows required by rational close planting. To ensure the quality of transplanting, a mud-skin water, that is, 1 to 2 millimeters deep, should be maintained on the field surface during the transplanting. In this way, rational close planting can be ensured, and the seedlings can be planted in a straight, shallow, stable, and orderly fashion, while avoiding seedling death from lack of water or their floating in water which is too deep. This raises the seedling survival rate. Experiments on early-rice irrigation in 1972 showed that mud-skin water transplanting raises the seedling survival rate by about 3 to 5 percent over deep water transplanting.

b) Revival of Green, Shoot-nourishing Water

When the young shoots are moved from the seedling bed to the main field, the roots all suffer a certain amount of damage. Their water absorption capacity weakens, and they may easily lose their water balance. At this time, a suitable water level must be maintained on the field surface to provide the shoots with a relatively stable water and temperature environment in order to facilitate an early renewal of root growth and to increase the revival of green as rapidly as possible. The temperature during the early-rice regreening period in Meichuan District is rather low. If the irrigation water is too deep, the mud temperature will fall. When the shoots are soaked in deep water, it is not conducive to new root growth, and the shoots become too supple. If the water layer over the field surface is too shallow or altogether absent, the soil solution concentration increases, leading easily to root scorching which is not conducive to the growth of new roots and may delay regreening.

The local peasant proverbs "If you neglect yellow seedlings for a while, they grow old without sprouting" and "Sun-drying yellow seedlings is the same as not transplanting them" clearly show the importance of maintaining an appropriate water level to promote shoot regreening. From the experience of the Meichuan Irrigation District, an irrigation water depth of about one cun [33 millimeters] is appropriate at this stage.

c) Tillering, Mud-moistening Water

Not long after shoot regreening, tillering begins. The promotion of early tillering is an important link in achieving a high rice yield. But early tillering requires sufficient sunlight and nutrients and comparatively high mud and air temperatures. Generally, the temperature during the early tillering period is still rather low. Low temperatures inhibit microbial activity and the decomposition of nutrients in the soil, and lower the nutrient-absorbing capacity of the root system. This causes the rice stand to absorb insufficient nutrients and affects early tillering. "Tillering, mud-moistening water" indicates a method of shallow irrigation and alternating dry and moist in order to maintain a regular water level of 0.5 to 1.0 cun [17 to 33 millimeters] on the field surface. Districts where water sources are relatively convenient adopt the method of "In the daytime, plenty of water to nourish the flowers; no water left by night" and "With one watering each day, vital water comes daily," which enables the field surface to maintain dryness and humidity, with humidity as the main condition. This method of irrigation, when adopted, can raise the mud temperature and increase the amount of air in the soil, promoting microbial activity, accelerating organic decomposition and raising the nutrient-absorbing capacity of the shoot root system. This allows the shoots to obtain sufficient nutrients and promotes early tillering of the rice.

d) Sprout Promotion, Let the Water out (Dry the Field)

Letting the water out to promote the sprouts indicates that when the number of tillers reaches a certain level (a high-yield field requires about 450,000 per mou), the water is drained instantly, and the field is dried in the sun. This inhibits the ineffective tiller and enables the rice plants to have "mid [period] stability" and "late [period] soundness" on a basis of early development.

Practice demonstrates that sprout promotion through drying the field has the following functions:

1) It can inhibit the ineffective tillers, allowing the number of sprouts per mou to remain constant in order to facilitate the movement of air and the penetration of light between the plants, causing the ears to enlarge and the grains to firm up, thereby increasing output.

2) It can promote the health and vitality of the old roots, the clustering of the new roots, and the deepening of the root system, enlarging the scope of activity of the root system so that it thoroughly absorbs the nutrients in the soil.

3) It strengthens the aeration function in the soil, oxidizing poisonous substances in the soil and increasing its capability for aerobic microbial activity, thereby promoting the decomposition of organic material and the storage of a large amount of nutrients during young spike differentiation.

4) It can inhibit excessive growth of stalks and leaves, promoting the health and vitality of the plants and increasing their capacity to resist bending and disease.

5) It increases the day-night temperature differential and lowers the relative humidity in the fields, decreasing the conditions for the development of disease.

Drying the fields must be done in accordance with concrete conditions by seizing opportunities and strengthening management. In drying the fields, one must make the three observations, that is, observe the sprouts, observe the fields, and observe the weather. Observe the sprouts: In general, about twenty-five to twenty-eight days after transplanting, when the basic number of sprouts has reached about 450,000 per mou, the water should be drained off and the fields dried in the sun. Observe the fields: In long* fields, marshy fields [deficient in potassium], clayey fields, cold waterlogged fields, and fields

---

*Long (垅 ) usually refers to a field ridge, but here appears to denote a small alluvial valley between mountain ridges. —J. E. N.

where shoot growth is overabundant, one must dry early and heavily, until hairline cracks appear in the field and the leaves turn yellow, generally six to seven days. In high fields, sandy fields, lean [soil] fields, and fields where growth is normal and leaf color a healthy green, one must dry lightly, until the field is dry but not cracked, no mud sticks to the feet, and the leaf color has faded. This generally requires three to five days of drying. Observe the weather: As much as possible, use clear days to dry the field. Before drying the fields, no matter whether the individual fields are large or small, ditches must be dug all around and through the middle, and they must be linked together so that no water will accumulate if it rains and once the rain passes, the fields will remain dry.

The fields must be dried until the shoots turn from green to yellow, the leaves straighten out, the shoots straighten up, the seedling root zone coarsens, and a large number of white roots and fibrous roots appear in the fields. If the fields have been dried enough, when water is released the sprouts will turn green.

e) Ear Formation and Flowering, Root-submerging Water

After the fields are dried, paddy rice enters the stages of ear formation, heading, and flowering. During this period, the shoot growth flourishes, air temperature is high, evaporation off the leaf surfaces is heavy, and photosynthesis becomes markedly stronger. Because of these factors, the amount of water required is the greatest of the entire growth period. One cannot [allow the crop to] suffer lack of water. If that happens, the rice ears will become small, and the kernel count will fall, with an increase in empty and half-filled kernels. The peasant saying "The tree fears the skinning of its bark, the paddy rice fears the drying of its husks" thoroughly demonstrates the importance of the water requirements at this stage. On the other hand, one must note that the irrigation water cannot be too deep. At present, most rice is densely planted and heavily fertilized, and the plants are also short. Excessive irrigation water depth can affect aeration and the penetration of light and can easily lead to disease. The so-called "root-submerging water" means to keep the irrigation water depth controlled at about 1 to 1.5 cun [33 to 50 millimeters].

f) Milky Ripening Stage, Field-crossing Water

The milky ripening stage is the later period of rice growth when the moisture demands gradually diminish and can be satisfied by simply maintaining dampness on the field surface. However, water cannot be cut off too early or the rice stalks and roots will weaken early, maturation will be restrained, and the attainment of full weight by the seed grains will be affected, reducing output. If there is too much irrigation water and the water level is too deep, the rice may stay green without maturing, delaying the harvest and hampering the rush transplanting of late rice. The "field-crossing water" means to maintain a condition of alternating dryness and dampness on the field surface, with primary emphasis on dampness.

g) Yellow Ripe, Drain Dry

At this time, the rice no longer needs moisture. Water should immediately be drained to dry the field and facilitate harvesting.

The irrigation of late rice is basically a frequent, shallow watering, but it has some special features. The temperature is high after late-rice transplanting. A water depth of about 1 to 1.5 cun [33 to 50 millimeters] may be maintained on the field surface to facilitate early shoot activation and revival of green. During the tillering period, watering should be frequent and shallow, in general maintaining a water depth of half a cun, relying on natural drainage before irrigating again. In this way, the moisture demands of the tillering period can be satisfied while speeding up the dispersion of heat in the soil at night, lowering the mud temperature, and promoting root development and tillering. When the total number of tillers reaches about

450,000 to 500,000 per mou, the water should be drained and the fields dried in the sun. But this should be done a bit more lightly and for a shorter period than for early rice. The ear-formation and flowering stage requires root-submerging water and the milky-ripening stage requires field-crossing water. When the spikes begin to dip, ditches must be dug at the appropriate time to drain the water and allow the field surface to maintain a condition of alternating dryness and dampness so that one can stand on it. This facilitates the intercropping of green fertilizer or wheat.

Over the past several years, the Meichuan Irrigation District has basically popularized shallow irrigation and sun drying of the fields. In the beginning, there were differing viewpoints. Some people thought that shallow irrigation would make it easy for weeds to grow. But they only looked at one aspect of the problem. Problems must be viewed dialectically. If shallow irrigation makes it easy for weeds to grow, it must also facilitate seedling growth. The contradiction between shallow water and weed growth can be solved by developing people's subjective initiative to weed the fields and using the weeds to fertilize in order to promote the growth of the shoots even better. The experience of Hongxing Commune is that shallow irrigation certainly requires a strengthening of field management, but all the weeds can be cleared. They originally weeded every ten days, but after introducing shallow irrigation, they changed this to every seven days. In the past, some people were of the opinion that shallow, frequent irrigation definitely requires favorable water conditions and that since there was little water in the Meichuan Reservoir and the water was not delivered on time, they could not carry out shallow and frequent irrigation. However, human will is the determining factor in doing things. The Meichuan Irrigation District has a large number of ponds. Simply by strengthening pond management and fully developing their role, the ponds could be closely linked to the reservoir water and their joint utilization could completely solve this contradiction.

It is necessary to point out, however, that shallow, frequent irrigation is not an absolute. In keeping with the differences in water conservancy conditions in the district and the different stages of rice growth and under the precondition of emphasizing shallow irrigation, during certain short periods of time it is also necessary to have moderate and deep storage, in order to raise the utilization rate of rainwater. For instance, in the Meichuan Irrigation District there are still some border districts with relatively few ponds which are also rather distant from the reservoir. During the revival of green in the late rice and the infantile-ripening and earing stages of paddy rice, the fields may store water a bit more deeply after a rainfall in order to make effective use of the fallen rain.

## IV. IMPROVE SOIL THROUGH DRAINAGE, CREATE FARMLAND THROUGH RIVER CONTROL

The Meichuan Reservoir Management Office Party Branch places great stress on drainage work in the irrigation district, in accordance with Chairman Mao's teaching "Have water when there is drought, drain water when there is flooding." The very fact that drainage has been made part of the management work of the irrigation district has involved a process of cognition. In the past, they only knew that water plays an important role in increasing farm output. They lacked the essential knowledge that too much water is harmful. They therefore "only cared about irrigation, not drainage" and "only knew enough to release water to irrigate the fields, but did not ask about the yields." Through investigation they discovered that yields within the irrigation district were very unbalanced. Some of the fields had low yields not because they were not irrigated, but because the field irrigation and drainage system was not sound, irrigation was plot-to-plot or by flooding, and flow loss of water and fertilizer was serious. In other cases, it was because they were topographically low and marshy with poor drainage and were thus flooded by natural rainfall, causing cold incursion in normal years. This made them realize that in order to make irrigation district management work better serve increased agricultural output, they must "grasp drainage and irrigation together," combine farmland water conservancy construction with farmland capital construction, and combine drainage and river control with soil improvement and field creation work.

## 1. Eliminate Plot-to-Plot Irrigation, Transform Long Fields

The hilly area has a variable topography with alternating ridges and alluvial spots. The long (alluvial) fields cover quite a large area. In the past, most of the long fields lacked a field irrigation and drainage system, and the phenomenon of plot-to-plot irrigation and plot-to-plot drainage was extremely serious. In addition to causing fertilizer loss through leakage and lowering the water temperature, plot-to-plot irrigation and drainage adversely affects rational irrigation in that it wastes water and it prevents the draining of water to dry the fields. When there is a rainstorm, there is no escape path for the water, so it covers the fields, floods the seedlings, and washes away the soil. During irrigation, the water flows around the high spots so that the irrigation is not timely and drainage does not dry the fields. Through investigation and study, the staff of the management office found that plot-to-plot irrigation and drainage is one of the main causes of low yields in the long fields. In order to eliminate the phenomenon of plot-to-plot irrigation and drainage it is necessary to construct an irrigation and drainage field ditch system and combine this with land leveling and the transformation of the long fields. The old long-field plots are small and irregular in shape, a vestige of the small peasant economy of several thousand years of feudal society. They are most unsuitable to the development of socialist agricultural production. We have to rebuild the original long fields.

Under the leadership of the qu Party committee, the masses were mobilized and relied on to operate a test point in the Wuli Brigade of Hongxing Commune. Figure 4a is a drawing of a long field in the No. 9 Team [production team] before it was rebuilt. Its total area was 12.5 mou, divided into thirteen plots of various sizes, with an average area less than a single mou. The shapes of the plots were most irregular and had no irrigation or drainage canal. With rebuilding, the original thirteen plots were combined into five relatively large plots with an average size of 2.5 mou and a regular shape (see Figure 4b).

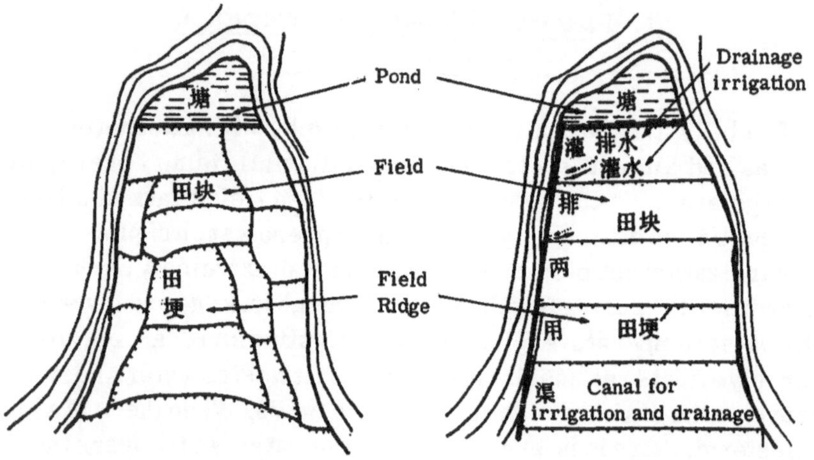


*a* Long field before reconstruction

*b* Long field after reconstruction

Figure 4

In keeping with the topographic conditions, a dual-use irrigation and drainage ditch was dug on the left side. During irrigation, the water depth on each plot can be controlled, and water can be drained to sun dry the fields as well. When it rains, the water has an escape path and no longer floods the seedlings or washes away the soil. Water is spared, fertilizer is preserved, the water and land temperatures have been raised, and the soil moisture, nutrient, and aeration conditions have been improved considerably, creating favorable conditions for high crop yields. With the enlargement of the plots, tractors can also be used in the fields. In the past, some comrades did not understand and thought that digging ditches in the long fields would reduce the acreage. In reality it even increases it. Statistics indicate that the leveling of the crisscrossing field ridges can increase the acreage by at least 3 to 5 percent.

From the test point at the Wuli Brigade, the masses have now come to realize the advantages of eliminating plot-to-plot irrigation and rebuilding the long fields. This is currently being extended throughout the entire district.

According to the experience of the Meichuan Irrigation District, when constructing a field irrigation and drainage network while rebuilding the long fields, the arrangement of the irrigation and drainage canals takes one of the following two forms:

a) Combined Placement of Irrigation and Drainage Canals

In level fields on long, narrow mountain ridge bottoms (with a width of about 100 meters), the field irrigation and drainage canals may be combined and situated on one side of the long field. The long side of the plots is perpendicular to a dual-use irrigation and drainage canal. Each plot has a water inlet-outlet for both irrigation and drainage (as in Figure 4b).

If the long field is rather broad (over 200 meters wide), with a gentle slope, a dual-use irrigation and drainage canal may be located in the middle. If the mountain ridge crest is rather high and the slope surface runoff great, drainage ditches (or dual-use irrigation and drainage ditches) may, in accordance with concrete conditions, be located on one or both edges of the low field. Figure 5 is of a long field in the No. 13 Team of the

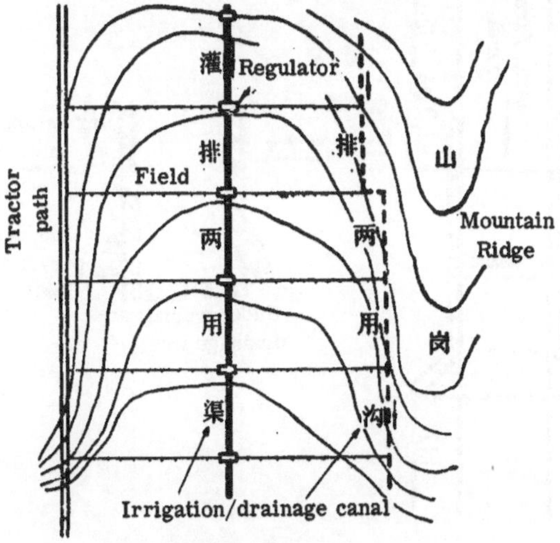


Figure 5

Wuli Brigade. The ridge bottom width is about 200 meters, with a total area of about eighty mou. After the land was leveled, it was rebuilt into eight regular plots, each about ten mou, which has facilitated machine cultivation. In the middle of the long field a dual-use irrigation and drainage canal was dug. Considering the rather large acreage of the long field, a dual-use irrigation and drainage ditch was dug on the right side of the mountain ridge bottom to intercept the surface runoff from the high mountain ridge crest on the right side. The dual-use irrigation and drainage canal located in the middle can drain both surface and ground water. This facilitates the lowering of the water level in the herbaceous seed fields after the harvesting of late rice. Regulating structures have been built on the canal for this purpose. In order to suit the needs of increasing farm output, the form of the structures allows them not only to irrigate and drain (surface water) but also to drain the ground water (see Figure 6). Before rebuilding, the yield of early and late rice was 700 jin per mou [5.25 t./ha.]. Now the yield for both crops is 1,000 jin per mou [7.5 t./ha.].

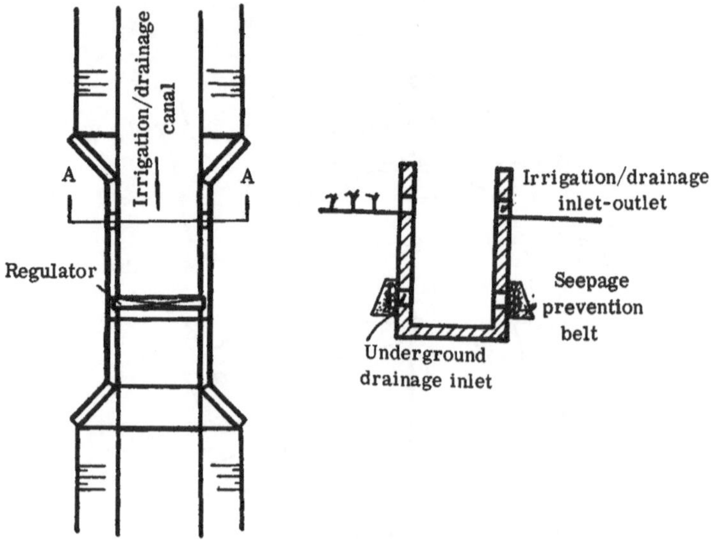


Figure 6. Regulator

b) Separate Placement of Irrigation and Drainage Canals

In relatively narrow ridge bottoms with a marked unidirectional slope, the irrigation and drainage canals may be located separately, with the irrigation canal on the elevated edge of the ridge bottom and the drainage ditch on the low edge (see Figure 7).

If the ridge bottom is broad with a marked natural trough in the middle, the irrigation and drainage canals may also be separated with the drainage ditch in the middle and irrigation canals along both edges (see Figure 8).

It must be pointed out that the separation of irrigation and drainage is not an absolute. If there is a relatively high mountain ridge crest near the side with the irrigation canal and if the surface runoff from the slope is rather large, the irrigation canal may be used to intercept the surface runoff and serve as a drainage ditch.

To sum up, when building a field irrigation and drainage

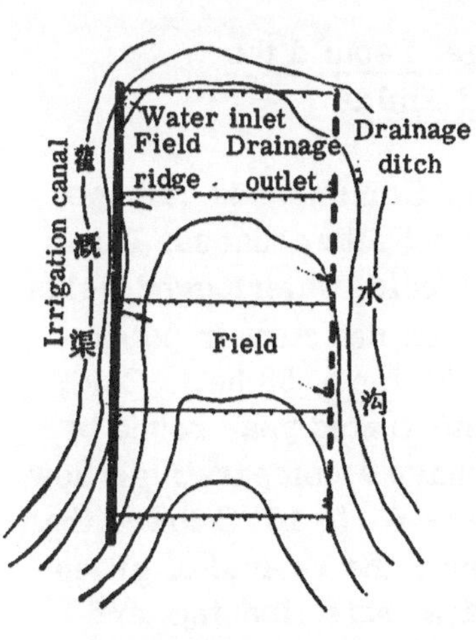


Figure 7

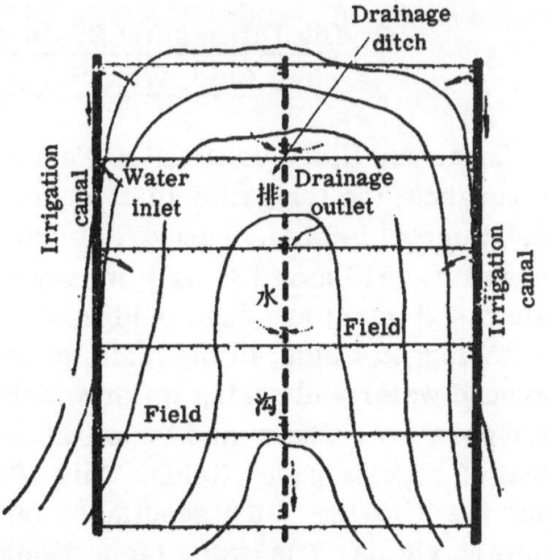


Figure 8

system, no matter what form of placement is selected, it must conform to the actual conditions of the locality and be combined with land leveling, the rebuilding of long fields, and the large-scale creation of garden-style fields in order to construct stable, high-yield fields with both irrigation and drainage and which accommodate machine cultivation. In leveling land, it is necessary to act according to topographic conditions and combine those plots which do not have a large vertical separation in order to reduce the amount of work. The multiple-cropping index on the land in the Meichuan Irrigation District is high, all of it devoted to continuous double-crop rice, with three crops a year in one portion, consisting of wheat, rice, and rice, or oilseeds, rice, and rice. Thus, the time during which leveling the land can take place is very short and must be carried out in stages according to manpower and animal power conditions. In construction work, do the easy projects first and the hard ones later; in enlarging the plots, do some enlarging and then do more. Standards may go gradually from low to high. Each stage should be completed and provide benefits within a single year so that production and field reconstruction do not interfere with one another.

### 2. Dig Ditches for Drainage, Rebuild the Cold, Waterlogged Fields

Guanshan Ridge Bottom in Nanquan Commune is famous throughout the irrigation district for its backwardness. It has 2,100 mou [140 ha.] of paddy, of which cold, waterlogged fields constitute 510 mou [34 ha.]; muddy fields deficient in potassium, 720 mou; and dead mud fields, 870 mou [58 ha.]. Cold, waterlogged fields, in the main, are infiltrated year round by ground water and spring water which have a comparatively low temperature. Their mud temperature is 6° to 10° C lower than that of regular paddy fields. This affects the revival of green and the tillering of the seedlings, delays their ripening, and lowers yields. The water table under the potassium deficient muddy fields is high, with cold infiltration. On their surface is a thick (about one meter) layer of surface mud, which covers a person past the knee and touches the skin of the belly of an ox. Cultivation is difficult, and it is hard for the seedlings to grow. Dead mud fields are impenetrable to water, do not aerate, and have a low organic content with many virulent substances. When shoots are transplanted, they turn from green to yellow, from yellow to red, and finally from red to black, and they all fall over dead. Guanshan Ridge Bottom is fifteen kilometers long, yet had not a single drainage ditch. After a big rain, the mountain floodwaters would drain directly, covering the entire ridge bottom. The seedlings would be flooded, and the fields washed away. The grain harvest would regularly fail. The masses described it in this way: "If you live on Guanshan Ridge Bottom, you must always be poor; if the sky is clear for three days, the fields crack; if there is heavy rain for a day it fills up the fields; when an ox goes into the field it bows its head [that is, it buckles forward]; when a person goes into the field, both hands stick in the mud and his or her clothes become wet; a whole year's human and ox power can be exhausted and the yield will only be 100 jin per mou [0.75 t/ha.]."

After liberation and the construction of the Meichuan Reservoir, the problem of drought was solved and the appearance of Guanshan Ridge Bottom changed somewhat. But the natural disasters of flood, excess surface water, and cold infiltration were not solved in a fundamental way, and farm output never increased. It remained a famous low-yield area in the district. In a normal year, the yield from a single crop would only be 200 to 300 jin per mou [1.5 to 2.25 t./ha.]. In 1963, a large rainstorm became a disaster, and over 200,000 jin [100 t.] of grain rotted.

Through investigation and study, the reservoir management office came to see that the principal contradiction of Guanshan Ridge Bottom was drainage. First they dug a drainage ditch in order to control drainage. Having eliminated water disasters, they then mixed fertilizer into the soil and step by step rebuilt the cold waterlogged and potassium deficient muddy fields. In 1966, the masses dug a small drainage ditch in the middle of the ridge bottom, but because the silt was deep, the ditch small, and the side slopes unstable, after a rainfall the soil eroded into the ditch, seriously collapsing the slopes and rapidly silting up the ditch. In 1968 they dug another one, but since the standards were too low it did not serve to drain water. The management office conscientiously summed up the lessons of the failure of the two drainage ditches. The principal causes were: one, the drainage ditches were too shallow and did not serve to drain off the cold intruding water or to lower the water table, and the cross section of the ditch was too small and not sufficient to drain away the surface runoff; and two, because the mud was too deep, the slopes along the sides of the drainage ditches would not hold and collapsed easily. By searching out the causes of the failures, the situation became clear, and their resolution [to change it] became great. In 1970, under the direct leadership of the qu Party committee, the entire district vigorously launched a "Learn from Dazhai in agriculture" campaign. A secretary of the qu Party committee went in person to Nanquan Commune to mobilize the masses extensively to thoroughly transform Guanshan Ridge Bottom. The broad masses of Nanquan Commune fostered the revolutionary spirit of "self-reliance and arduous struggle" and worked hard for one winter. Braving serious cold they worked in waist-deep mud fields and transported a large amount of stone from Guanshanzhai for supporting the base and bricking up the slopes. They finally conquered the cold infiltration and mud and dug a main drainage ditch 4,895 meters long, 2 to 3 meters deep, and with a base width of 1.5 to 3.5 meters, and branch ditches with a total length of 9,465 meters (see Figure 9). The total earthwork was 337,152 cubic meters, the total stonework, 1,500 cubic meters. The over 2,000 mou [167 ha.] of cold waterlogged mud fields which were preliminarily rebuilt produced benefits that year. Single cropping was changed to double cropping, and the yield increased from the former 200 to 300 jin per mou to over 800 jin per mou [6 t./ha.]. Over 1,000 mou of winter fallow land was planted in safflower for the first time. The masses expressed their deep

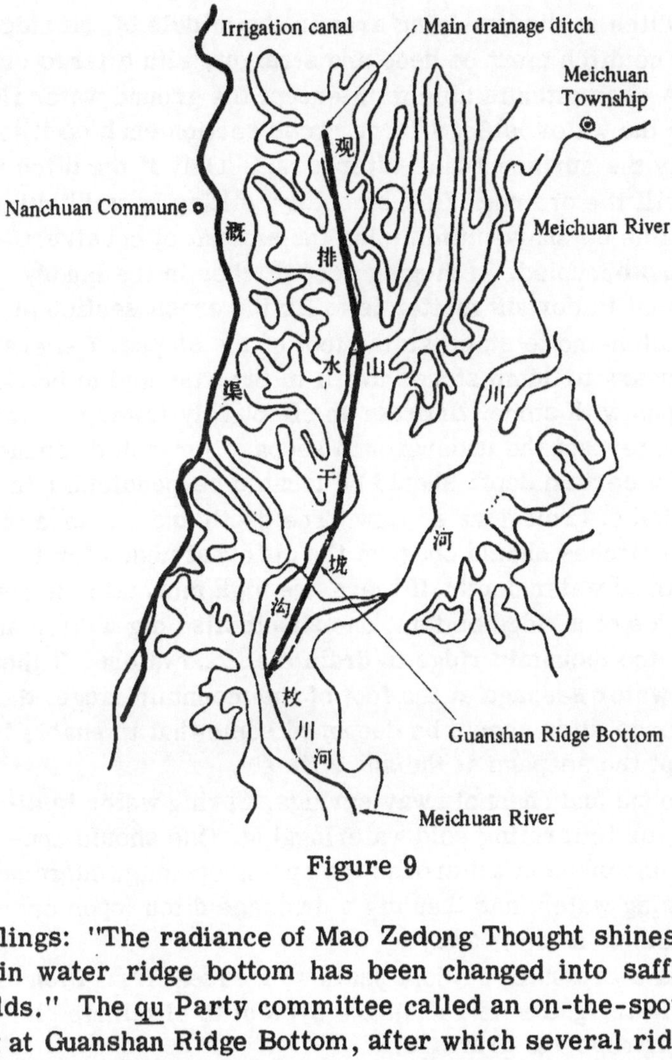


Figure 9

feelings: "The radiance of Mao Zedong Thought shines. The plain water ridge bottom has been changed into safflower fields." The qu Party committee called an on-the-spot meeting at Guanshan Ridge Bottom, after which several ridge bottoms in Hongxing and Duqiao communes were brought under control through the rebuilding of their cold waterlogged and muddy fields.

According to the experience of the Meichuan Irrigation District, improving cold waterlogged and muddy fields mainly involves the following measures:

1) Digging ditches to drain the water. They locate the main

drainage ditch in the low-lying area in the middle of the ridge bottom. The ditch must be deep and straight, with a large cross section. A deep ditch is able to intercept the ground water flows and lower the water table; a large cross section enables it to drain away the surface runoff after a rain. Only if the ditch is straight will the drainage flow smoothly, silting be unlikely, and the canal line be short, minimizing the amount of construction and the land occupied. In digging deep ditches in the muddy fields a most important matter is to fix the cross section of the drainage ditch and to stabilize the foot of the slopes. Generally it is necessary to dump stones to fill in the base and to brick in the slopes with stone. In order to effectively lower the water table and intercept the underground seepage, branch drainage ditches of a certain depth should be located perpendicular to the direction of ground water flow. The depth and distance of the branch ditches should observe the different needs for lowering the ground water depth. If there are high mountain ridges on both sides of a ridge bottom, one should also dig a ditch at the foot of the mountain ridge to drain the floodwaters. If there is ground water seepage at the foot of the mountain ridge, the flood drainage ditch should be deepened somewhat to enable it to intercept the seepage at the same time.

2) Surround and channel away springs. Spring water is always a factor in forming cold waterlogging. One should construct an embankment all around the spring opening, surrounding the spring water, and then dig a drainage ditch (open or underground) to drain it away.

3) Irrigate rationally. Adopt shallow, frequent irrigation and build a field irrigation and drainage system to eliminate plot-to-plot irrigation and drainage.

4) Mix sand to sink to the bottom in order to make fields with a deep mud base become shallow. About 1,200 to 1,500 <u>dan</u> [60 to 75 t.] of sand were mixed into each <u>mou</u> on Guanshan Ridge Bottom. The results of the sand mixing were especially good on the dead mud fields which were impermeable to water and air. In 1972, the Songyang Commune alone improved over 2,000 <u>mou</u> of land through mixing in sand.

5) Grow green fertilizer to increase the organic matter.

6) Fertilize rationally. Utilize thermal fertilizers such as a compost of ox and horse manure, wood ash, or lime to raise the mud temperature and satisfy the nutrient requirements of rice.

### 3. Rearrange the River Course and Rebuild the Farmland through Drainage

With the construction of the Meichuan Reservoir, the Meichuan River's flow was basically cut off. The masses, acting on their own, narrowed the old riverbed by creating some farmland along the banks. But since the old river course was quite crooked and the riverbed was narrowed too much, drainage was not smooth during rainstorms, and the farmland was flooded. In addition, the Meichuan Irrigation District also had some natural gullies. Drainage was affected because these gullies were also crooked and had an insufficient cross section.

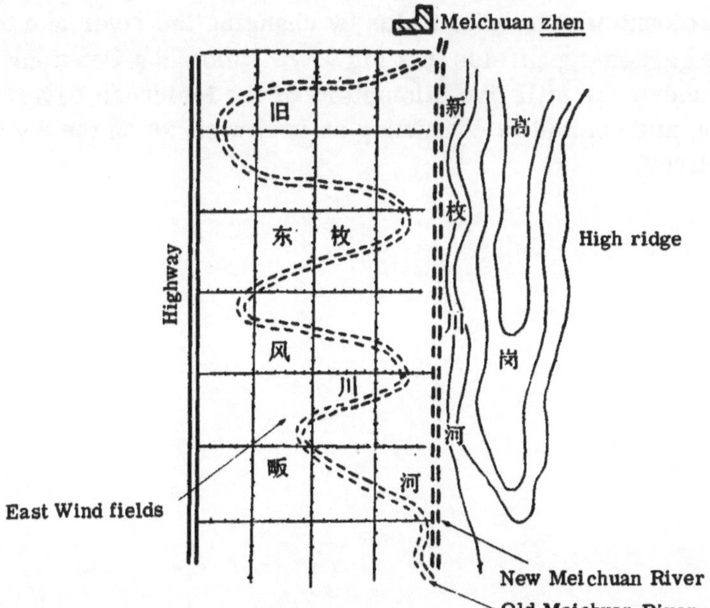


Figure 10

The Meichuan Management Office, while grasping irrigation work well, has also paid serious attention to drainage in the irrigation district. Under the leadership of the qu Party committee, they began by grasping a test point in the Dongfeng No. 1 Brigade of Hongxing Commune where they combined the straightening of the river course with creating garden-type fields in a big way. Figure 10 is a representation of the rebuilding of the fields and river course in Dongfeng. The old crooked Meichuan River has been basically filled in and turned into farmland, while a new five-kilometer Meichuan River course has been constructed. This course is smooth and straight, and drainage is easy. The land has been leveled, allowing the formerly irregular plots of various sizes to be combined and enlarged into orderly shaped plots averaging about ten mou [0.67 ha.] each. They have also constructed a field irrigation and drainage system and a road network and have in a preliminary way realized the creation of garden-type fields. The qu Party committee called an on-the-spot conference in the Dongfeng fields, and now a mass movement is presently unfolding in a profound way to build fields by changing the river and to create garden-type fields in a big way. Below the Dongfeng fields there are still five kilometers of the Meichuan River course, and control is continuing on it as well as on the Songyang River.

# V. PARTY LEADERSHIP AND THE MASS LINE

## 1. Strengthen Party Leadership, Be a Good Party Officer

The key to how the Meichuan Reservoir could "make large contributions though the reservoir is small and do many things though the people are few" lies in Party leadership. The Meichuan Reservoir Party branch realizes from its practical experience that if it is to do a good job in reservoir irrigation district management it must strengthen the unified leadership of the Party and actively take the initiative in being good Party officers.

In the beginning, individual leading cadres of the reservoir paid insufficient attention to respecting the leadership of the local Party committee. They paid attention to line leadership and neglected area leadership, so at times contradictions over water use arose between them and the qu Party committee. Afterward, they studied Chairman Mao's teachings on strengthening the unified leadership of the Party, understood the relationship between line and area, and strengthened the qu Party committee's leadership over the work of the reservoir irrigation district, with the planning, policy, management, and activities of the latter unified by the qu Party committee. Several times each year, the reservoir management office submits a report to the qu Party committee on water stored, meteorological conditions, and plans for fighting drought and using water. The qu Party committee attaches utmost importance to the work of the reservoir irrigation district and appoints one of its secretaries to hold the additional post of head of the management committee of the irrigation district. It also assigns a responsible comrade of the qu Party committee to oversee work in this area. To strengthen concrete leadership, a Party branch secretary of the reservoir management office participates on the qu Party committee. The reservoir irrigation district work is entered in the daily agenda of the qu Party committee, which makes arrangements and inspections and personally handles key problems.

For example, at the key moment in the 1972 drought resistance, the qu Party secretaries and the secretaries of the reservoir Party branch personally went to the seriously affected Taosi Commune to check out the drought conditions on the spot. They went to the lake to investigate and measure the water sources and visited the poor and lower-middle peasants and summed up their experience in fighting drought. They then assisted that commune in a concrete way in using the lake water to fight the major drought. This motivated the drought resistance struggle throughout the irrigation district. In the latter part of June, a medium rain fell. The qu Party committee immediately convened a radio broadcast conference to mobilize people to organize the masses to "lead the water from the ponds, lift water with machines, block the flows in riverbeds, and store water in the fields." They opened up new water sources in every way they could. For the period of drought resistance they established a headquarters for that purpose under the unified leadership of the qu Party committee. Responsible comrades of the qu Party committee and of the management office went together to the commune sector and divided up the area to inspect the drought and organize the masses to carry out a struggle against drought.

The Party committees at all levels in the irrigation district also pay utmost attention to irrigation district management work and place it on their daily agenda. Secretaries of the commune Party committees participate on the irrigation district management committee. Each administrative section pays attention to honoring the leadership of the local commune Party committee and reports to it at regular intervals. Different management squads set up under the irrigation district management committee with the management sections as their basic unit are led by commune Party committee secretaries, while responsible comrades of the management section and brigade Party branch secretaries participate in the organization.

In this way, all the management work of the reservoir irrigation district is carried out under the unified leadership of the qu Party committee.

In order to strengthen the Party's leadership, the Party branch of the reservoir management office has brought its role into play as a militant bulwark. Responsible comrades of the branch can all set good examples and take the lead in getting things done. Every year during the most intense days of the drought resistance at double rush, they are fighting day and night along the canals. They go wherever there is trouble. During the 1971 drought resistance at double rush, the Huangjiapang Aqueduct on the East Canal was damaged and could not deliver water to two communes in the lower reaches. The late rice could not be transplanted on time in the affected 9,000 mou. Comrades in the qu Party committee responsible for managing water conservancy and responsible comrades of the management office all hurried to the spot and mobilized the masses to do some rush construction using local methods. They battled for three days and nights and finally fixed it so that water could flow through smoothly. A responsible comrade of the Shichuan Reservoir, fifty-year-old Comrade Qin Laishan of the Party branch committee, regularly goes out to the commune sector to study the situation and grasp what the drought condition is. During the drought resistance, he continued to struggle despite an illness, and when it rained, he braved the rain to lead the water into the ponds. The masses of Nanquan Commune praise him: "Every plot of land in our commune has Old Qin's footprint, every pond his sweat."

The Meichuan Reservoir Management Office has come to realize from many years of practice that in order to strengthen the unified leadership of the Party it is necessary on the one hand to strengthen the Party concept and overcome the one-sided thinking which stresses the special nature of functional departments; on the other hand, one must actively take the initiative in being a good Party officer and bring into play one's own role in increasing agricultural output throughout the district. For the past several years, the Meichuan Reservoir Management Office have striven to be good officers of the qu Party committee in the three areas of weather, construction work, and water use. They have taken the initiative in handling their own work well and in sending timely reports to the qu Party committee to ask for instructions. For instance, after the beginning of summer in 1972, the rainfall was quite sparse. The water stored in the Meichuan Reservoir only came to 12 million cubic meters, compared to 18 million at the same time in 1971. Moreover, on over 100,000 mou of farmland in the irrigation district, it was necessary both to guarantee a bumper harvest of early rice and to protect the rush transplanting of late rice. At that time, a number of people lacked confidence in the proposal of the xian Party committee to "resist drought for a long time, everywhere, and to the end in order to seize a bumper harvest." Some people said: "This year the drought came early and little water is stored in the reservoir. If we guarantee the bumper harvest of early rice, we cannot protect the rush transplanting of late rice. We can only rescue one of the two." Some people also advocated: "This year there is little water in the ponds which raise fish. If we save the grain, we lose the fish; if we save the fish, we abandon the grain. Of the two heads, we have to lose one." The masses of the upper, middle, and lower reaches of the irrigation district each made their own calculations; some demanded that the gates be opened a bit early, while others hoped that water would be released a bit late. How should they solve the contradiction between scarce water and resisting the major drought? The management office acted according to Chairman Mao's teaching that "to investigate is to solve problems" and carried out an investigation of the water stored in the small reservoirs and ponds and the conditions of water deficiency in the fields throughout the irrigation district. The 5 small reservoirs, 16 very small reservoirs, and over 5,000 ponds had a total of 20 million cubic meters of water. Water from Malong Lake, the 12 rivers, underground water and unearthed springs could add 2 million cubic meters of water. With this total of 22 million cubic meters, calculating on the basis of 101,000 <u>mou</u> of early rice in the district, each <u>mou</u> could receive 200 cubic meters of water, essentially enough to guarantee that the early rice would not be affected by the drought. Moreover the water of the main Meichuan Reservoir could be used until the "knife's edge" of protecting the rush transplanting of late rice, thereby guaranteeing bumper harvests in both early and late rice and increasing all-round output in agriculture and fishery. The reservoir management office analyzed its investigation of the situation in time and submitted a report to the <u>qu</u> Party committee to ask for instructions. The <u>qu</u> Party committee accepted its suggestions and quickly convened a broadcast conference to call upon the commune sector to try in every way to open up water sources and engage in a great people's war against drought. They built over 50 embankments across the rivers throughout the irrigation district, found over 40 places in the mountain river valleys to tap underground water, dug 6 tunnels and 13 kilometers of new canals, and installed over 200 water-lifting machines with over 4,000 horsepower. Because they were good officers of the Party committee, they mobilized the masses to carry out "store, lead, lift" in a big way to satisfy the water-use needs of the early rice and guarantee a bumper harvest. The Meichuan Reservoir did not release any water until July 16, guaranteeing that the rush transplanting tasks for the over 100,000 <u>mou</u> of late rice would be fulfilled ahead of time and that the 3,100 <u>mou</u> of ponds would have water for the fish, and ensuring an overall bumper harvest in cotton and other multiple-operation economic crops.

## 2. Rely on the Masses for Democratic Management

Chairman Mao teaches us that "all work must entail a mass movement; without a mass movement, it won't work." Chairman Mao has always taught us to have faith in and rely on the masses, and this is the Party's basic line. If we are to properly manage and use water works, we must have faith in the masses and thoroughly mobilize and rely on them, combining mass management and professional management. However, concerning this question, the Meichuan Reservoir has also gone through several processes. In the beginning, some people asserted that since the irrigation district had expanded and its tasks had grown heavier, the professional organs were understaffed, and they should be increased accordingly. Moreover, they viewed professional management as something very mysterious and did not tell the masses things like the amount of water stored and the amount released when the gates were opened. The masses had minimal understanding of the conditions of the reservoir. Every time they used its water to resist drought, they became anxious. Some people even hurried to the reservoir from several dozen li away to see how much water was left. Water fees were collected from a purely economic viewpoint, at the rate of .008 yuan per cubic meter of water, but little was done to popularize the idea of using water sparingly and uniting to resist drought. A few in the commune sector believed that as long as they paid for it, water should be released to them regardless of other circumstances. They demanded too much water. They did not consider that there was little water in the Meichuan Reservoir, that the irrigated area is large, and that they should heed the balanced use of water throughout the irrigation district. A small number of communes and brigades upstream along the canal would not request water at the appropriate time, but waited to use the water which seeped through as it passed by. Others did not request reservoir water at all and only used pond water, causing their fish to die and affecting both agricultural and fishery production. Therefore, collecting water fees according to the cubic meter was only carried out for two years and then discontinued. Afterward, to strengthen water management, a total of seventy-five people in the irrigation district were selected from the various production teams to be worker-peasant water management personnel. Under the leadership of the management office, they assisted the management sections in managing and releasing water. On paper, this looked like the mass line, but in actuality it still emphasized the need to have professional management. The broad masses still did not understand the importance of good management and use of water projects; nor could they become self-consciously motivated to use water sparingly or rationally.

From continuously summing up its experiences, the comrades of the management office have come to realize that to properly manage and use a Meichuan Reservoir-type irrigation district where "the water is sparse, the fields many, the canal lines long, and the works scattered," they must have faith in the masses and thoroughly mobilize and rely on them to carry out combined democratic management by the masses and management by professional organs.

From the experience of the Meichuan Irrigation District in carrying out democratic management by the masses, three points must be grasped:

First, there must be a sound leadership group, that is, an irrigation district management committee composed of responsible people of the qu and commune Party committees as well as the management office. The "management committee" carries out its work under the leadership of the qu Party committee and is responsible for convening conferences in the irrigation district, putting into operation the water distribution plan, determining the system for water use, establishing water management organizations, exercising unified management over water projects of various sizes within the irrigation district, unifying arrangements, utilizing [water] jointly, and adjusting surpluses to make up deficits. The leadership of the various management sections and affected commune sector units have organized joint management groups.

Second, there is a 692-member mass water management contingent in the district with the poor and lower-middle peasants forming its backbone. This contingent is composed of activists sent from the beneficiary communes. Their thoughts are good, they are full of energy, and they are acquainted with the conditions. They play a significant role in "rectifying danger by plugging leaks, doing maintenance and repair, protecting and defending the canals and gates, and maintaining the system." For instance, one day toward evening, Comrade Wang Huixing, branch secretary of the Youth League in Wangsheng Brigade, Hongxing Commune, discovered a fissure at the side of a ditch gate. He led five water managers to sleep at the side of the gate on protective watch. On the following day in the early morning, they began the repair work and rushed until it was finally finished at noon, preventing an accident. Once Shujia Pond broke through its embankment. More than ten water managers leapt into the water to block the flow with their bodies. They dropped in trees and grass to repair it very rapidly and guarantee the transport of water to the lower reaches.

Third, there is a unified management system. The management office regularly submits reports to the qu Party committee and the "management committee" concerning the amount of water stored, the water requirements, and the progress of irrigation. Before the gates are opened to release water, they send the various levels the water allocation plan and the water-use targets, handing them down to the communes and popularizing them broadly among the masses, thus lending a high degree of unity to the water-use plan for the entire irrigation district. When water is allocated, they hold to the "three first, three later" principle; when they irrigate, they carry out the "Four Fixed" system, that is, fixing personnel, acreage, flow, and time. Moreover, they have set up a "four-anti, six-forbidden" management system. They have achieved "water use as on a chessboard, with water management a whip." In carrying out the system of collecting water fees according to acreage, they set the water fee standards according to concrete conditions. They are based on the standard of an ordinary bumper harvest year. Less is collected in poor years, and none is collected when there are natural disasters. In addition, they distinguish between pumped water and gravity flow and look out for the lower reaches in a suitable way. The masses of the irrigation district are satisfied and can be mobilized each year to pay the fees.

Because they have had faith in the masses and relied on them, bringing into full play the role of democratic management by the masses with the close uniting of mass management and professional management, the irrigation sequencing throughout the entire district in recent years has been excellent, and no major disputes have arisen over the release of water. The masses can consciously observe the management system, pay attention to using water sparingly, and develop a "Dragon River" spirit of unity in resisting drought.

In the area of project management, the main Meichuan Reservoir and the five small reservoirs are managed by professional management organs. The sixteen tiny reservoirs are managed separately by full-time personnel sent by the benefited communes or brigades, with leadership over their operations being carried out by the management office. The ponds are managed by the teams. For the maintenance and repair of the reservoir and canal works, a unified distribution of labor force is made throughout the district.

### 3. Train a Contingent of Peasant Technicians

Ever since the Meichuan Reservoir was constructed, they have mobilized the masses to construct a large number of small on-farm water projects. Generally speaking, the quality of the projects basically matches the needs. The professional management personnel of the Meichuan Reservoir are few and the technical personnel even fewer. How were they able to solve this contradiction? They heeded Chairman Mao's teachings on having faith in the masses and relying on them and selected a core from among the peasants and, using the method of impart [knowledge], help, and lead, they trained a batch of peasant technicians. Statistics show over 160 trained to date throughout the irrigation district. They have already basically grasped the building methods and survey techniques for small water projects such as earthfill dams, canals, and gates. Some can do the design and construction on their own. All the peasant technicians are worker-peasants who engage in farm activities during ordinary times and use their know-how when water projects are constructed. They have played a major role in the commune sector's own implementation of small waterworks.

## VI. PERSIST IN FOCUSING ON WATER WHILE DEVELOPING MULTIPLE OPERATIONS

Chairman Mao attaches utmost importance to the comprehensive utilization of water conservancy projects. Before the Great Cultural Revolution, Chairman Mao sharply criticized the phenomena of neglecting aquatic products, transportation, and trees in water conservancy construction. Therefore, with the preconditions of guaranteeing the safety of the projects and persisting in serving increases in agricultural output, an important task in water management work is to make complete use of water and soil resources and forcefully carry out comprehensive utilization.

The Meichuan Reservoir has also undergone a continuous struggle over comprehensive utilization and multiple operations.

After the construction of the reservoir in 1958, they raised over 40 million fish, reclaimed over 80 mou of land, and operated a livestock farm. The enterprises of the reservoir were all thriving. However, the counterrevolutionary revisionist line ruthlessly carried out by the renegade, traitor, and scab Liu Shaoqi blew up an evil wind of "get off the horse." The land was transferred down to the production teams, and the livestock farm was broken up. In 1964, when Chairman Mao raised the great call "In agriculture, learn from Dazhai," the broad masses of personnel, under the guidance of Chairman Mao's revolutionary line, worked hard for one winter to bring 4 mountaintops under control, plant over 10,000 trees, fill in over 10 deep gullies, and open up over 7 mou of farmland.

During the Great Proletarian Cultural Revolution, the broad masses of the personnel held fast to Chairman Mao's revolutionary line, pushed aside the interferences from the "Left" and the Right, and further developed multiple operations. Especially since the founding of the new Party branch in 1970, in order to put Chairman Mao's "May 7" Directive into further operation, they mobilized the masses to draw up brand-new plans and proposed to attain self-sufficiency in grain, cotton, and funds within three to five years. But there were also a small number of people who said, "[Those who beat] drums and gongs sell sugar — each has his or her own profession. We manage water, the peasants plant grain," or "Grasping multiple operations will affect project management." The class enemies also jumped out to stir up trouble. The Party branch led the employees in recalling the history of the struggle between the two lines which had occurred since the construction of the reservoir over the issue of developing multiple operations, and it educated the broad masses of Party members and workers in thought and political line. Everyone assembled the historical facts and vigorously criticized the revisionist contraband of "single operations" spread around by swindlers like Liu Shaoqi. In grappling with the class enemy, they strengthened their confidence in properly carrying out the tasks of a socialist reservoir.

At the same time, they also conscientiously summed up their experiences and lessons in developing multiple operations. They came to recognize that in the relationship between water conservancy and multiple operations, they must clearly focus on water and combine the two so they would promote each other. The main task of a reservoir management department is to properly manage the water projects to serve improvements in agricultural output. This cannot be neglected or relaxed at any time. Practice proves that, as long as water is taken to be the main task, forcefully developing comprehensive utilization and multiple operations not only does not harm management work, but can also promote the ideological revolutionization of the management personnel and make water conservancy management work even better.

After clarifying the direction of developing comprehensive utilization and carrying out multiple operations in a big way, the key to solving the problem of insufficient manpower lies in bringing into play the activism of the broad masses of the employees. When the Meichuan Reservoir was constructed, the state planned that it would have thirty-three cadres and workers. Later, the five small reservoirs were built one after another, yet there was no increase in the manpower allocation. The dependents of the employees were then mobilized to participate in production, and this added some temporary labor during the busy season, with the total being no more than sixty to seventy persons. The people were few, the tasks many; how could they resolve this contradiction? Most important was to thoroughly bring into play the revolutionary activism of the broad masses of the employees, to go all out and aim high, and to have everyone become a "jack-of-all-trades." Not only were they management and building personnel, but also animal breeders. With the precondition of keeping the irrigation district in mind and serving increases in agricultural output, they rationally arranged their labor power, which involved both a division of labor and cooperation, to carry on the tasks of the reservoir with one heart and united efforts. For example, when water is used to ward off drought, they do not separate water conservancy from fishery, but concentrate forces to go out to the different front lines of the irrigation district and unite with the cadres and masses of the commune sector to release and use water properly. During the peak season for fishing, the water conservancy cadres also participate in catching fish, working hard day and night. For instance, Su Hannian, a member of the Communist Party, is by profession a cashier, but he is also in charge of opening of the sluice gates, measuring the flow, observing the water level, and measuring the amount of rainfall. He is conscientious and responsible and fulfills all of his tasks.

"Water" is the largest resource for reservoir enterprises. Thus, multiple operations must be centered on that word. Among the five activities of agriculture, forestry, animal husbandry, sidelines, and fishery, fishery should be taken as the foremost key, and fish raising should be vigorously developed in the reservoir. In order to enable reservoir fish raising to achieve high and stable yields, they have raised the fish in an experimental and scientific way, raising fish at different levels and with rational density, so as to utilize the water surface fully. Moreover, they have engaged in their own hatching, using local methods, and have reached self-sufficiency with a surplus in minnows. In developing a fishery, it is necessary to solve the problem of fish food. In the past, they relied on having the personnel cut the grass and pick up the manure and on having the state supply feed such as soybeans and bean cakes. This wasted both labor power and funds, and fishery output did not increase. They analyzed the internal relationships of things and vigorously developed domestic pigs. They feed the fish and fertilize the fields with pig manure, using pig rearing to promote fishery and agriculture. Originally, they lacked land for raising grain. Now they transplant one season of early rice into a two-season minnow pond. The fish pond produces grain, and the rice stalks fertilize the fish pond. The grain has had bumper harvests, there is feed for raising pigs, and with the pig manure, there is feed for raising fish. So much grain means many pigs, and many pigs mean much fertilizer: they rely on each other and promote each other.

For the past several years, the broad masses of personnel in the Meichuan Reservoir have held fast to Chairman Mao's revolutionary line and persisted in traveling the glorious "May 7" road, persisting in taking water as the key link and developing multiple operations. The area of the irrigation district has continuously increased, and agriculture and fishery have had bumper harvests year after year. The irrigated area has already expanded from 70,000 mou to 120,000 mou. In 1971, there were eighty days of drought, yet the irrigation district's grain yield reached 1,017 jin per mou [7.63 t./ha.]. In 1972, there were another eighty days of drought, and then after autumn, there was 300 millimeters of continuous rain. In addition, the late rice was attacked by pests. Yet the district's grain yield reached 910 jin per mou [6.83 t./ha.]. The Meichuan Reservoir had a total of 270,000 jin [135,000 kg.] of adult fish, with each mou of fish-rearing surface area producing an average of 108 jin. There were 6.97 million artificially raised minnows, more than enough for self-sufficiency. The management office raised 303 pigs, an average of 4 per capita, and sold 100 to the state. The total pork was 21,500 jin. In each season, the rice yield exceeded the "Program," with a total of 35,000 jin. They planted over 20,000 trees and joined with the commune sector in planting an additional 130,000. Economic income from reservoir enterprises (not including water fees) was 130,000 yuan for the entire year, or 40,000 yuan above expenditures. In addition, they achieved self-sufficiency with a surplus in grain, cotton, and oilseeds. Thus far, the Meichuan Reservoir has had a luxuriant development in its multiple operation enterprises centering on fishery and combining agriculture, forestry, animal husbandry, and fishery. They have self-reliantly used the reservoir to sustain the reservoir.

## Conclusion

Chairman Mao has taught us: "Take the line as the key link; once it is grasped, everything falls into place." For the past several years, the broad masses of employees of the Meichuan Reservoir have gradually improved their knowledge through repeated practice and have made remarkable achievements in reservoir management. They have been in quest of a set of experiences and have grasped some laws to correctly handle the relationship between management and construction, the mutually coordinated relationship between medium-scale projects and small-scale ones, the relationship between managing water and using it, the relationship between controlling water and controlling soil, and the relationship between water control and comprehensive utilization. In the final analysis, this is the result of consistent adherence to Chairman Mao's proletarian revolutionary line.

However, things are always characterized by one divides into two. If we measure them against the demands of higher yields or compare them with advanced reservoir irrigation districts, there remains a definite gap. For instance, in project management, they must continue to fortify installations and improve them, and they must strengthen ancillary work. Some canal systems and construction works still need rebuilding and improvement. Within the irrigation district there are still many thousand mou of water conservancy "dead corners" which must be taken care of and fields affected by cold which must be improved. In addition, Learn from Dazhai in Agriculture campaigns must continue to be unfolded in the reservoir district, such as tree planting along the canals. The broad masses of personnel of the Meichuan Reservoir, encouraged by the spirit of the Party's Tenth Congress, are resolved to further deepen the campaign to criticize Lin Biao and Confucius, to seriously read and study and to elevate their awareness of thought and line. They are radiating revolutionary spirit and are working hard to raise their water management work to a new level in order to promote high and stable yields in agriculture and to make greater contributions toward putting into practice Chairman Mao's great call to "store grain everywhere."

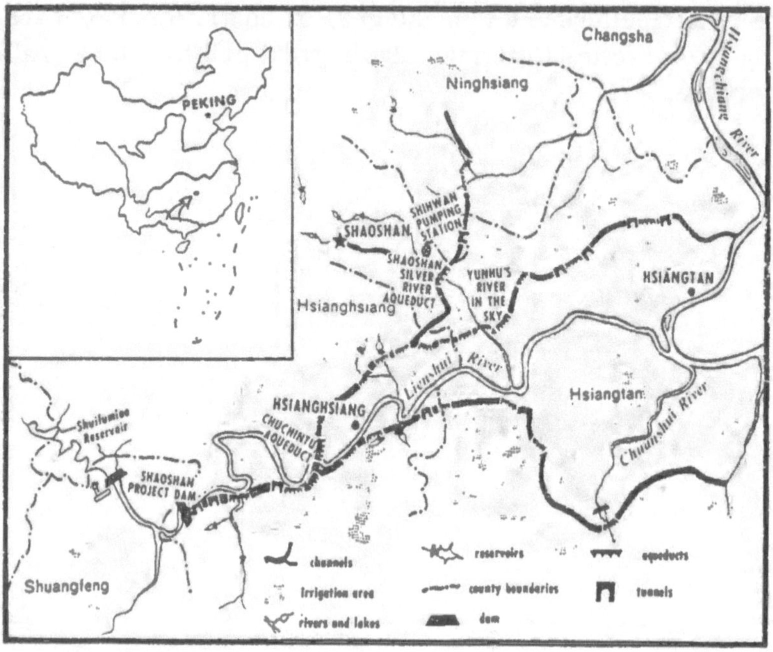


The Shaoshan Irrigation Project (Source: China Reconstructs. October 1977, p. 11).

Note: Place names in this figure are in the Wade-Giles transcription used in the original source. Most of the names here are spelled the same as in the pinyin system adopted in the text. In other cases, the differences are slight (e.g., Lien = Lian, Hsianghsiang = Xiangxiang). — J. E. N.

*Reading 4*

# SHAOSHAN'S CANAL WATERS ARE CLEARER THAN CLEAR: CHAIRMAN HUA'S AND THE PEOPLE'S HEARTS ARE NEAR

The waters of Shaoshan Irrigation District! They are clear and sweet, drop-by-drop moistening the fields for the welfare of the millions of people in the irrigation district. The hearts of the millions of people! They are closely linked with the wise leader Chairman Hua.

On this happy day when everyone high and low is celebrating the fact that the great, glorious and correct Chinese Communist Party again has its own wise leader, Chairman Hua, when it is celebrating the great victory of the Party Central Committee with Chairman Hua at its head, crushing with a single blow the anti-Party clique of the "gang of four," the people of Shaoshan Irrigation District, viewing the bumper harvests of fragrant, waving rice and wheat and the full development of the vast irrigation district, hold grateful memories in their pounding hearts of our great leader and teacher Chairman Mao and unanimously praise Chairman Mao's great concern for the people of the irrigation district.

---

*"Shaoshan qushui qing you qing, Hua zhuxi he renmin xin lian xin." From Hua zhuxi zai Hunan [Chairman Hua in Hunan], Beijing, 1977, pp. 25-35.

## I

The majestic Shaoshan Irrigation District Project is a large-scale comprehensive water project used primarily for irrigation. It was built speedily with high quality in only ten months' time by the people of the irrigation district under the guidance of Chairman Mao's revolutionary line and the personal leadership and direction of Chairman Hua. Its construction shines with the brilliant illumination of Mao Zedong Thought. Its construction permanently memorializes the great achievements of Chairman Hua in loyally implementing Chairman Mao's revolutionary line.

Shaoshan Irrigation District includes an extensive 2,500-square-kilometer hilly area in Shaoshan District; Xiangtan, Xiangxiang, Ningxiang, Shuangfeng, and Changsha xian; and the suburbs of Xiangtan Municipality. Before liberation, because the reactionary ruling classes did not tend to water conservancy, the high fields of this area lacked water during the drought season, and the low fields were prone to flooding. During the great drought of 1934, in Wangmei Production Brigade of Nanzhushan Commune, Xiangtan xian, most of the entire village's more than 1,400 mou of rice fields reaped not a single kernel of rice. In the Hanjiashan area, more than forty families, totaling seventy-three people, had to go begging for rice, while some sold their sons and daughters and fled to other villages as the drought brought misery to the suffering masses. Beside a plum tree, the people constructed a "Wangmei [watching the plum] Pavilion," and just as one watches the plum to alleviate one's thirst, they hoped for springs of sweet water to moisten the earth. After liberation, although a number of small-scale water conservancy projects were built under the leadership of the Party and production and living conditions changed somewhat, the requirements for the development of agricultural production still could not be satisfied. The people earnestly hoped to lead in waters "of good fortune" to water the 10,000 hectares of fields and thoroughly eliminate the threat of disasters caused by drought and excess water.

In the Great Leap Forward year of 1959, our great leader Chairman Mao returned to Shaoshan and wrote in superb poetic verse, "Dare to teach the sun and the moon to change to new skies." This stimulated in the sons and daughters of Chairman Mao's native village bold hearts and strong wills to build socialism. During this very year, the Hunan Provincial Committee decided to build the Shaoshan Irrigation District project, leading the people of the irrigation district to drum up a battle to draw the waters of the Lian Shui [River] into irrigation canals. Within a very short time they also completed the Shuifumiao Reservoir dam to capture the waters of the Lian River. Just when the people were victoriously building the Shaoshan Irrigation District canals, the black wind of Liu Shaoqi's counterrevolutionary revisionist line blew in, and the construction plans for the Shaoshan irrigation canals died an early death. The efforts for progress made by the people of Chairman Mao's native village, however, could not be impeded. In 1964, Chairman Mao issued the great call "In Agriculture Learn from Dazhai," and the broad masses in Xiangtan, Xiangxiang, Ningxiang, Shuangfeng and the suburbs of Xiangtan Municipality, harboring strong hopes for the strengthening of Chairman Mao's native village, once again demanded the construction of the Shaoshan irrigation canal. This demand by the masses immediately received the highest consideration and enthusiastic support of the provincial committee. At that time, Comrade Hua Guofeng, who was serving as a secretary in the Secretariat of the Hunan Provincial Committee, personally assumed the post of chief director and political commissar of the project command headquarters. On July 1, 1965, construction formally began on the Shaoshan canal project. This happy and exciting news was like a spring breeze blowing in every commune along the irrigation canal. People danced with joy and ran about telling each other the news. Their fond hopes of many years were about to be realized. A construction corps of 100,000 under the direct leadership and command of Comrade Hua, overcoming many difficulties and dangers, played one heart-stirring victory song after another.

Open up the first issue of the Shaoshan Irrigation District News, July 1965, to the inscription penned by comrade Hua Guofeng himself. "Be a good model of a water diversion project which conforms to the spirit of the General Line."* These brilliant gold characters shine in a special way before one's eyes. When looking at them, how can one avoid thinking back to those laborious days and nights spent building the irrigation district? How can one not recall how Chairman Hua personally directed the 100,000 civilian workers to battle heaven and earth to attain this great accomplishment?

During the entire construction of the Shaoshan Irrigation District project, Comrade Hua Guogeng always raised high the great red banner of Mao Zedong Thought, using Mao Zedong Thought to lead everyone to battle and using proletarian politics to exercise control over the construction of the irrigation district project. He personally organized every level of leadership cadres to conduct study classes, to teach everyone to use the political work experience of the Liberation Army in the construction of the project, and to train a revolutionized construction corps that dared to fight hard battles and was good at fighting them, truly accomplishing the slogan "Build the canals to forge good people and yield bumper harvests both spiritually and materially." At the time, in every civilian workers' company a communist night school was created, thus turning the entire work site into a huge school for the study of Mao Zedong Thought. Setting an example, Chairman Hua Guofeng also personally made inspections, three times visiting the civilian workers' company of Chengqian Commune of Xianghsiang Municipality, earnestly listening to everyone's reports, inspecting the reports written by the civilian workers on what they had learned in their studies, and promoting their experiences in political work throughout the entire work site with great fanfare. Under the direct promotion of Comrade Hua Guofeng, the entire work site also organized two reporting

*The General Line is to build socialism with greater, faster, better and more economical results. — J. E. N.

groups of activists in the study of Chairman Mao's works. He personally listened in and took notes, while giving enthusiastic direction and earnest encouragement. Even though very busy with his work, Comrade Hua still regularly visited the front line of the projects, studying Chairman Mao's writings with the workers, fighting shoulder to shoulder with them, and leaving behind him in many places traces of his achievements, the results of his sweat and hard work. Comrade Hua's lofty character and loyalty to Chairman Mao's revolutionary line and his glorious revolutionary practice in fighting shoulder to shoulder with the masses have greatly encouraged the broad masses of civilian workers to use the spirit of the General Line to overcome difficulties. There have accordingly cropped up at the work sites many heroic model persons who "fear neither hardship nor death." The "never-grow-old" He Guihua of Shebu Commune, Xiangtan, at the age of sixty-seven, went to the work site to set an example for the foolish old men. He exerted great effort on constructing the irrigation district and, at the work site, gloriously joined the Chinese Communist Party. The young woman Dai Zhonggui, who was always in the fore in difficult, heavy or dirty jobs and who had three times delayed her marriage, also joined the Party as a model worker. The secretary of the Shaoshan Production Brigade Party branch, Mao Diqiu, recalled his past and related many ideas and feelings. During the period of the democratic revolution, our great leader Chairman Mao had taught his father, Mao Fuxuan, to engage in revolutionary activities and had also personally trained and introduced his father into the Chinese Communist Party. During the period of socialism, Mao Diqiu himself grew up healthfully under the nurturing of Mao Zedong Thought and, under the leadership of Comrade Hua, happily participated in the construction of the Shaoshan Irrigation District project. In this great melting pot, he grew up to be a glorious Communist Party member. Mao Diqiu recalled his own path of growth and in boundless appreciation said: Chairman Hua has always loyally carried out Chairman Mao's revolutionary line and has always had enthusiastic concern and love for the people. His heart and the heart of the people of Shaoshan Irrigation District are united.

Comrade Hua has, with the outstanding ability of a proletarian revolutionary, firmly carried out the spirit of the General Line of socialist construction in the innovative spirit of having faith in the masses, relying on them and respecting them, and carrying out construction carefully, while making a great effort to work quickly. The broad masses of cadres and civilian workers, in order to complete the construction in Chairman Mao's home village and with strong determination and fervent ardor, braved the fierce day and extreme cold, difficulties and danger to build aqueducts and excavate tunnels. In only ten months' time, they opened up 110 mountaintops, filled in over 90 valleys, dug 10 tunnels, erected 26 aqueducts, built structures of different sizes in over 2,400 places, and completed 240 kilometers of main canals, victoriously completing the main part of the project, providing benefits in the year of construction, and setting a good example in building socialism with greater, faster, better and more economical results. With the personal concern and leadership of Comrade Hua, they earnestly implemented Chairman Mao's directive that it only counts when there is high production, overcoming the erroneous thinking of "stressing construction while neglecting management" and "stressing the main work while neglecting the ancillary work." The people of the irrigation district also spent three winters digging 2,520 kilometers of branch canals and building many electrical irrigation stations, dams, and reservoirs, and other ancillary projects, thereby gradually forming a large-scale irrigation system that combines the storage, diversion, and lifting of water. They have received the great benefits of comprehensive use; irrigation is the major consideration, but they can also engage in electric power generation, fish raising, navigation, agricultural and sideline products processing, and so on.

In the short space of ten years, the irrigation district has gained a new appearance. Under the guidance of Chairman Mao's revolutionary line and under the direct leadership and command of Comrade Hua Guofeng, the heroic people who participated in constructing the Shaoshan Irrigation District during that year, after undergoing the baptism of battle during the Great Proletarian Cultural Revolution, continued to march forward with great strides and created new achievements. Each of them has used his own two hands to struggle arduously; each has portrayed the land of Shaoshan Irrigation District as a beautiful picture of a new and prospering socialist countryside. Now, in the million mou of farmland in the irrigation district, the average grain output per mou has risen from 480 jin before the construction of the irrigation district to over 1,000 jin for three successive years. Cotton, vegetable oil, live hogs, tea, fresh fish and Hunan lotus have grown many times in output, leading to a prosperous situation of "all-round development with grain as the key link." The canals are open throughout the year, the grass on the dike embankment slopes is a profusion of greenery, the trees along the canals have become like forests, the silvery river reflects the green mountains, and the flowing waters sound as if they are laughing happily. As they observe this excellent situation which causes the birds to sing and dance, the people of Shaoshan Irrigation District are all the more stirred by the incomparable love of our great leader Chairman Mao and our beloved Chairman Hua, and they are all the more stirred by a deep hatred toward the anti-Party clique of Wang, Zhang, Jiang and Yao. The Fenbiwuchang Production Team of Daqiaobu Production Brigade, Dongjiao Commune, Xiangxiang xian, has an elderly poor peasant named "Old Man Huang" who worked for thirty years under the old society. When he heard the especially happy news that Comrade Hua Guofeng had become the leader of the Party, he was so excited that he could not sleep for nights. He assembled all the members of his family and, in front of the picture of Chairman Mao, talked glowingly about his happiness in seeing Chairman Hua at the irrigation district work site during that year. He praised Chairman Hua's lofty quality of always planning for the people's benefit, complained of the sufferings in the old society, praised the happiness in the new society and severely criticized the conspiracy of the "gang of four" to usurp the Party and seize power and their grave criminal acts to restore capitalism. He said excitedly: Without Chairman Mao's leadership, there would have been no liberation for us poor and lower-middle peasants; there would be no Chairman Hua to carry out faithfully Chairman Mao's revolutionary line and no day such as today for the people of our irrigation district. Chairman Mao had boundless trust in Comrade Hua Guofeng. The people of the irrigation district know him the best. Comrade Hua is the leader of our Party. We poor and lower-middle peasants love him dearly and put our complete trust in him.

## II

By working day and night to build the irrigation district, Comrade Hua Guofeng reached into the hearts of the masses. Comrade Hua Guofeng was extremely concerned about the interests of the masses. He regularly taught the cadres that in management and in thinking through problems the interests of the people have to be used as the point of departure.

When Lao Yin, a cadre of the management bureau of the irrigation district project, saw Comrade Hua's personal inscription on the large aqueduct "Yunhu tianhe" [Lake of Clouds, River of Heaven], it stimulated in him a happy memory. During that year, Lao Yin was leading a battalion of civilian workers and was in charge of a section of the large embankment at the inlet part of the "Yunhu tianhe" Aqueduct. At the time, the higher-level design departments of the project proposed lengthening the embankment and shortening the span of the aqueduct, but the local masses preferred to shorten the embankment and lengthen the span of the aqueduct in order to reduce the amount of land occupied and retain the fish ponds. Furthermore, this would not affect the rail and highway transportation below the aqueduct. The wishes of the masses were not accepted at first by the design departments, so more than a hundred poor and lower-middle peasants cosigned a letter reporting the matter to Comrade Hua Guofeng. While the poor and lower-middle peasants were hopefully waiting for Comrade Hua Guofeng's approval, he personally went to inspect the work site. He wore a straw hat, and dust-covered and tired, he accompanied the provincial and prefectural leaders and the design personnel of the project in an on-the-spot examination and study of the problems involved. He walked beside Comrade Lao Yin, putting his hand on his shoulder and intimately soliciting opinions. He developed an understanding of the situation from all different aspects, and after assembling the varying viewpoints, Comrade Hua Guofeng fully affirmed and enthusiastically supported the wishes of the poor and lower-middle peasants. This happy news spread quickly, and the poor and lower-middle peasants said: "Secretary Hua is really good. He has approved the report of us poor and lower-middle peasants." In accordance with the views of the masses, the "Yunhu tianhe" Aqueduct was lengthened by $2\frac{1}{2}$ spans as compared to the original plans. Thus today under this "Milky Way," the broad fields are wide and expansive, the fertile land yields high production, and the railway and highway are open to through traffic. When Lao Yin and the poor and lower-middle peasants think of all this, they are deeply grateful that whenever Comrade Hua handles things he meticulously studies the situation and always has the interests of the masses in mind. Everything he deals with is exactly what is in the hearts of the poor and lower-middle peasants. Every item is in conformity with the revolutionary line of Chairman Mao. Comrade Hua Guofeng is the leader of our Party. How can the people of the entire nation refuse him their boundless trust and heartfelt love?

It was Comrade Hua Guofeng who took the bounty and sunshine of Mao Zedong Thought and spread it in the hearts of the heroic sons and daughters of Shaoshan Irrigation District. It was Comrade Hua Guofeng who rearranged the mountains and rivers of Shaoshan Irrigation District in accordance with the requirements of Chairman Mao's revolutionary line. People will never be able to forget how in that year along the several-hundred li work site for the construction of the irrigation district, Comrade Hua Guofeng and the construction workers on the project studied together, worked together, lived together, and together experienced extraordinary times. During the crucial period of development of the project, it was Comrade Hua Guofeng who guided everyone to overcome countless difficulties and dangers. Under the hot sun and through wind and rain, it was Comrade Hua Guofeng who gave everyone his meticulous concern and intimate encouragement. The heroes who saw the dust of battle at the great Zaolinchung "Gate of Heroes" Tunnel still clearly remember that Comrade Hua Guofeng came many times to this difficult and dangerous work section which had complicated topographical conditions with large inundated areas and cave-in areas. He led them to study Chairman Mao's glorious works "On Contradiction" and "On Practice," giving everyone great courage and increased strength. Comrade Hua Guofeng even wore a hard hat and put on galoshes, personally going into the tunnels to take part in the labor. He presided over and conducted three-in-one technical breakthrough meetings to concentrate the wisdom of the masses and adopt the methods of "digging at two levels," "shooting fireworks," and other effective measures, ultimately bringing under control as many as sixty-one serious cave-in areas. Thus, the "Gate of Heroes" Tunnel became firmly inlaid into the magnificent left branch-canal of the irrigation district. During that year, fighters who battled on the "Fei lian guan wan qing" [Flying Lian River Waters Irrigate 10,000 Hectares] Aqueduct still remember that it was Comrade Hua Guofeng who led the workers and technicians to study and practice repeatedly, to depend on the wisdom of the masses, and to respect the creativity of the masses in order to solve the task of installing the prefabricated reinforced concrete piece weighing hundreds of tons. It was Comrade Hua Guofeng who went personally to the work site many times to stir up the fighters' revolutionary fervor and boundless enthusiasm to break out of foreign molds and travel our own road, forcibly lifting the waters of the Lian River more than twenty meters into the air, flying across the swift torrents of the Zhu [Pearl] Ferry Crossing. The comrades who worked on construction at Maoxingshan work site recall how once, just when Comrade Hua Guofeng had arrived at the site to inspect the work, there was a huge blast, and the work site was covered with smoke and flying dust. As soon as he arrived, he inquired with great concern: "Are the workers safe? Are the commune members in the surrounding areas safe?" Upon leaving, he repeatedly urged that attention be paid to the safety of production and that a careless and negligent attitude never be adopted. Comrade Hua Guofeng also regularly led the cadres to study Chairman Mao's saying, "Always be concerned about the livelihood of the masses and pay attention to methods of work." When in the course of an inspection he discovered that the civilian workers had brought dried vegetables from home to eat with their rice, he encouraged everyone to emulate the spirit of Nanniwan and raise pigs, plant vegetables, operate good mess halls, and prepare good meals. He greatly cherished the revolutionary initiative of the masses and taught the workers to pay attention to striking a proper balance between work and rest.

In his direction of project construction in the irrigation district, Comrade Hua Guofeng always implemented the principles of occupying as few fields as possible and tearing down and moving as few of the people's homes as possible. In both big and small things, he was always very considerate of the masses. When constructing the canals, in addition to providing irrigation, electric power generation, and navigation, even all the soil that was discarded was put to good use, and there was a big campaign to use the waste soil to create new fields. In the entire irrigation district waste soil was used to create 6,800 mou of new fields, or over 1,500 mou more than the 5,300 mou of farmland occupied by the canal itself. Along both sides of the canal wherever people lived, wharves were built so they could wash their clothes and fetch water. Where necessary and possible, faucets for running water were also installed for the convenience of the masses. At intervals of less than one kilometer, pedestrian bridges span the canal. Below, boats can pass through, while the people can cross above. Thinking in terms of the long-range interests of the masses, Comrade Hua Guofeng also personally led the commune members to go to the mountains to plant trees in order to spread greenery on the barren mountain ranges. After the irrigation district was completed, Comrade Hua continued to show concern for its people. He made many inspections of the irrigation district and gave his personal concern and direction from the operation, maintenance, and management of the irrigation district down to each specific item of work related to the interests of the masses. One day in July 1966 when he was inspecting the irrigation district's Yintian Management Office, Chairman Hua Guofeng asked two of the commune members who were there for their opinions of the irrigation district project. After some reflection, the two commune members said: "The canal is well and good, but the embankment of the canal is too high. When we go to the other side to do our work it is very inconvenient. It needs a flight of steps." Comrade Hua Guofeng smilingly nodded his head. He then immediately asked the management office to fetch some of the comrades of the project's crew, and he personally ordered them to build a flight of steps for the commune members. In the afternoon of that very day, construction was begun on the steps. Afterward, the commune members asked who that comrade had been. When the comrades of the management office told them it was Provincial Committee Secretary Comrade Hua Guofeng, everyone excitedly said: "Secretary Hua is truly a good secretary, fostered by Chairman Mao. His heart is linked to ours."

The leader of the people loves the people, and the people love their leader. The people of Shaoshan Irrigation District, from their own personal appreciation, feel that Chairman Hua adheres to Chairman Mao's revolutionary line, is loyal to the Party, is public spirited and unselfish and is closely linked with the masses. He is concerned about the hardships of the masses and firmly stands with them. He is a warm person in whom the broad masses of laboring people have boundless trust.

## III

"The red sun in Shaoshan never sets. The mountains and rivers of our homeland are ever in the season of spring. We are forever loyal to Chairman Mao and closely follow our leader Hua Guofeng!"

At this moment of celebrating a great historical victory, in the broad expanses of the great lands of Shaoshan Irrigation District, songs of praise fly about, and the red flag is unfurled. The people of Shaoshan Irrigation District have just taken some firm steps, and under the leadership of Chairman Hua Guofeng, they are courageously marching forward. They have used loud and forceful language to express their firm conviction: In the past, Chairman Hua was commander-in-chief of construction in the irrigation district. Now and in the future, he will forever be our commander-in-chief to carry out a new Long March of 10,000 li. In everything, we must comply with the order of Chairman Hua and the Party Central Committee. Wherever the Party Central Committee led by Chairman Hua points, we should fight and vow to carry through to the end the cause of the proletarian revolution initiated by Chairman Mao!

During that year in Shaoshan Irrigation District when they were under Comrade Hua's personal cultivation and guidance, the 100,000-man construction corps comprehended especially deeply and indelibly marked in their hearts the first article of the "Three Main Rules of Discipline and the Eight Points for Attention," namely, "Obey orders in all your actions; only by marching in unison can we achieve victory." They studied this article and put it to use in overcoming one difficulty after another. During that year on the work site, a "mutual-love campaign" in which "the civilian workers love the commune members, and the commune members love the civilian workers" was launched everywhere.

In observance of Comrade Hua's directives, the civilian workers learned a great deal from the Liberation Army and regularly helped the residents of the area fetch water, sweep floors, harvest sweet potatoes, and plant wheat. The masses also voluntarily helped the civilian workers by making room for them in their own houses, serving them tea, and mending and washing their clothes. They truly had deep and fond feelings for each other. The civilian workers' corps of Xiaduopu, Ningxiang xian, whom Comrade Hua Guofeng praised for their exemplary conduct, were once engaged in construction at Sanjiao [Triangle] Pond, Xiangxiang. When the project was completed, they made an on-site summing-up and checked how their discipline was carried out in their dealings with the masses. They successively visited 399 poor and lower-middle peasant commune members, extensively soliciting their opinions. They discovered that they had damaged a hoe belonging to one of the commune members. The workers' corps immediately forged another hoe of the Xiangxiang type to compensate this commune member. Later, when the civilian workers left, the masses enthusiastically saw them off for part of the way again and again. They also presented them with many embroidered banners and awards and continuously praised Comrade Hua Guofeng's direction of the workers' corps, saying their discipline was strict and there had been no violations. The sixty-one-year-old Communist Party member Lao He assumed the role of teacher of the civilian workers' battalion of the Daping Commune when working on the construction of Shaoshan Irrigation District. This contingent which he led was a model in implementing the "Three Main Rules of Discipline and the Eight Points for Attention." Wherever this contingent went, it blended in with the masses. Its members helped the production teams to crash plant and crash harvest. They cleared wasteland and gathered fertilizer, chopped wood and carried water for the commune members, planted vegetables, and built houses. Whenever something had to be done, they did it; wherever it was busy, they helped. They thought as the masses thought and were concerned over the concerns of the masses. The commune members called them the good civilian workers whom Chairman Mao had taught and thought of them as their own relatives. This contingent was especially conscientious in "obeying orders in all its actions." They were mobilized five times and transferred to fight in five different battlefields. Each time, they fulfilled their tasks ahead of schedule, both in quality and quantity. Their exemplary actions and deeds won the praise of Comrade Hua Guofeng. Comrade Hua made four successive personal inspections of the Daping Battalion's work site, and did the "Three Togethers" [san tong: eat, live and work together with the masses] with the workers. He listened many times to Instructor Lao He's reports. At the conference of advanced delegates convened at the general headquarters for construction of the irrigation district project, Comrade Hua also personally conferred on the Daping Battalion a large red flag embroidered with the words "A Liberation Army not dressed in army uniform." At the meeting, closely concurring with Chairman Hua's angry condemnation of the "gang of four," Lao He recalled the previous conditions of battle and with boundless depth of feeling said: "The reason why we were able to complete such a tremendous project as Shaoshan Irrigation District during that year in only ten months' time was because we had a great labor corps of 100,000 which was armed with Mao Zedong Thought and which in all its actions listened to the commander."

The Party Central Committee led by Chairman Hua, carrying out the behest of Chairman Mao, with one blow has crushed the conspiracy of the anti-Party camp of Wang Hongwen, Zhang Chunqiao, Jiang Qing, and Yao Wenyuan to usurp the Party and seize power. In a time of crisis, they have saved the Party and the revolution and have made a signal contribution. The 800,000 people of Shaoshan Irrigation District are all delirious with joy and smiles have broadened their faces. By crushing the "gang of four" and winning victory in production, the red flag is fluttering and dancing in the several hundred li of this extensive irrigation district, and reports of success keep pouring in. The people of the irrigation district firmly believe: No matter how many difficulties and crooked bends we meet on the road ahead, if we only follow Chairman Hua step by step and in everything heed the orders of the Party Central Committee, then we shall certainly be able to achieve even greater victories.

He Guihua, a veteran model and a civilian worker of Xiangtan xian who has met with our wise leader Chairman Hua many times, has enthusiastically sung this song:

Not afraid of the wind and not afraid of the rain;
Not afraid of goblins and devils;
The people closely following Chairman Hua
Can overturn the rivers and the seas,
So why should they be afraid?

This simple ditty expresses the faith of the people of the irrigation district that victory is theirs if they adhere firmly to Chairman Hua's support of continuing the revolution. It also reflects the fearless heroic spirit of the people of the irrigation district. Under the leadership of the Party Central Committee led by Chairman Hua and with such heroic and incomparably strong people, the future of our country is boundlessly promising. The proletarian revolutionary cause which Chairman Mao initiated will certainly become even more prosperous and flourishing!

*Reading 5*

# PROPERLY MANAGE THE IRRIGATION DISTRICT TO SERVE TO INCREASE AGRICULTURAL OUTPUT

## Management Bureau, the Shaoshan Irrigation District Project, Hunan Province*

On the glorious day of July 1, 1965, work was begun on the construction of the Shaoshan Irrigation District project on the basis of the great call from Chairman Mao "In agriculture learn from Dazhai" and under the direct leadership of the provincial committee. In April 1966, the primary projects of the irrigation district, which included the key project for water diversion at Yangtan and the feeder and north main canals totaling 174 kilometers, were victoriously completed. During that single year, construction, benefit, and increased yields were achieved for 400,000 mou of irrigated fields. In 1967, the south main canal was completed. At the same time, ancillary projects of the irrigation district were firmly grasped, and benefits were gradually expanded.

During the past seven years, under the guidance of Chairman Mao's proletarian revolutionary line, we have closely relied on the leadership of the various levels of Party committees and the broad masses and cadres of the irrigation district who have been self-reliant and industrious in both management and construction to continually consolidate and improve the main

---

*Hunan sheng Shaoshan guanqu gongcheng guanli qu, "Guanhao guanqu gongcheng, wei nongye zengchan fuwu." From Shuili guanli gongzuo jingyan huibian [Compilation of Experiences in Water Management], Beijing, 1973, pp. 69-78.

canal projects and to make the ancillary projects of the canal system more complete. At present, the irrigation district is capable of diverting water at the rate of 46 cubic meters per second from the Yangtan Water Diversion Dam. The water flows through 240 kilometers of main canals and 1,600 kilometers of branch canals with 193 electrical irrigating stations with [total] installed capacities of over 10,000 kilowatts to irrigate 830,000 mou of farmland in the seven xian and municipalities of Shaoshan, Xiangxiang, Xiangtan, Ningxiang, Changsha, the suburbs of Xiangtan, and the Shuangfeng xian Reservoir District. It also supplies part of the water used by industry and mining and by the cities and towns. The feeder and north main canals can be navigated by ten- to twenty-ton wooden sailing vessels, while fishery can be greatly developed on the 100,000 mou of ponds and reservoirs of the irrigation district. At the Yangtan Water Diversion Dam, a hydroelectric power plant with an installed capacity of 1,500 kilowatts has been built. Using hydraulic and electric power, agricultural and sideline processing plants have been put into operation in over 180 places. The irrigation district has developed over 15,000 mou of tea plantations and has reclaimed 150,000 mou of reforested land. Various enterprises in agriculture, forestry, animal husbandry, sidelines, and fisheries have all become more developed. During the past few years, on the two banks of the Lian River, 183 kilometers of flood prevention dikes have been built, and more than 60 kilometers of flood diversion canals have been dug, so that 150,000 mou of farmland along both banks are free from the threat of floods, thus creating the conditions necessary for high and stable agricultural yields. In 1970 grain yields exceeded the goal set by the "Program." In 1971 the average yield per mou reached 957 jin, double that of 1965. In 1972 a great drought, rarely seen in 100 years, occurred, but the people of the irrigation district, under the leadership of the various levels of party committees, using Dazhai as a model, promoted the "Dragon River spirit" and launched a mass campaign to resist the great drought, reap a bumper harvest, and strive to make contributions [to the state]. Thus the irrigation benefits of the project were expanded, and the grain output of the irrigation district again showed an increase over 1971. The people of the irrigation district, their hearts filled with joy over the bumper harvest, stirringly sang in praise:

Shaoshan's canal waters are clearer than ever.
The Party's kindness is as deep as the ocean.
We increase yields, increase water, and increase our contributions.
For this good fortune, we shall not forget Chairman Mao.

## Firm Support for Line Education Is the Guideline for Effective Irrigation District Project Management

Chairman Mao has taught us, "The correctness of the ideological and political line determines everything."

During the past few years, in the rectification campaign to criticize Lin Biao, we have seriously studied and repeatedly come to understand Chairman Mao's directives concerning water conservancy, and in accordance with the spirit of "only when there is high production does it count," we have initiated education in the "three destructions and the three establishments" [san po san li], that is: destroying the idea that "releasing water is all that counts" and establishing the orientation of water management serving to increase agricultural yields, destroying the idea that water management is difficult and establishing the belief that complete devotion should be given to managing water for the revolution, and destroying "the theory of a priori idealism" and establishing the revolutionary work style of reliance on the masses, going deep into the realities of things, and investigation and study. By recognizing that we should take good project management and good water utilization and raise them to the high level of the struggle between the two lines and the two world views, we shall accordingly be raising the awareness of all the cadres of the struggle between the lines as well as their consciousness in firmly carrying out Chairman Mao's revolutionary line. The director of the Management Office of Yintian Temple, Comrade Yin Kaisheng, originally felt that good water management was for the welfare of the people, so that any problems which would arise would be a crime against the people. He thus felt that the responsibility was very great and that it was a difficult matter to manage water. He repeatedly studied Chairman Mao's great directive that "water conservancy is the lifeline of agriculture" and recalled how he himself had suffered from class opression and the disasters of flood and drought in the old society, thus deeply appreciating the great significance of "lifeline." He was determined to put every effort into managing water and thus make a contribution toward high production. He served wholeheartedly as a good poor and lower-middle peasant water management official. He set his mind on the overall situation and conscientiously fulfilled the duties of his position. Relying on the leadership of the Party committees, he established close contacts with the masses, engaged in investigation and study, and continually put things into practice. He searchingly summed up the idea that prevention and cure are of equal importance, with prevention being the main consideration. Through coordinating engineering and biological measures, he solved the problem of preventing collapse, seepage, and silting of the canals, and thus continually strengthened and raised the standards of the projects and rapidly expanded the irrigation benefits. For the several communes within the area of this management office, the irrigation benefits exceeded the demands of the plan, and grain yields rose to more than 1,000 jin. This was a great contribution to the people, so the masses called him the "red water-management official."

We also closely relied on the various levels of Party organization in the irrigation district and repeatedly conducted propaganda campaigns among the broad masses and cadres of the irrigation district concerning the political and economic significance of the Shaoshan Irrigation District project, making a great effort to advocate the implementation of the spirit that only with high production does it count. Using our reminiscences, we engaged in education by contrast, developed in a thoroughgoing way revolutionary mass criticism and relentlessly criticized Lin Biao's counterrevolutionary revisionist line. We clearly distinguished between having the management of the irrigation district project rely on the masses and relying on a small minority; between basing policies on our own strength and solely relying on state investment; and between being mindful of the overall situation and united in the management of water and "profiting ourselves at the expense of others" or "just minding our own affairs." We raised the awareness of the broad masses and cadres of the irrigation district concerning class struggle, the struggle between the lines, and continuing the revolution under the proletarian dictatorship. We stimulated the spirit of self-reliance and arduous struggle, and we brought into full play the activism of the masses in consciously and properly managing and utilizing the irrigation district project. During the past few years, more than 1.3 million cubic meters of earthwork and stonework, more than 800,000 cubic meters of masonry, more than 8,000 cubic meters of concrete, and mortar lining on more than 109,000 cubic meters of canals have been completed for maintenance of the main canal project. Over 300,000 square meters of grass has grown on the canal slopes. More than 3.8 million labor days have been put in. Thus the irrigation district project has been continually strengthened, irrigation benefits have expanded year after year, and grain output has increased year after year. "The people's canal is managed by the people. Self-reliance has turned things around."

## To Rely on the Masses and Respect Their Creative Spirit Is the Foundation of Good Management of the Irrigation District Project

Nanzhushan Commune has obtained rich experience with respect to reliance on the masses to self-reliantly manage the canal. This commune is situated on the upper reaches of the left main canal. Although the canal passes through 19 li of the commune, which constitutes a fourth of the total length of the left main canal, the area it irrigates there is only a fifth of the farmland benefited. The Party committee of Nanzhushan Commune considered the overall situation, however, and did not bicker about the length of the canal, the difficulties of maintenance, or the size of the tasks. Persisting in relying on the masses, they raised their own expenses, provided their own materials, and bore the cost of their own tools and provisions. During the busy farming season, there are professional personnel; during the slack season, mass movements are promoted. As a result during all four seasons of the year there is someone to maintain the canal, and thus the maintenance of the project each year can be completed properly. During the past few years, they have completed a total of over 50,000 cubic meters of earth and stonework and over 5,300 cubic meters of masonry work, built 4,200 meters of new flood diversion ditches, dug over 1,500 meters of additional canal inlet ditches, and completed 2,600 meters of embankments on their section of the canal. They have applied over 3,500 cubic meters of mortar, planted over 3,600 mou of the canal's banks with false indigo [amorpha fructosa] trees and planted over 33,000 square meters of grass to protect the canal slopes. Altogether over 85,000 labor days were used, an average of 11 for each person in the commune. Thus within the 19-li area of the main canal, they accomplished embankments without leaks, masonry work without collapses, reforestation of the two canal banks, canal slopes covered with green grass, a level walkway for pedestrians, and a canal in which the water flows freely.

The experience of Nanzhushan Commune was a great lesson for us, but some comrades raised the question of whether their experience can be promoted throughout the entire irrigation district. If the responsibility for maintenance of the canal were divided by section according to commune, tasks could not easily be balanced. Was this in contradiction with the policy of rational assumption of burdens? We asked the opinions of the poor and lower-middle peasants of Nanzhushan Commune. The poor and lower-middle peasants of the Xianfeng Production Team of Wangmei Production Brigade said that before the irrigation district was built, they had relied on the waters of a small river inlet to irrigate the fields. "The cows went down to the fields, and the people went up to the treadmills." In any one year, the labor for treading water constituted one-half to two-thirds of the labor used in farming. Now there is total gravity-flow irrigation. It is not necessary to worry about water, and grain yields every year exceed a thousand jin. The expenditure of labor on maintaining the canal is not even a small fraction of the labor formerly spent on treading water. Besides, as the quality of the canal has increasingly improved and the labor required on it has diminished, so our contributions to the state have become greater and greater. We are all unendingly grateful to Chairman Mao. Who wants to haggle over this little bit of labor? This has made us realize that on the question of water control, we must consider the rational assumption of burdens and avoid favoring or burdening [one place] inordinately, but "rational" is also relative, and we must avoid overemphasis on it because this could lead to thinking about narrow personal gains and losses and deviation toward departmentalism, thus restricting the initiative and activism of the masses.

We have relied on the various levels of Party committees in the irrigation district quickly to promote the experience of Nanzhushan within the irrigation district. Beginning in 1968, we adopted the system of managing the maintenance of the main canals and their small-scale structures along xian (or municipal) boundaries. The xian (or municipality) subdivides its tasks by section among the local communes for the management of maintenance. The water fees and "water grain levies" [shui liang] are collected and managed on our behalf by the finance and grain departments of the xian (or municipality). The maintenance expenses are uniformly arranged by the xian (or municipality). We merely coordinate with the communes in the district to establish good maintenance plans, formulate construction designs, carry out technical guidance, organize quality inspection and certification, properly handle the recording of labor time and account settlements, and patrol the canal for security in order to guarantee the normal passage of water. The advantages of this system are: (1) It enhances the leadership of the local Party committee over management work, fully promotes the activism of the masses in managing the canal, and increases the glorious sense of responsibility of the masses in their love and protection of the canal. (2) When the communes are responsible for maintenance management, their arrangements have demonstrated flexibility and initiative, and problems have been handled promptly. During the busy farm season, professional people have been used; during the slack season mass movements have been promoted. Maintenance is carried out during all four seasons of the year, guaranteeing that work on the canal is done well. (3) It strengthens the professional management contingent so that the professional management departments have more time and energy to go out among the masses, investigate and study, and carry on scientific experimentation, continually raising the standards of management.

The experience of Nanzhushan Commune also demonstrated that in the management of irrigation district projects, maximum results can be obtained with minimum effort both by carrying out the policy of stressing both prevention and remedy, with primary emphasis on prevention, and by adopting the method of attack which achieves "early remedies, small remedies and good remedies." During the past few years, we have relied on the masses to carry out diligent management and careful maintenance of the irrigation district project, and we have adopted a large number of engineering and biological measures. We have effectively prevented cave-ins of the canal slopes, reduced erosion losses, and guaranteed the safety of the project through such methods as slant-cutting the slopes to reduce pressure on deeply cut canal sections, draining inundated areas, protecting the slopes with masonry, planting trees along the canal, laying sod, and planting false indigo trees on the slopes of both banks. We have summed up and utilized the experience of the local masses in mixing mortar and, using it to line the over 100 li of embankments along the canals, have greatly reduced seepage losses. Surveys have proven that use of the mortar can reduce seepage losses by over 80 percent. If the embankment of the entire section of the canal were lined with mortar, the reduction in seepage could irrigate about 50,000 mou of farmland (calculated on the basis of water being released five months a year). Furthermore, the coefficient of roughness of the canal would also be reduced, thus increasing the water flow and preventing water-flow scouring. By stabilizing the canal slopes, we have greatly reduced the amount of maintenance on the canal. During the past few years, we have mobilized the masses to line the canals with over 108,000 cubic meters of mortar, so that 80 percent of the embankment section of the main canal has been completely reinforced. Through the above measures, the standard of the project has been strengthened and raised, allowing the water-carrying capacity of the main canal to reach 46 cubic meters per second, 1.5 cubic meters per second over the designed usable flow of 44.5 cubic meters per second, thus increasing the irrigation of the farmland. Moreover, the security of project operation has been guaranteed.

## Actively Stressing the Ancillary Works of the Canal System Is an Important Measure for Speedily Promoting the Benefits of the Irrigation Project and Guaranteeing Increased Agricultural Output

During the past few years, under the leadership of the various levels of Party committees, we have relied on the revolutionary spirit of the people of the irrigation district for being self-reliant, diligent, and creative. We have used the method of concentrating our efforts to fight a battle of annihilation, speedily completing the task of building ancillary works for the canal system. In the construction of the ancillary works for the canal system, we have accumulated some rich experiences. Fengjia Production Brigade of the Shaoshan District is a very good example. This production brigade is located at a place which historically has experienced the most severe droughts. The 1,055 mou of farmland in the entire production brigade are spread over "five gulleys, one gulch, and one beach." In the past, it always depended on several dozen mountain ponds and several small river dams for irrigation, and its capacity for resistance against drought was very low. In 1964 its yield per mou was only 530 jin. After construction was completed on the irrigation district, the canal passed through this production brigade, and a source of water was guaranteed. The Party branch of the production brigade carried out the spirit that only with high production does it count, and with Dazhai as a model, they worked self-reliantly and struggled arduously, firmly grasping water management and construction. They adopted the methods of centralizing water rights, as well as overall planning, unified preparations for construction, and unified management. They coordinated the use of the ponds, dams, electrical irrigation stations, and canals, tapping the latent strength of their original water facilities and accelerating water conservancy construction on their farmland. In a period of one or two years, they built 6 electrical irrigation stations, dug over 30 li of canals, and opened up more than 50 meters of tunnels, so that the more than 1,000 mou of fields in the entire production brigade received irrigation. Water was also diverted to the mountain areas, and over 250 mou of new fields and land were created. In 1967 the yield per mou of grain of this production brigade exceeded the "Program."* The yield per mou has been over 1,000 jin every year since 1968. Because of the increase in grain production in each successive year, the collective economy developed rapidly. For the past few years, more than 20 kinds of machines have been introduced, including tractors, threshers, and transplanters. They have planted over 130 mou of fruit trees, tea plants, and bamboo forests, and every family has a radio and electric lights, thus presenting a scene of flourishing prosper-

*The "Program" target for Hunan was 800 jin/mou. —J. E. N.

ity. The Shaoshan District has conscientiously summed up and promoted the experience of Fengjia Production Brigade so that the total area benefited by irrigation increased from the more than 17,000 mou which had been planned to 25,000 mou. Last year, a great drought occurred such as is rarely seen in a hundred years, but the irrigated area again increased from 25,000 mou to 35,000 mou, to double the planned irrigation benefits. In 1966, Lianghu Commune in Xiangtan xian had an irrigated area amounting to over 3,700 mou. By studying Fengjia Production Brigade, they increased it to over 8,700 mou.

The poor and lower-middle peasants of the Daolin district in Ningxiang xian, taking advantage of the momentum created in completing the building of the main canal, firmly supported taking the struggle between the lines as the key link. They thoroughly initiated a competition of the "four competes and the four sees": To compete in placing politics in command and to see who studies Marxism-Leninism and Chairman Mao's works; to compete in being self-reliant and to see who can work hard to be creative; to compete in the ancillary work of the canal system and to see who can do more, faster, better and more economically; and to compete in project benefits and to see who can contribute the most to increase production. In two years, 55 branch and distributary canals, totaling 742 li, were built in the entire district; 34 tunnels, totaling 5 li, were dug; and 14 aqueducts, totaling over 2 li in length, were set up. In addition, 273 small-scale sturctures were built on the canal system, and 17 electrical irrigation stations were set up with an installed capacity of 1,726 kilowatts. The canal links the mountain ponds, the reservoirs, canal water and river water to form an interconnected irrigation system combining storage, diversion, and lifting; and large, medium and small. This network serves 82 percent of the more than 80,000 mou of farmland in the entire district, so there is no worry about flood or drought, there are high and stable yields, and grain output is continually on the rise.

## Grasping Objective Laws and Carrying Out Scientific Irrigation Are Important Links to Making Good Use of the Irrigation District Projects and Promoting High Agricultural Output

How are we to make management in the irrigation district implement the spirit that only with high production does it count and better serve increased agricultural output? In the past, we only knew "whether or not there is a harvest depends on water; how large depends on fertilizer"; we only understood that water is the lifeline of agriculture. We lacked the understanding that too much water is harmful. Thus, "everyday we moved about on the edges of the fields, not questioning how deep or how shallow the water was." In 1969 we went to inspect and study Changfeng Commune at Xiangxiang and visited and conversed with the cadres and poor and lower-middle peasants, engaging in a comparative analysis of the irrigation methods for rice fields with different topographic features. We discovered that, due to seepage in the branch canal, the 150 mou of farmlands along the Dingtuo branch canal of Dingtuo Production Brigade were flooded with water all year long, and the yield per mou was only 400-500 jin, while on a plot of farmland higher up on the bank quite distant from the canal, the water in the fields was just sufficient, and the average yield per mou was 100-200 jin more. This production brigade has over 3,200 mou of fields on the banks adjacent to the Lian River. The topography is low and marshy. In the past, 20 percent of the fields were usually "winter rice paddies," and 60 percent of the fields did not even grow grass. Every year much effort was expended, but output was always in the range of 600 jin. The poor and lower-middle peasants said: "There is too little fertilizer, the soil is thin, and the flooding is harmful." This was one of the main reasons why output could never improve. Through investigation and analysis, we more deeply understood the dialectical relationship that water, while being the "lifeline" of agriculture, could also be a "disease." However, "we cannot immediately understand things when we perceive them. Only when we understand these things can we develop a deeper perception of them." In order to grasp the laws relating to the water requirements of rice during its various periods of growth and development and to understand the relationship of water to soil improvement, the increase and promotion of fertilizer utilization, and the prevention of disease and control of insects, during the past three years, we have worked at the offices of Dingtuo Production Brigade, Changfeng Commune, Xiangxiang. We, the cadres of the commune sector, and the poor and lower-middle peasants have jointly participated in the three great revolutionary movements of class struggle, production struggle, and scientific experimentation. We have laid great stress on managing water for the revolution and farming scientifically; have engaged in a big way in the construction of dual-use drainage and irrigation farm canals; have developed independent field canal networks for each field with well-controlled drainage and irrigation linked to the various [off-field] canals and ditches; and have also launched a mass scientific experimentation movement. Sixteen scientific experimentation groups comprised of cadres, experienced farmers and technical personnel have been organized. Over 220 mou of experimental fields have been planted, and experimentation has been conducted in the rice fields, comparing rational irrigation and the old customary irrigation method of maintaining deep watering for long periods. Experimentation with seven similar conditions [controls] (soil quality, fertilizer, seed type, cropping system, density of planting, season, and cultivation management) and one different condition (irrigation method), has yielded two different outputs. According to the 1970 experiment with early rice, by using the rational irrigation method, the yield per mou can be increased by 137 jin as compared to the old customary method. In 1971, on the basis of past experience, the yield of early rice was 950 jin per mou using the irrigation method of "shallow water for revival of green; less water for tillering; when the rows are full, sun dry the fields; deep water for ear formation; and dampness for healthy seeds." With adequate and plentiful fertilizer, the yield per mou reached 1,112 jin. Using the old customary irrigation method of maintaining deep water in the fields for long periods, the yield per mou was 825 jin. For late rice, using the irrigation method of "deep-flowing water for revival of green; shallow water for tillering; sun drying the fields at the right time; some water for ear formation; and dampness for healthy seeds," the yield per mou was 927 jin. With the old customary irrigation [method] of maintaining deep water of the fields for long periods, the yield per mou was 804 jin. The rational irrigation method resulted in an increase of 248 jin per mou for both early and late rice over the customary deep water method. In general, the increase in yield per mou was 100 to 140 or 150 jin. At the same time, the amount of water consumed was reduced. For early rice, the experimentation on the amount of water consumed in the fields showed that by using the old customary irrigation, 362 cubic meters were used, while by using rational irrigation only 302 cubic meters were used, a reduction of 60 cubic meters. The Dingtuo Production Brigade lowered the water table in more than 3,000 mou of rice fields by extensively building dual-use drainage and irrigation field canals. By using the method of frequent shallow irrigation and sun-drying the fields, the yield per mou of green fertilizer was over 10,000 jin, and the yield per mou of grain increased from 681 jin in 1969 to 1,008 jin [in 1971]. In the course of practice, we came to a preliminary understanding of the objective laws for water utilization to obtain high rice yields, and we grasped the following three links: In the first period, promote early growth and quick development; in the middle period, control the seedlings and strengthen the stems; and in the last period, push push ahead fiercely for fruitification and healthy seeds.

## Strengthening Party Leadership Is the Key to Proper Management

Chairman Mao has taught us: "With respect to these seven, industry, agriculture, commerce, education, military affairs, politics, and the Party, the Party is the leader of them all."

Water management must be placed under the unified leadership of the Party. The provincial and prefectural committees pay great attention to the Shaoshan Irrigation District project and regularly direct our work. The main leadership comrades of the prefectural and provincial water conservancy and electric power bureaus also assume leadership responsibilities in the irrigation district management committee. The various levels of Party committees of the irrigation district have also incorporated in their agendas the management of the Shaoshan Irrigation Bureau. In addition, there are important responsible comrades who have divided the management duties of this aspect of the work, thus strengthening the actual direction. They arrange, inspect, and sum up, and exercise leadership with regard to key problems. We especially educate the people of the irrigation district, helping them deeply appreciate from the lofty aspect of the line the spirit that only with high production does it count, and put this into practice in their activities. This is the key to good management of Shaoshan Irrigation District. Under the unified leadership of the Party, the irrigation district, in accordance with the principles of united leadership and management by level, formulated regulations for management of the irrigation district project and set up an irrigation district conference of delegates, as well as a three-level management committee composed of the xian (or municipality), qu, and communes. The production brigade has a management group, while the production team has full-time water watchers. Each commune, in accordance with the size of its irrigated area, has provided one or two cadres to take charge of managing the work of the canal system. The vast majority of these comrades are selected from among the important responsible cadres of the production brigades; their political qualifications are good, and they have practical work experience, can relate closely with the masses, and constitute the backbone force for the management of the irrigation district. We closely coordinate our work with the qu and the communes, convene classes at regular intervals, exchange and sum up our experiences, educate them politically, help them in their work, show concern for their livelihood, and fully develop their positive role. Practice has told us: With Mao Zedong Thought as our compass, by strengthening the Party's leadership in water management work, by the management organizations at every level strengthening and with a mass water management contingent which has the canal-system cadres as its mainstay, we can guarantee that our management will victoriously march forward along Chairman Mao's revolutionary line and continually make new achievements.

We are determined to take the rectification movement to criticize Lin Biao as our key link, "seriously read and study in order to understand Marxism clearly," and firmly support the viewpoints that practice comes first and that the masses are the true heroes. As we face the irrigation district and production, we shall closely rely on the broad cadres and masses of the irrigation district, redouble our efforts, and take further steps in effectively managing and using the Shaoshan Irrigation District project. Thus we shall better serve to increase agricultural output, fight for the glory of our great leader Chairman Mao, and make a contribution to the Chinese revolution and to the world revolution.

## *Reading 6*

# THE THOUSAND-*LI* CANAL IS MANAGED BY TEN THOUSAND PEOPLE*

## By Relying on the Masses to Manage the Qianli [Thousand *Li*] Canal, Yingshan *Xian*, Sichuan Province, Achieves Initiative in Work

In whatever we undertake, we must mobilize the masses and rely on them. Water conservancy construction benefits the masses and protects them from harm. Because the broad masses are very much concerned about it, we should all the more mobilize and rely on them. The experiences and lessons of the management of Qianli Canal in Yingshan xian are a vivid explanation of how difficult it is to operate effectively by relying only on a few professional personnel working in an isolated fashion. We must follow the mass line, fully mobilize the socialist activism of the broad masses, and get everyone organized before we can get things done well. [In Yingshan xian] they originally relied only on a minority of people in specialized teams and could not manage well. During busy times, they added temporary labor, but still could not manage well. Later, they carried out coordinated management by both professionals and the masses. Then a stirring situation arose in which 10,000 people manage the 10,000-li canal. This report is worth reading.

Editor, Renmin ribao [People's Daily]

---

*"Qianli chang qu wanren guanshui." From Yikao qunzhong, guanhao shuili [Rely on the Masses to Manage Water Conservancy Well], Beijing, 1973, pp. 65-70. This article originally appeared in Renmin ribao, April 4, 1973.

The management personnel of Qianli Canal, Yingshan xian, Sichuan Province, observing Chairman Mao's teachings on the mass line, have relied on the broad masses of cadres and commune members of the irrigation district and have pooled the wisdom and efforts of the masses to manage the canal and to manage water, fully developing the benefits from the project in order to vanquish the disaster of drought, promote production, and make a contribution. In 1972, although the Qianli Canal Irrigation District suffered a severe drought, the total grain output was still 9.5 percent higher than that of 1971, exceeding the highest level in the history of local grain output.

## Management by the Few; Often in a Passive Position

The Qianli Canal project, begun in 1958, is the product of a big mass movement by the people of Yingshan xian under the glorious brilliance of the General Line of the Party for building socialism. After more than ten years of continuous construction and building of ancillary works, the entire irrigation district now has a total of more than 300 canals with a total length of more than 1,200 li. Qianli Canal connects 9 reservoirs and more than 300 ponds and weirs to form a "melons-on-a-vine" style gravity-flow irrigation network which is able to irrigate an area of over 140,000 mou constituting approximately a third of the total area of the rice paddies in the entire xian.

On whom does Qianli Canal rely for management? The people have improved their understanding of this question through a process of repeated practice.

During the earliest few years, in the more than 400-li section of the three large main canals, the project maintenance, irrigation management, and other related work were entirely monopolized by the 180 professional personnel of the management organization. These comrades came regularly, rain or shine, and were diligent and earnest. They accepted the hard labor and the problems and were dedicated to getting the job done well. But things did not turn out as they wished. The more they monopolized things, the more problems arose and the more their work became passive. Each year they failed to finish removing all the sand from the canal and to finish repairing all the embankments and levees that had collapsed. They were also unable to find an easy solution to some contradictions regarding water use. When drought became serious and everyone wanted to use water, the contradictions became even sharper: The communes in the lower reaches wanted to release water, but the communes in the upper reaches wanted to block it off. The communes at the canal head could use water with ease and sometimes wasted it, while the fields at the tail of the canal were terribly dry, and sometimes when water was released, it could not get through. The masses criticized: With this kind of management, even if you added some more professional personnel, you could not manage well.

Later, the management personnel thought of another method. Whenever it was the season for using water, they invited some temporary laborers to help in the work. Each of the water distribution gates of the main canal sent personnel to take turns being on duty to stand guard at the "dragon's den," that is, to stand watch at the sluice gates and keep people from freely blocking or releasing water. Whenever a problem was discovered, they would ask some temporary laborers to go and make the repairs. During one year, although they used more than 150 temporary laborers, the irrigated area was even reduced. The masses also complained about this method of doing things.

When neither the first nor the second method can be carried out, then what can one do?

Some people suggested turning it over to the masses to manage:

"We ourselves have worked strenuously to manage it, but for several years have been unable to manage it well. We have invited temporary laborers to help us, but still have been unable to manage it well. How can we now say that if we turn it over to the masses, they will be able to manage it well?" At the time, many of the management personnel thought this way.

Some experienced poor peasant commune members said to them: Qianli Canal was built by the masses. The masses receive its benefits. Who among them would not be concerned? If just the few of you monopolize it, you cannot handle it all. This is not to say that we don't want professional personnel to manage, but that the professional personnel should manage it with the masses. Only then can there be good management.

At the Shishanpu branch canal of the main north canal, production brigades Nos. 3, 4 and 5 of Chengfu Commune were jointly benefited by the canal. In the past, No. 4 Production Brigade in the middle reaches and the No. 3 Production Brigade in the lower reaches received comparatively fewer benefits. No. 5 Production Brigade in the upper reaches would often block off the canal water during periods of drought. Much of this water would be used for flood irrigation, and there would be losses and waste. Subsequently, they jointly organized a branch canal management committee and adopted the method of joining the professional personnel and the masses. By relying on the masses to manage water, the situation was changed. When the water-using season arrived, they first organized the cadres and mass water-management personnel of each production brigade to check up on the maintenance conditions of the canal. They surveyed the area of farmland to be irrigated and the amount of water needed and gave this information to the canal management station for unified planning and overall arrangement. When the time came to release water, the professional personnel of the management station worked with the water-management personnel of the masses. On the basis of the principle of "first the distant and then the near, taking care of the most urgently needed," they first irrigated the lower reaches, then the middle reaches, and finally the upper reaches, achieving planned water use, rational water use, and thrifty water use. This not only guaranteed that the farmland of the various brigades which were benefited could be irrigated, but also strengthened revolutionary unity.

This lively example was very enlightening to the management personnel of Qianli Canal. They truly understood that it is necessary to rely on the masses in the management of water projects as well as in their construction and in ancillary works. Only by persisting in the mass line and concentrating the wisdom and strength of the masses will we be able to seize the initiative in water management.

## Rely on the Masses; Their Latent Strength Is Limitless

At Qianli Canal, an irrigation district representative conference system was set up, thus organizationally guaranteeing the implementation of the mass line. Every year before the spring irrigation and winter repairs, the conference of representatives is convened to discuss problems related to management. At the conference, the opinions of the broad masses in the irrigation district are made known and the Party's water conservancy policies and the conditions in the irrigation district are communicated to the masses so that everyone will be concerned about the overall situation and know what is going on.

In order better to combine mass management and management by the professional personnel, the entire irrigation district also set up more than 140 joint irrigation-management groups. At designated sections of the canal, the local production teams elect one commune member to be the water management officer, breaking down the administrative boundaries and unifying water management and water use. After the tasks are completed, these water management officers return to their teams. As compensation for their labor, the method of evaluation of work and allotment of points [pinggong jifen] has been adopted, and they participate in the distribution of benefits within their teams. In the whole irrigation district, there are now a total of more than 70 such water management officers who are both workers and farmers. They are familiar with the people and the area, and they join with the water management officers of the various production teams benefited, forming a water management contingent of the broad masses. In this way, although the professional management personnel of Qianli Canal have been reduced from the original 180 people to 44 people, their contacts with the broad masses are much closer than they were in the past, and their work has penetrated much deeper than before. In the past, the professional personnel just managed the one line of the canal. Now they manage the whole large area below the canal. In the past, they only managed the canal and the water. Now they also manage the ponds and the fields. The masses have responded very well to this.

In the years when Qianli Canal was first used for irrigation, the various teams benefited paid water fees uniformly based on the size of their irrigated areas regardless of whether they used water or not, or how much water they used. In this way, the communes in the upper reaches sometimes used their convenient conditions to release more water, while the communes in the lower reaches were unwilling to pay the water fee and lacked concern for management work because they received insufficient water. The present method is rational responsibility. In addition to a small basic water fee based on their irrigated area, all those in the communes benefited pay their main fee according to the actual amount of water they use. This encourages those in the communes benefited to be sparing in the use of water to reduce their expenditures on water fees. At the same time, it also mobilizes their activism in carrying out small-scale water conservancy on their own. According to statistics, every year since this method was put into effect, the entire irrigation district has been able to save more than 1.5 million cu. m. in water for irrigating an additional 5,000 or more mou of farmland.

The improvement in management also aroused the enthusiasm of the masses to maintain the project. Responsibility for annual repairs and regular maintenance on the main and branch canals was determined by the management stations which delineated sections of land and parceled responsibility for them out to the various teams benefited according to the size of their irrigated areas. In addition, a rational assessment of work done was made in accordance with the size of the project. The teams benefited by the small canals under the branch canals assume the responsibility for their maintenance. In the past few years, all the teams benefited have been able consciously to complete their maintenance tasks for the projects in accordance with considerations of time, quality and quantity. Also, on the back slopes of the canal they have dug water storage pits and sand-settling ponds and have planted trees to protect the dikes and reduce losses from erosion. In the past, annual repairs required 100,000 labor days a year. Now they require only 50,000-odd labor days to complete.

## 10,000 People Engaged in Water Management; Harvests Are Guaranteed in Spite of Drought and Excess Water

The severe drought of 1972 gave the management of Qianli Canal its first serious test. Quite early, when the drought was just becoming obvious, the professional personnel of the management station explained it to the management officers of the masses to let everyone make good preparations in thought as well as in action. During the months of July and August, the sun was scorching hot, the heat was oppressive, and the drought was extremely severe. The sluice gates of several large reservoirs were opened. A maximum volume of clear reservoir water flowed rapidly along the three large main canals, through the branch canals, the dou [subbranch], nong [farm] and mao [field] canals and onto the farmland. At this time, the rice was just budding and earing, and it was necessary to have large amounts of water. One drop of water meant one grain of rice, and drop by drop, the water flowed into the hearts of the people of the irrigation district. The professional personnel of the management station and the water-management personnel of the masses fought together, and at Qianli Canal, there appeared a lively scene of 10,000 people engaged in water management, resisting the drought and protecting a bumper harvest.

It only took the flow of water from the north main canal 3 days and 3 nights to reach the tail of the canal 130 li away.

The Chapan main canal took only 2.5 days to deliver water the 100 li from its head to its tail at Qingyanpu in Xiaoqiao Commune.

Huilong Commune is situated at the head of the south main canal. The commune members said: We are situated below the mouth of Xinfu Reservoir and have good conditions, so we must be of lofty character and show more concern for those in the communes at the tail. In August when the drought conditions were the most severe, on their own initiative they let Zengchan Commune irrigate its fields. In Zengchan Commune, the No. 5 Production Brigade mobilized more than 120 people and helped the No. 7 Production Brigade make emergency repairs on 90 meters of canal to divert water to save the rice seedlings. The No. 7 Production Brigade of Chengfu Commune had 300 mou of late rice which were subject to drought. They originally had canal water for irrigation, but when they heard that a production brigade at the lower reaches had 500 mou of late rice fields seriously lacking water, they immediately released the canal water. Then, to irrigate their own late rice, they took the leftover water from the hard-slab fields from which they had just harvested the intermediate rice.

All this made the people think back to preliberation times — to the tragic events in 1937 when there was a great drought for 50 days. The earth was dry for 1,000 li, and people fled to escape calamity. The people also thought of the early postliberation period — of the scene of arduous struggle against the drought of 1952 in the muddy ditch area of Dayakou, Huilong xiang [township], when more than 800 people used more than 400 waterwheels to lift water for over 20 days straight. The people thought of how several years ago, there were various kinds of contradictions stemming from conflicts over water which prevented unity among the communes of the upper and lower reaches. Now these phenomena are gone, never to return. "Water conservancy is the lifeline of agriculture." Under the guidance of Chairman Mao's revolutionary line, the broad masses have built Qianli Canal and have managed it well, thus firmly seizing the initiative in their own hands.

*Reading 7*

# AN ANCIENT IRRIGATION DISTRICT CHANGES ITS APPEARANCE; SUCCESSIVE YEARS OF BUMPER HARVESTS OF GRAIN AND COTTON

**Management Bureau, the People's Yingjing Canal, Shaanxi Province***

The People's Yinjing Canal Irrigation District is situated on the Guanzhong Plain. Its natural conditions are relatively good. It is one of the ancient irrigation districts of Shaanxi Province.

Since liberation, under the guidance of Chairman Mao's revolutionary line, democratic reforms have been carried out, the projects have been repaired and improved, a drainage system has been dug, water utilization has been done according to plan, and irrigation management has been strengthened. All this has gradually expanded the irrigated area from 500,000-odd mou during the period of liberation to over double that, 1,270,000 mou. The output of the irrigation district has also increased from year to year. Due to the interference and sabotage of Liu Shaoqi's counterrevolutionary revisionist line, however, farmland capital construction has progressed slowly; the standards of resistance to drought have not been high; coordination of water and agriculture has not been good; grain output has hovered around the 400-jin mark; and the output per mou of cotton has also only been between 50 and 60 chin. The criticism by the masses is: "The old irrigation dis-

*Shaanxi sheng Renmin Yinjing qu guanli ju, "Gulao guanqu huan xinmao, liang mian liannian huo fengshou." From Shuili guanli gongzuo jingyan huibian [Compilation of Experiences in Water Management Work], Beijing, 1973, pp. 79-86.

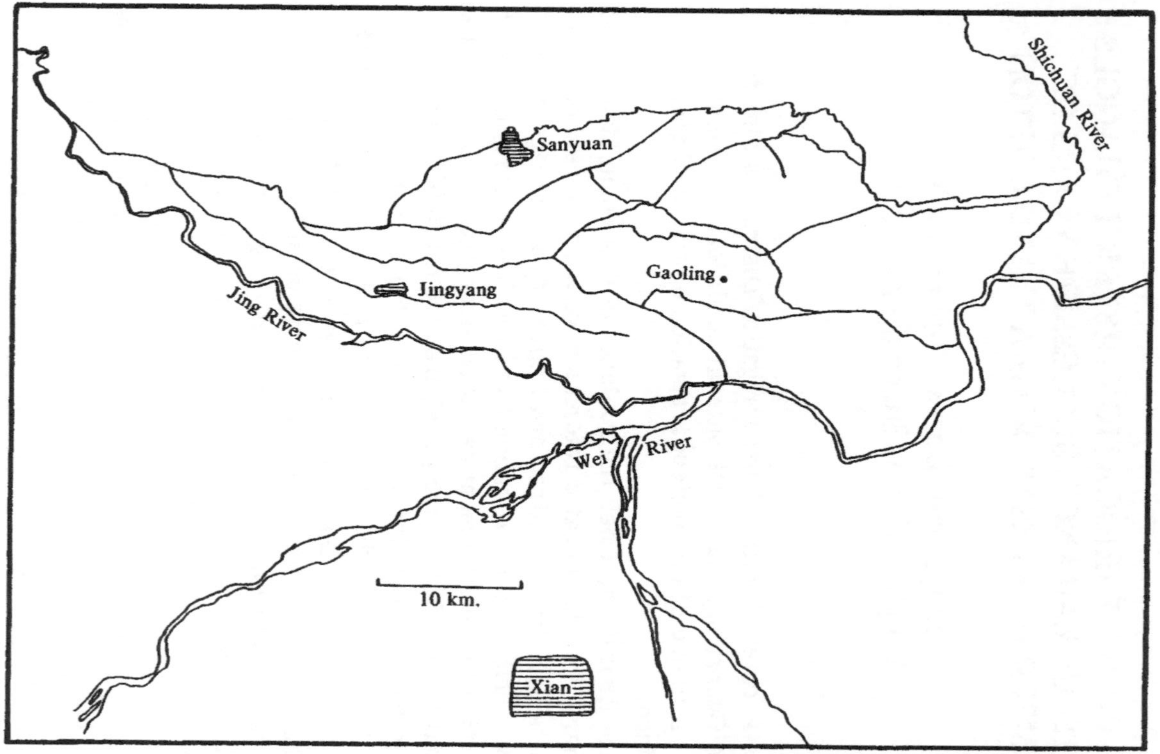


The Jinghui Project in the 1950s (Now the People's Yinjing Canal).

trict has the same old appearance and the same old output."

In 1964, Chairman Mao issued the great call "In agriculture learn from Dazhai," and the irrigation district launched a new upsurge in farmland capital construction. Through the Great Proletarian Cultural Revolution, the broad masses of cadres and commune members relentlessly criticized Liu Shaoqi's counterrevolutionary revisionist line and resolved to build farmland which would have high and stable yields despite drought or flooding, continualy advancing toward depth and breadth in production. During the past few years, they have successively carried on improvement of the canal system projects and farmland capital construction, energetically grasping soil improvement through deep plowing and strengthening their ability to resist natural disaster, in order to create conditions for the realization of high and stable yields. Since 1965, for seven successive years, grain yields have "crossed the Yellow River."* Through the rectification campaign to criticize Lin Biao, the criminal sabotage of management work by the anti-Party clique of Lin Biao has been exposed and criticized. Output has developed further. In 1971, even with summer and autumn drought, the output per mou of the 700,000 mou of grain land was 770 jin, and the output per mou of the 500,000 mou of cotton land was 73 jin. Throughout Gaoling xian, grain yields "crossed the Chang Jiang [Yangtze]." Seven communes in Jingyang and Sanyuan had grain yields exceeding 1,000 jin per mou. In 1972, they suffered an onslaught of frost, drought, and hot winds, but still had a comparatively good harvest, the output per mou for grain being 649 jin. The more than 10,000 mou of wheatland in Jinggan Commune,

*The "National Program for Agricultural Development" target for the area between the Yellow and Huai Rivers is 500 jin/mou (3.75 T./ha.). Yinjing is north of this, so when its per mou grain yield reaches 500 jin, it is said to have "crossed the Yellow River." Similarly, one "crosses the Chang Jiang" with yields of at least 800 jin/mou (6 T./ha.). — J. E. N.

Jingyang xian, had a yield of 589 jin per mou, while for the entire year, the output per mou for grain was 1,028 jin.

## Simultaneously Store, Divert and Lift to Solve the Shortage of Water Sources

Yinjing Irrigation District depends mainly on gravity-flow water diversion. Following the continued expansion of the irrigated area, there was a severe shortage in the quantity of water from river sources. In the past, the average amount of water diverted was only 60 percent of the amount of water needed. Of this, the water supply for summer irrigation constituted not even half of the water needed.

How were they to solve this contradiction? Should they blame it on nature and on other people and stop progressing, or should they struggle against nature and expand their water sources? The broad cadres and poor and lower-middle peasants were determined to struggle against the right-wing conservative thoughts of following the established routine and being unwilling to progress. They earnestly carried out the policy of "stressing small-scale projects, ancillary works, and work carried out by the commune sector." Starting from the reality of the irrigation district, they opened up many kinds of water sources in order to accommodate the development of the irrigation district and satisfy the water requirements of the crops.

Through the improvement of the canal head and the canal system, the total amount of water diverted in 1972 reached 490 million cubic meters, an increase of nearly 100 million cubic meters over the annual average amount of water diverted before the improvement was made. At the same time the main canal was lined. So far, 30 kilometers have been completed, reducing the loss from seepage.

The water quality of the ground water of the irrigation district is comparatively good. Investigation has shown that there are about 130 million cubic meters of ground water which could be used, but in the past it was seldom employed. Since 1964, the broad masses have criticized that idea of relying on nature and on the canals which is typified by the saying "Much water passes by our door, so why should we dig any wells?" Thus many in the commune sector situated in the upper reaches have upheld the slogan of using more well water in order to save canal water to support fraternal communes and teams in the lower reaches. As a result, a mass movement for self-reliantly digging mechanized wells quickly unfolded in the irrigation district. It developed very rapidly, especially in recent years, and by now 12,000 mechanized wells have been dug, 9,800 of which have already been provided with ancillary works, controlling an area of nearly 900,000 mou. In the summer of 1972, 2,160,000 mou were irrigated [in several waterings]. Of these, 880,000 mou, or 40 percent, were watered by wells. Now combined irrigation by canals and wells has become an important method of solving the problem of water sources.

The masses in the lower reaches of the irrigation district also used marshlands and gullies to build over 100 ponds and reservoirs according to local conditions. These can store over 1.7 million cubic meters and water more than 20,000 mou.

Many in the commune sector also utilized drainage ditch water, river water, and accumulated water to develop lift irrigation. The entire irrigation district already has 109 small-scale pumping stations, irrigating an area of approximately 60,000 mou.

The entire irrigation district has now taken preliminary steps to form an irrigation and drainage system which combines canals and wells, with canals feeding the wells; canals and reservoirs, with canals supplementing the reservoirs; and irrigation and drainage, with wells substituting for drainage.

## Control Alkalinization to Improve the Soil; Engage in Large-Scale Farmland Capital Construction

Before liberation, due to the long periods of heavy water use in flood irrigation and irrigation without drainage, the water table rose and the soil deteriorated. In the irrigation district, an area of about 100,000 mou was threatened with salinization, and planting was abandoned on nearly 10,000 mou. After liberation, preventive measures were adopted such as the digging of ditches to drain away water, the use of both canals and wells for irrigation, doing winter irrigation to suppress salinity, and the application of more organic fertilizer. Altogether 5 drainage systems, 35 main and branch ditches and 285 distributary and field ditches, totaling over 790 kilometers in length, were dug. In addition, through recent well irrigation, the heavy drawing of groundwater has caused the water table to be brought under control at a depth of 1 to 2 meters or below. All these things help prevent salinization of the soil. During the early period after liberation, more than 60 percent of the farmland of Xianfeng Brigade of Jinggan Commune, Jingyang xian, was saline, and its grain yield was around 100 jin per mou. After drainage ditches were dug and both canals and wells were used for irrigation, the water table was controlled, eliminating the danger of salinization. In the most recent years, these techniques have been linked with land leveling, deep plowing and scientific farming, so there have been bumper harvests of grain and cotton year after year. In the eight years since 1965, grain has "crossed the Chang Jiang." In 1972, the output of grain was 1,250 jin per mou, making this one of the high-yield collectives of the irrigation district.

The irrigation district's original canal system network and the physical arrangement of field projects were confused; the canals were crisscrossed and could not meet the requirements of mechanized cultivation, rational water use or high and stable yields. In the movement to "learn from Dazhai in agriculture," the broad masses of commune members built up a strong resolve "to transform the appearance of the irrigation district and construct new gardenlike fields." Through overall planning based on test points, they took canals, roads, and drainage as a framework and marked off specified areas for the planting of trees and the spreading of greenery. After successive years of struggle, they completed the initial formation of rectangular plots of farmland by means of "one leveling, three straightenings, and six combinings" (the leveling of land; the straightening of roads, canals and rows of trees; and the combining of canals, roads, trees, drainage, wells and electricity). The 454 subbranch canals throughout the irrigation district have been completely improved, with a total of over 15 million cubic meters of earthwork completed, over 8,300 structures newly built, and 476,000 mou of land leveled. At Anle Commune, Sanyuan xian, which is situated in the middle reaches of the irrigation district, the soil is fertile and the land level, but output had not increased for a long time. In recent years, through overall planning, over 30 subbranch and distributary canals and over 80 kilometers of canals and roads have been built, with more than 300,000 cubic meters of earthwork completed. This was combined with the leveling of land and increased digging of mechanized wells to realize the double insurance of canals and wells. Increases in farm output have been strongly promoted, and in 1972, the grain yield reached 813 jin per mou.

Although the macrotopography is level, the microtopography is uneven. Moreover, irrigation was done irrationally for many years. Therefore, the soil was hard and could not retain water and fertilizer. This is one of the main reasons why the irrigation district was unable to achieve any large increases in output for many years. In 1970, the Gaoling xian Party Committee seized deep plowing to improve the soil as a key measure in implementing "learn from Dazhai in agriculture." They mobilized the masses, and criticized the conservative idea of following the beaten path. Leading comrades of the xian committee personally went to squat at a point and "grasp the point to lead the area," thus promoting a mass movement for deep plowing to improve the soil. Within two years, more than half of the cultivated area of the entire xian has been deep plowed, changing the plowing depth from the five to six cun [16.5-20 cm.] of the past to more than one chi [33 cm.] and thus deepening the cultivated layer of soil. This changed the structure of the soil and promoted a large increase in the output of grain and cotton. In 1971, the output per mou for grain reached 810 jin, making this the first xian in our province to "cross the Chang Jiang." In 1972, their harvest was even better. Gaoling xian's deep plowing of the soil has become a model of large increases in output and has been popularized throughout the entire irrigation district.

## Planned Use of Water and Rational Irrigation

In 1954, Yinjing Irrigation District began on a trial basis to plan water use. Through continuous practice and the summing up of experience, the district has successively overcome the tendencies toward scholasticism and being divorced from reality which were prevalent during the early period of planned water use. Especially through the Great Proletarian Cultural Revolution, we have taken class struggle as the key link and have penetratingly criticized Lin Biao's counterrevolutionary revisionist line. Under the guidance of the correct line, we have further distinguished between learning professional techniques and planning water use well and having "professional work in command" and "technical skills come first." We have also drawn a clear boundary between a system of rational rules and regulations and "control, check and suppress." We have persisted in carrying out planned water use, gradually firming it up and raising its level, and basically guaranteeing more evenly distributed benefits throughout the irrigation district.

In accordance with such characteristics as the area of the irrigation district, the length of the canals and the insufficiency of water, in implementing the water use plans, we have done our utmost to propagandize the spirit of Dazhai. We have made unified, planned arrangements of the various water sources, such as canals, wells, ponds and drainage, and have strongly advocated that the irrigation district be thought of as a chessboard and that the overall situation be considered in the use of water. This has fostered a lofty style of unity in water use. At the same time, with respect to water distribution of the canal system, we have adhered to the principles of centralization of water rights, three-level allocation, and management at different levels. Water rights for the canal system have been centralized in the management office, and water allocation in the stations; water rights for the main and branch canals have been centralized in the stations, and water allocation in the subbranch canals; water rights for the subbranch canals have been centralized in the management committee, and water distribution in the production teams. When the volume of water from river sources is sufficient, water is allocated according to need. Larger allocations are not reduced, and smaller usage is not supplemented. The leftover water is channeled to ponds and reservoirs for storage. When the river sources have been unable to supply sufficient water, water has been allocated proportionally, with reductions for those who draw more and supplements to those who draw less. Accounts are settled on the amount of water each day. When the water from river sources has been extremely limited, we have carried out rotational irrigation. At the same time, we have strengthened our surveys and reports on water, rainfall, soil-moisture, crop-growth, and disaster conditions so that water allocations can be quick, accurate, lively, stable, and closely linked to the realities of production.

In our practice, we have come to realize that the allocation of water within a subbranch canal should be in accordance with the needs of the crops. "We should observe the skies, the earth, and the crops," link ourselves to reality, and make allocations in a lively way. The cadres of the commune sector accompany the water management personnel to the fields to inspect the soil moisture of every piece of land and to look at the seedlings, classifying, arranging and clearly distinguishing the more urgent from the less urgent. They then arrange the water use plan, carry out democratic distribution of the water, and irrigate rationally. In order to preserve the sequencing of water use and to ensure evenly distributed benefits, we have persisted in waging battle [against nature] under the red flag, measured water at fixed intervals, and allocated in a timely fashion, carrying out the "two no-reductions" (no reduction [in allotment] if water is spared and more land watered and no reduction if water allocated according to need is used further) and the "three no-supplements" (no supplement after voluntarily relinquishing water rights, no supplement after wasting water and watering less, and no supplement after discrepancies arise from not measuring the water). We have sought to have the "three exact fits" (branch canals, subbranch canals, and fields) with respect to water volume. We have definitely had to do a good job in the key subbranch canal work. In the present situation, the more than seventy key subbranch canals that the bureaus and stations grasp have, on the whole, achieved the "four carry outs" of leadership, organization, planning, and operation. In addition, we have gained experience in self-reliantly building ancillary works, managing by quotas, guaranteeing the sequencing of water use, improving the method of water distribution, and uniting in water use, and we have gradually promoted these experiences throughout the irrigation district.

After many years of practice, there has been an overall promotion of winter irrigation. The masses have universally reflected the saying that "in order for wheat to grow well, one cannot depart from winter irrigation." In the past, the entire area of wheat fields of the irrigation district has one winter irrigation, while half the cotton fields had a winter irrigation, and half a spring [late winter, by the western calendar] irrigation. For the last several years, there has been no interruption in the flow of water through the Spring Festival, and the spring irrigation has immediately followed the winter irrigation. Great efforts have also been made to promote irrigation both before and during the wheat harvest. This has played a significant role in advancing the autumn crop planting season and promoting high production.

To coordinate canals and wells, such experiences as "using wells to water cotton and canals to water the autumn crops" and "when the canals irrigate the wells are covered" have also been popularized extensively.

Unfolding mass scientific experimentation activities is an important measure for raising the level of irrigation management and promoting increased output of grain and cotton. In addition to the professional experimental stations, we have asked the basic-level cadres to cultivate experimental fields on a large scale. In 1971, the Yueyang, Yanliang, and Gaomiao Management Stations cultivated seventy-seven experimental plots, totaling over 800 mou. The output per mou for corn was 800 to 1,200 jin. Last year, Sanhe Production Brigade's 12-mou furrow-irrigated cotton experimental fields had an average output per mou of 141 jin, thus becoming a model for popularization which was welcomed by the masses.

## Do Well at Spreading Greenery in the Irrigation District and Develop Multiple Operations

Under local Party and state leadership, we have grasped in a big way the planting of trees on both sides of the canal system and the roads, and in the entire irrigation district we have extensively popularized Chairman Mao's directives on spreading greenery. We have also carried out related policies which have greatly promoted the work of spreading greenery. In 1972, more than 800,000 trees were planted along the main and branch canals, and more than 2.8 million trees were planted along the subbranch and distributary canals. Over 650 mou of seedlings were cultivated, and the rate of survival was over 90 percent. Many sections and subbranch canals developed multiple operations, and purple locust trees, day lily, fruit trees and so on were planted along the subbranch canals. The feeder and main canals and the fourteen subbranch canals last year used the income from canal output to purchase two frame carts and fourteen tons each of cement and white plaster and to outfit the subbranch and distributary canals with twenty-five iron gates. Huojian Brigade of Gaoling xian and Dongmao Brigade of Sanyuan xian chopped down every other tree within the jurisdiction of the production brigade to get lumber. Each brigade purchased two tractors and thereby strengthened the collective economy.

Since the Chuanliu hydroelectric power station operated by the management office was completed in 1960, it has generated at least 2,000,000 kwh. of electricity each year. In 1972 it generated 2,560,000 kwh., an increase of 320,000 kwh. over 1971, thus supporting local industrial and agricultural production. The self-operated repair plant and cement plant have provided a portion of the materials needed for maintenance and ancillary works of the canal system and have increased the income [ of the office ].

Every year, management and maintenance expenses constitute approximately 40 percent of the income from water fees and canal property, so even with investment in capital construction, there is self-sufficiency and a surplus.

## Strengthen the Unified Leadership of the Party; Rely on the Poor and Lower-Middle Peasants to Manage Water

After the revolutionary committee of the office was set up, we closely combined education in the line with the struggle-criticism-transformation movement in irrigation management work, and by deeply unfolding revolutionary mass criticism, we further came to realize that persisting under the unified leadership of the local Party organizations and thoroughly relying on the poor and lower-middle peasants are the basic guarantees that irrigation management will continuously progress along Chairman Mao's revolutionary line.

The various levels of Party organizations of the irrigation district also included water management in their daily agendas of important items regarding farm output. The important management problems have been subject to unified study and discussion with prefectural, xian or commune leaders participating in the irrigation district's irrigation committee, thus guaranteeing the initiation of the various items of management work.

In order to do a good job of management, it is necessary to believe in and rely on the masses and to combine mass management with professional management. Our irrigation district has a total of 483 section and subbranch canal leaders, over 230 subbranch canal technicians, and over 280 canal patrol squad members. They are not only the basic-level water cadres of the professional organizations, but also water-management personnel of the units benefited. During the past few years, observing Chairman Mao's great teaching "carry out education in the ideological and political lines," we have organized the entire body of management cadres seriously to study Marxism-Leninism-Mao Zedong Thought, to unfold a rectification campaign for criticism of Lin Biao, to establish gradually the thought of serving agricultural output increases, and to take the initiative to coordinate the management of water, soil, and even increased output in the commune sector so that management can be more closely linked to the realities of production. The poor and lower-middle peasants say: "In the past, the water conservancy cadres and ourselves were quite aloof from each other; now our hearts have been brought together."

From now on, in order to promote new achievements of high and stable yields of grain and cotton in the irrigation district, we resolve to take the struggle between the lines as the key link, to do our various jobs effectively, to seize models properly, to work from point to area, to engage in farmland capital construction in a big way, to exploit fully the latent strength of water sources by developing well irrigation and pond irrigation, to complete the projects for improving the canal system, to strengthen planned use of water, to upgrade irrigation techniques, to promote small strip check and ditch irrigation and to carry out scientific farming.

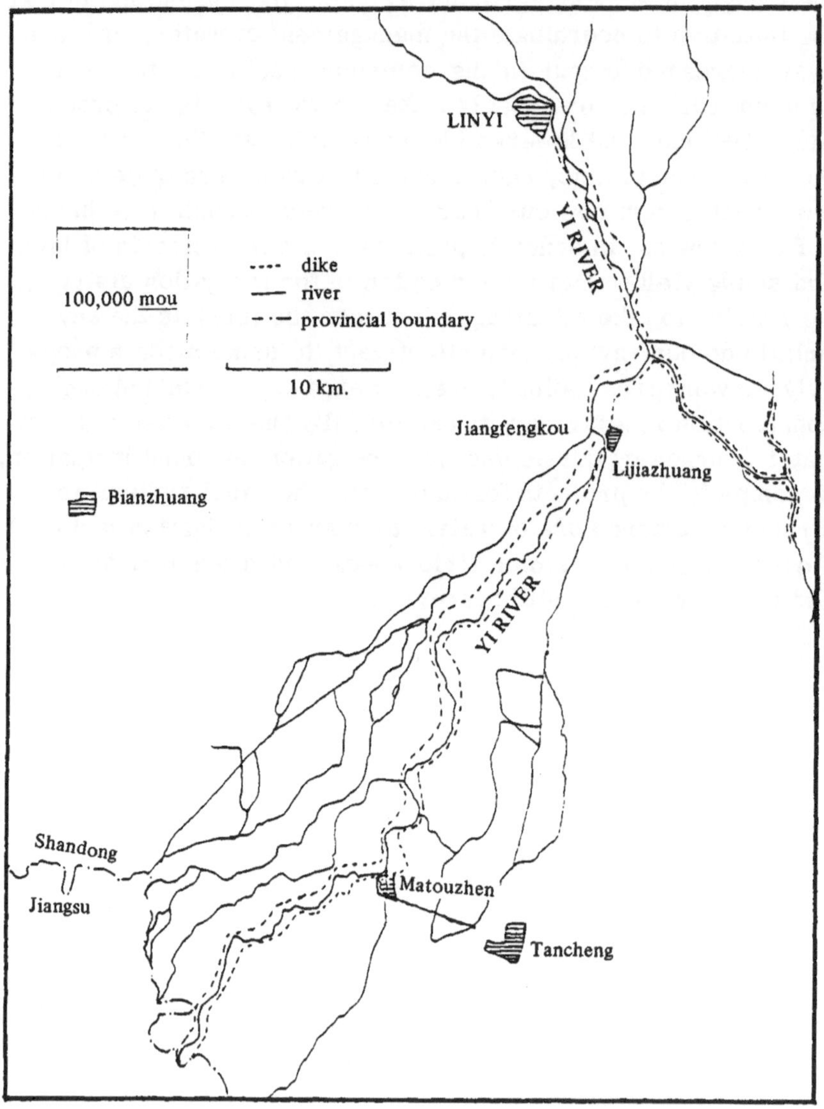


Middle Reaches of the Yi River in Shandong.

*Reading 8*

# PROPERLY MANAGE THE BIG FLOODGATE FOR THE REVOLUTION

## Water Construction Headquarters, Linyi Prefecture, Shandong Province*

The Jiangfengkou Flood Diversion Gate is located at the entrance of the Wu River flood diversion channel along the middle reaches of the Yi River. In addition to managing the Jiangfengkou Gate and the dikes along the Yi and Wu Rivers, the Yi and Wu River Management Office is also responsible for allocating water to the canal headworks of four river diversion irrigation districts at Gegou, Chashan, Xiaobudong and the Wu River. For the past ten or more years, all the staff and workers of the office have earnestly studied Chairman Mao's works and have held to their orientation of managing the gate for the revolution and of working for farm output increases. They have made regular inspections of the gate and embankments, scheduled surveys, punctually maintained the gate and dikes, and kept the machinery and equipment in good running condition so that the gates open and close smoothly. They have thus victoriously completed the task of flood diversion in past years and have changed a gate used only for flood diversion into a dual-purpose drainage and irrigation gate, promoting the development of agricultural production along the two banks of the Wu River. Simultaneous with doing a good job of managing the project to bring

*Shandong sheng Linyi dichu shuili jianshe zhihuibu, "Wei geming guanhao dazha." From Shuili guanli gongzuo jingyan huibian [Compilation of Experiences in Water Management Work], Beijing, 1973, pp. 110-114.

its benefits into full play, they have used their spare time to fill in hollows to create farmland in a planned way and to plant trees, spread greenery and develop orchard production. The area around the big gate, with its jagged, rock-strewn, sandy beaches, has become a flowery forest of orchards. The over 2,800 trees which have been planted produce over 300,000 jin of different kinds of fruit each year.

## Work Hard and Seriously; Properly Manage the Big Gate

When the idea of strengthening the management and maintenance of the gate and the dikes was first stressed, some people felt that the gate was exclusively for flood diversion of the Yi River. It was only to be opened when that river's flow reached the diversion level during the peak flood season. Since, in their view, the gate was not needed in ordinary times, it made little difference whether it was managed or not. When the Party branch discovered this problem, it felt that the negligent thinking among the management personnel was very dangerous. On the one hand, they organized everyone to study Chairman Mao's teaching that "The Huai River must be harnessed," while on the other hand, they invited the local poor and lower-middle peasants to come to the office to educate the personnel there by contrasting past miseries with present happiness. They used their own experiences to recall the bitterness of the old society and to discuss the sweetness of the new society. In the past, Jiangfengkou was the greatest door to disaster, bringing harm to people's lives and property along the Yi River. In the reaches above Jiangfengkou, the bed of the Yi River is much wider than in the lower reaches. Thus, a "throttle" exists. When floodwaters overflow, they inundate a large area. After liberation, the Party and the state put a great deal of manpower and materials into "leading the Shu and fixing the Yi." In 1955, the Jiangfengkou flood diversion gate was built to sluice off excess floodwaters from the Yi River. The broad masses of the people joyously said: "Because of the construction of Jiangfengkou, the water follows the people's will, lives are safe, and rich harvests are protected from drought and flooding." Chairman Mao's teaching and the people's hopes taught each member of the management personnel a great lesson. The office director, Comrade Zhao Xinhe, though elderly and frail, led the way into the water to do exploratory drilling in the stilling pool. He led the way in climbing up to the roof of the machine building which is over twenty meters high to carry on high altitude operations, and he also led the way in patching up the dike slopes. When he discovered rust spots on part of the gate, he immediately organized the staff and workers to remove the rust and paint over it and a also to caulk cracks in the gate which were leaking water before they worsened.

Under the leadership of the elderly office director, the more than twenty management personnel worked hard and seriously to manage the big gate for the revolution. A guard, Comrade Liu Pingsheng, has watched the gate faithfully for sixteen years through wind and rain and has been conscientiously and earnestly responsible. Once he discovered spots of mold appearing on the roofing of the machine building so he tied a rope around his waist and climbed up onto the roof which was about twenty meters high. He checked and found that part of the tile was loose and leaking, so he personally proceeded to repair it. In strict accordance with regulations, a technician named Zhang Chengyi and other comrades have earnestly carried out surveys on subsidence, shifting, osmotic pressure, embankment face pressure, circular flow permeability [raoliu shentou], hydraulic jump, and so on. In addition, on their own initiative, they have increased the number of items surveyed, such as cracks in the concrete, cracks due to expansion and shrinkage, and scouring and silting caused by river diversion in the upper and lower reaches. They have discovered problems and have taken timely measures to solve them. Once, after floodwaters had been diverted, in order to find out any changes in the condition of the project, they spent more than two days meticulously checking the entire stilling pool. They discovered that both the stilling pit and the downstream spillway apron [haiman]* had been washed out by the flood. They promptly took measures to fix it and eliminate the potential disaster. They planted willow trees to protect the dangerous section created by the washing out of the corner of the protective dike on the left side of the gate by floodwaters during the flood season. The results were good, saving the state over 400,000 yuan in maintenance expenses. In such ways, they have regularly taken independent action to carry out such work as project maintenance, spreading greenery on the dikes, and planting trees for protection against danger, thus guaranteeing the integrity and security of the project.

## Expand Benefits by Every Means

In order fully to develop the benefits of the flood diversion gate, and on the basis of practical experience, they have strengthened their investigation and research, grasped the hydrological forecasts, and accurately carried out controlled operation of the gate. One evening during the flood season in 1963, the Yi River floodwaters had already risen to the top of the gate. The higher levels notified them that when the river water ap-

*"The base of the outlet section [of a distribution gate] is dry-laid stone which can continue to dissipate the surplus energy of the water flow. This kind of permeable base is also called a haiman. It and the stilling pool [xiaoli chi] form a complete system for dissipating energy and preventing scouring." — Nongtian shuili jichu zhishi [Basic Knowledge of Farm Water Conservancy], Beijing, 1977, p. 167. The haiman is item 3 in the accompanying illustration. — J.E.N.

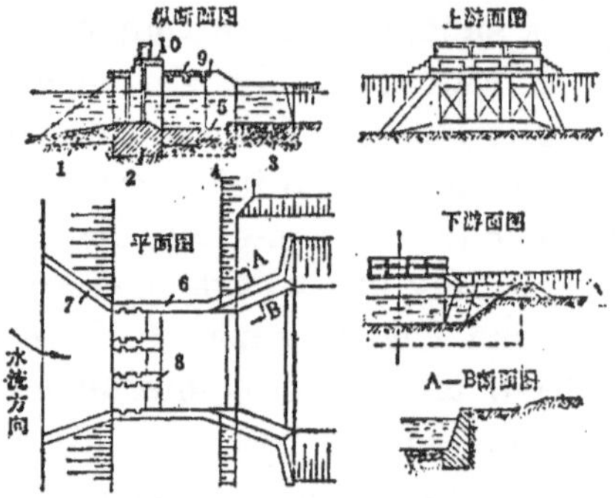


图 7—8 分水闸结构图

1.铺盖 2.闸底板 3.海漫 4.齿墙 5.消力池 6.闸墙 7.翼墙 8.闸墩 9.交通桥 10.工作桥

proached the flood diversion flow volume, then immediate preparations should be made to open the gate and divert the floodwaters. For several successive nights, the management staff and workers of the entire office, in spite of having insufficient sleep, kept strict watch at their posts. The elderly office director Zhao Xinhe waited for phone calls while he monitored the water level at the proper times. He thought: it would be a very easy matter to open up the gate to divert the floodwaters. A pull of the electric switch, and it would take only four or five minutes to open the big gate completely, but once the gate was open, the more than 100,000 mou of farms in the flood diversion channel would be wiped out with a single stroke. If the peak flow flood mark was exceeded, however, and the floodwaters were not diverted, the lower reaches of the Yi River would be threatened by flood, so the entire situation had to be considered. At this critical juncture, taking into consideration the pattern of rise and fall of floodwaters of the Yi River which had existed for many years and the water conditions at the time, he and the workers and technicians earnestly analyzed and studied the situation, making a firm decision to exercise accurate control. If the flood diversion flow was not reached, they would definitely not open the gate for flood diversion. At the same time, in order to guarantee the security of the reservoir and dikes, they further strengthened the observation of water conditions in front of the gate and took the initiative to maintain close contact with the hydrographic monitoring stations in the upper reaches of the Yi River, punctually analyzing the changes in rain and water conditions. When they verified that the floodwaters in the upper reaches were beginning to subside, the clouds were thinning out, and the rain had stopped, they promptly presented the higher levels with these grounds for not opening the gates for flood diversion. The higher levels accepted their rational suggestion and did not [order them to] open the gate for flood diversion. In this way, they not only protected the more than 100,000 mou of crops along the flood channel but also guaranteed the security of the dikes in the lower reaches.

In recent years, with the increase in the number of water storage projects in its upper reaches, the Yi River's floodwaters have gradually diminished, so that the necessity for flood diversion at Jiangfengkou Gate has also greatly diminished. However, the Party branch of the management office believes that whether the chance of needing flood diversion is large or small does not determine the significance of the management task. Just because no flood diversion has been needed for three or five years, one cannot say that there will not be a fierce one soon. No matter when it comes, there should be no negligent thinking. At the same time, water management should serve increased farm output. Helping the people on the two banks of the Wu River to develop production is a responsibility that should not be shirked. Beginning in 1964, in order to develop irrigation activity in the lower reaches, this gate used only for flood diversion was changed into a dual-purpose [flood] discharge and irrigation gate, and the channel used only for flood diversion was changed into a dual-purpose canal for drainage and irrigation. They successively helped Tancheng and Cangshan xian open up four river diversion irrigation districts, delivering water to over 100,000 mou of land. The management office regularly organized its personnel to go down into the communes in the vicinity of the river to help them survey canals, repair culverts, and build electrical irrigation stations. The masses have greatly welcomed these actions. Because its land is high, Wangjiashagou Brigade cannot use gravity flow. With the assistance of the management office, it built an electrical irrigation station, allowing its farmland to get suitable irrigation. This brigade sometimes only needs a flow of 0.2 [cu. m./sec.] to water its land; yet the staff and worker comrades conscientiously control the opening of the gate for release in order to satisfy the brigade's irrigation needs. In addition, for the past few years, they have successively helped fifty-two brigades along the flood channel to build over forty drainage culverts, changing more than 20,000 mou of flooded marshland into fields with high and stable yields.

## Work Hard to Start New Undertakings with Self-Reliance

Originally, all around the water gate there were sand dunes and ponds. The Party branch of the management office mobilized the masses to move the sand and fill in the watery expanses, moving silt to create land and cultivating seedlings and trees to develop orchard production; they were determined to travel the road of self-reliance and realize self-sufficiency in management expenses. At the time, some people said: "This is a flood diversion gate. We do not collect water fees; nor do we collect electricity fees. We are totally surrounded by sand dunes and vast ponds. Self-reliance is no easy matter for us." The Party branch organized everyone to study Chairman Mao's teachings "be self-reliant" and "struggle arduously" and his glorious works such as "The Foolish Old Man Who Moved the Mountains." Through study, they raised their ideological consciousness, and many of the worker comrades said: "Whether we travel the road of self-reliance is a major question of whether we carry out Chairman Mao's revolutionary line. Although our natural conditions are inadequate, they are much better than the conditions of Nanniwan during the War of Resistance. We should propagate the spirit of Nanniwan, and no matter how inadequate the conditions or how great the difficulty, we must become self-sufficient." On the second day of the Spring Festival in 1963, the elderly office director Zhao Xinhe led the comrades to brave the cold winds and begin the battle to move the sand and fill in the water. In only four days' time, they filled in a pond of more than 1 mou and fixed up more than 3 mou of level sandy earth. Everyone happily named this plot of land "Good Beginning." Now this plot has been transformed into a peach orchard with an annual production of 10,000 jin. In the same way, year after year, they moved one sand dune after another, filled in one pond after another, built one canal after another, and leveled over 100 mou of sandy land. One after another, they planted over 2,800 fruit trees, including apples, peaches, and pears, changing a barren sandy beach full of dunes and furrows into a flowery fruit orchard.

To provide fertilizer for the fruit trees, the staff and workers not only developed hog raising for manure, but they also used their rest periods to dig out the river sediment to make green compost [da'ou lüfei]. Also, whenever they went out, they shouldered a basket to pick up manure. From the winter of 1964 to the winter of 1965, they gathered over 500 carts of barnyard manure, collected over 100,000 jin of nightsoil, and dug out over 950 carts of river silt. On the average, over 300 jin of fertilizer was applied to each fruit tree, thus ensuring the growth needs of the fruit trees.

Owing to the emphasis placed on the development of multiple operations, from 1959 to 1972 this management office harvested a total of over 2 million jin of different kinds of fruit and over 3,800 jin of medicinal herbs; it sold over 40,000 jin of fat hogs to the state and raised over 500 head of piglets for commune members. Beginning in 1963, it has been more than self-sufficient in management expenses for ten consecutive years.

*Reading 9*

# FIRMLY GRASP LINE EDUCATION; STRENGTHEN MANAGEMENT OF THE DIKE


## Dike Maintenance Section, Yellow and Qin Rivers, Wuzhi *Xian*, Henan Province*


Our section is situated at the confluence of the Yellow River and the Qin River. It is in charge of the dike maintenance tasks along 65 kilometers of the Yellow and Qin river dikes. There are 6 communes and 54 brigades along these dikes. The mass and professional personnel who protect the dikes and gates total 130 persons.

Because of its relatively poor work in dike management, our section was a backward unit within the Xinxiang [Prefecture] Dike Maintenance Department before the Great Proletarian Cultural Revolution. During the past few years, we have firmly grasped line education, strengthened management of the dike, and accomplished a certain amount. Now, along the dikes there are a million trees, and 32 kilometers of dikes have been pressure grouted. Various kinds of potential calami-

---

*Henan sheng Wuzhi xian Huang Qin he xiufang duan, "Henzhua luxian jiaoyu, jiaqiang difang guanli." From Shuili guanli gongzuo jingyan huibian [Compilation of Experiences in Water Management Work], Beijing, 1973, pp. 128-133.

The term "line education" (luxian jiaoyu) in the title is from the period of the Cultural Revolution. It refers to educating people about the difference between the mass-oriented "proletarian revolutionary line" of Chairman Mao and the elitist "counterrevolutionary revisionist line" attributed to Liu Shaoqi and, subsequently, to Lin Biao. — J. E. N.

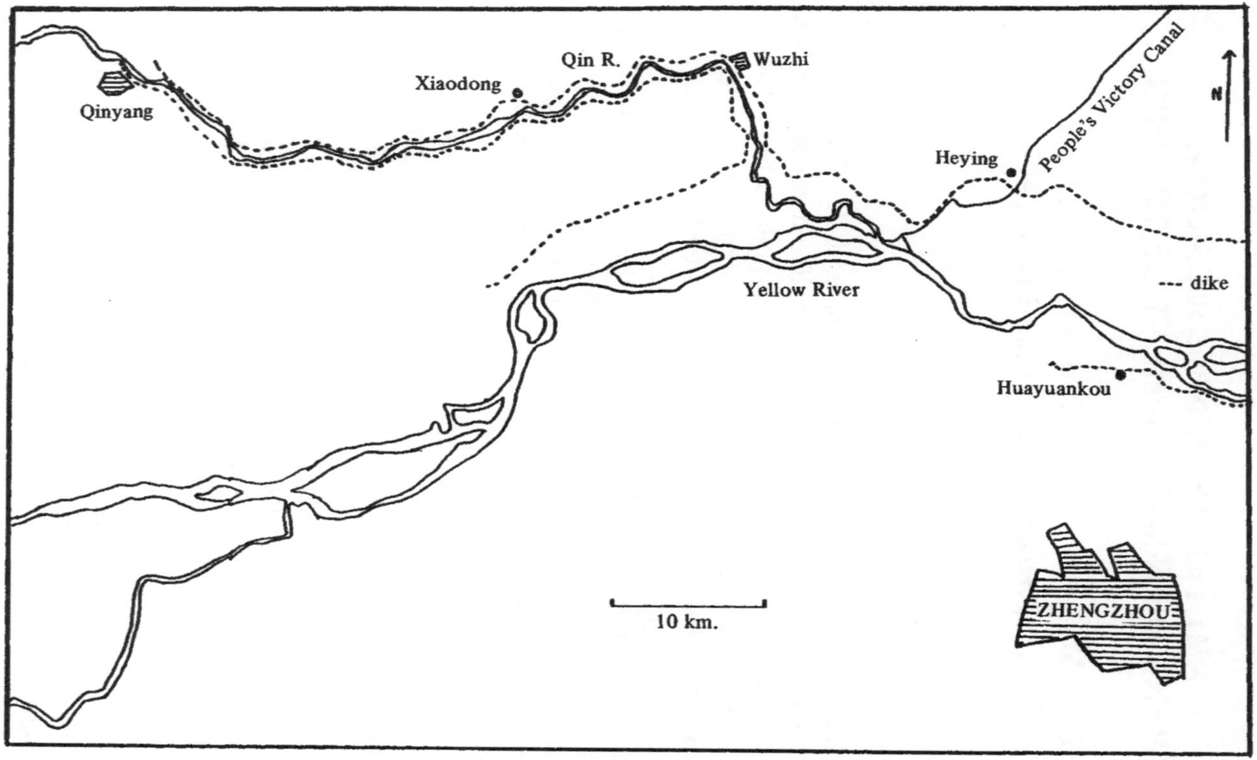


The Yellow and Qin River Dikes.

ties have been eliminated in 5,142 places, changing the appearance of the dike project. The masses of commune members [who live] along the dikes have shown great concern and love for the dikes, and the orderliness of management is getting better and better.

## Firmly Grasp Line Education; Go Down to Mobilize the Masses

"The line is the key link; once it is grasped everything falls into place." In 1969, after our dike maintenance section's new Party branch was established, we persisted in educating our Party members, staff and workers, and dike maintenance personnel in the ideological and political lines. We repeatedly studied Chairman Mao's teaching that "work on the Yellow River must be done well," and we organized the staff and workers to study diligently the works of Marx, Lenin and Chairman Mao. We closely combined serious reading and study with the rectification movement to criticize Lin Biao, penetratingly exposing and criticizing the sabotage and interference of the counterrevolutionary revisionist line of Liu Shaoqi and Lin Biao in dike management work and drawing a clear boundary between the correct line and the erroneous line. Everyone further realized that dike maintenance is the foundation and management is the key and that our goals are to guarantee no breaches [in the dikes] and to protect the lives and property of millions of people along the Yellow River, as well as to construct socialist industry and agriculture. The management of the Yellow River and Qin River dikes is extremely important work. There should not be the least bit of carelessness or neglect. During the past few years, the channel of the Yellow River has continuously accumulated silt, and a new situation with new characteristics has appeared. The task of flood prevention on the Yellow River and Qin River dikes has become more complex, so great efforts must be made to strengthen management.

In order to strengthen dike management, we must rely on the masses and mobilize them. It will not do to rely merely on a few professional management personnel to handle the matter in a cool and aloof manner. We have broadly and intensively publicized and implemented Chairman Mao's great directive that "work on the Yellow River must be done well" among the broad masses in the communes along the river. We have publicized the new situation and new characteristics of the Yellow River and the great significance of managing the dikes well, and we have mobilized the masses to unfold a campaign concerning the "three recollections and the three bringing outs" (that is, recollecting the oppression of the ruling classes suffered by the people in the old society and bringing out the happiness given to the people through the new society and Chairman Mao; recollecting the disaster of having two breaches in the dikes every three years before liberation when the dikes were dilapidated and bringing out the great achievements of the people in taming the Yellow and Qin rivers after liberation; and recollecting the danger to the dikes from the counterrevolutionary revisionist line of Liu Shaoqi and Lin Biao and bringing out the decisive role of Chairman Mao's revolutionary line in dike management work).

Both through rectification to criticize Lin Biao and various forms of education, we have used Mao Zedong Thought to arm the broad masses; we have raised the consciousness of the broad masses of workers and commune members in managing the dikes well and have strengthened their sense of revolutionary responsibility. Many good people and good deeds have appeared which have drawn the dike management work of our section to a new stage. A dike maintenance officer named Comrade Guan Xiaoxue, observing Chairman Mao's teaching that "in technology we should not rest on our laurels," studied technology intensively for the revolution; he seriously summed up his experience in pruning trees and contributed to the good management of the dikes' trees. A sixty-four-year-old dike maintenance officer named Comrade Wu Tongran, "fearing neither hardship nor death," in one day carried more than 140 loads of water on a shoulder pole to resist drought by watering trees. He also led three dike maintenance officers to gather fertilizer; they spread over 300 dan [15 metric tons] of fertilizer on more than 300 trees of the dike. Many dike management officers conducted home study classes and led members of their families to cooperate in maintaining the dikes.

## Strengthen Party Leadership; Rectify the Dike Maintenance Organization

Party leadership is the basic guarantee for properly doing the various items of work. Dike management work had to be placed under the unified leadership of the local Party committee. The advisory role of the dike maintenance section had to be fully developed. We made timely summary reports to the xian committee, giving our opinions of how to improve dike management work, and we received the xian committee's leadership. The xian revolutionary committee also especially promulgated "Regulations on Strengthening the Management and Maintenance Work for the Yellow and Qin River Dikes and Culvert and Gate Projects." At the same time, the section's Party branch clearly designated a deputy secretary to take special responsibility for dike management, and it appointed eleven staff and workers to go down into the commune sector throughout the year to be responsible for the daily work of dike management. The Party committees of the communes and the Party branches of the production brigades along the dikes also placed a deputy secretary or committee member in charge of dike maintenance work. In this way, they placed the dike management work under the direct leadership of the various levels of Party committees, who incorporated it into their daily agendas. This turned around the situation of the past in which dike management was carried out solely by the dike maintenance section.

At the same time, we earnestly reorganized the [mass] dike maintenance contingents. We consulted with the commune sector Party organizations, and in accordance with the basic conditions of good political ideology, good physical health, and a fervent love for dike maintenance work, we made readjustments in the full-time mass dike maintenance personnel. To create the conditions for good dike management, we selected thirty-nine commune members to shore up the dike maintenance contingents and strengthen them both qualitatively and quantitatively.

In addition to [selecting] the full-time dike and gate maintenance personnel, we adopted a management method which combines dike maintenance by the full-time contingent and the masses. In the communes and brigades, we revived the dike management committees. The commune dike management committee consists of five to seven persons, while the production brigade dike management committee consists of three to five persons. The Party deputy secretary or committee member assigned to dike maintenance acts as director. At the meetings, which are not at fixed intervals, the dike management work is checked up on and arranged. We also marked off sections of the dike and allocated them to the production teams, to carry out a mass "one prevention and four maintenances" [flood prevention; and maintenance of the dikes, the gates, telephone lines, and materials] effort. We widely popularized dike maintenance for the revolution, teaching the masses to recognize clearly that dike management work is a component of socialist construction, thus ensuring the political and economic significance of security from floods. The masses of commune members of Qinyangcun Brigade said: "Chairman Mao has issued the call that 'work on the Yellow River must be done well.' We certainly will manage the dike well, so that old Chairman Mao's heart will be at ease." A responsible comrade of the Xiaodong Commune Party Committee took the initiative to inspect dike maintenance work. He personally called a meeting of the dike maintenance personnel of the entire commune. Each production brigade in the commune was able on its own to organize the masses after a rain to go up to the dike and nip any trouble in the bud by filling in the ditches and the "wave pits."*

With dike management strengthened, they scored big new achievements in planting trees and spreading greenery, thus following the dual principles of preventing wave action on the river side of the embankment and of obtaining materials from the land side. Now there are a million trees along the entire section, about 16 trees for each meter of the dike line. The trees are continuously being renewed, and the benefits increase from year to year. In 1971, 156 cubic meters of timber were chopped down, with more than 30,000 willow tree trunks bringing in an income of over 60,000 yuan. This averaged 1 yuan per meter of the big dikes. The state and collectives divided this up according to the following policy: the state's share of the lumber supports the xian in operating its "five small" industries;† and the teams' share constructs collective buildings or goes to support commune members. Many production brigades have also used the income from the trees to purchase agricultural machinery. In this way, dike maintenance and agriculture have promoted each other, and there has been a close relationship between dike maintenance and the livelihood of the masses. This has further aroused the enthusiasm of the cadres and masses for maintaining the dike.

---

*"Wave pits" (langwo) appear to be portions of the embankment which have been gouged out by the wave action of floodwaters. These would weaken the structure of the dike if left alone. Likewise, ditches may be carved too close to the dike by floodwaters. These might provide a dangerous rechanneling of the mainstream in subsequent high water periods. The dikes along the Yellow River are usually set well away from the main channel. — J. E. N.

†The "five small" industries are cement, chemical fertilizer, iron and steel, agricultural machinery and coal. These have usually been developed by the xian, together with other types of local industry such as textile production. — J. E. N.

## Grasp a Point to Lead an Entire Surface;* Be Continuously Creative

Observing Chairman Mao's teaching that "we must grasp good models," we adopted the method of grasping a point to lead an entire surface. We chose Xiaodong Commune, which has a comparatively good foundation, as a trial point. We helped it develop its dike management work, while we engaged in investigation and study on the spot, formulated measures, and summed up the commune's experiences in strengthening its leadership and relying on the masses to maintain the dike for the revolution, by leveling of the big dike, completing projects, [planting] trees in abundance, and increasing the dike's resistance to flood. Once we had grasped a model, we made great efforts to organize its propagation. Our concrete methods were to print and publish Xiaodong Commune's experiences in dike maintenance for the revolution, to organize those in other communes to visit it, and to send out forces to make concrete adjustments in light of reality in various areas. This gave everyone an example to study, a direction for change, and a goal to pursue. "Brighten a lamp, so that it will illuminate a large area." The experience of Xiaodong motivated the backward units. Heying Commune had some dike sections which originally were basically inadequate and were weak links in the entire section. The dike maintenance section organized personnel to go down into the brigades of this commune and widely publicize Chairman Mao's great directive "Work on the Yellow River must be done well." They studied Xiaodong Commune's advanced experience and, with the commune and brigades, summed up lessons and formulated measures. By pooling everyone's wisdom and strength, they threw off the label of backwardness. In two years' time, they planted more than 100,000 trees on Heying Commune's dike, nearly half of the number assigned to the entire section. The survival rate

---

*<u>Zhuadian daimian</u>. This means to draw upon the experience of a selected unit to promote overall work. — J. E. N.

reached over 90 percent, thus eliminating vacant patches in the dike's greenery. They filled in over 300 ditches and "wave pits," to make the body of the dike whole and unbroken and the dike face level, thereby raising the ability of the dike to resist flood.

Now, the leadership method of having the model example show the way and of grasping a point to lead an entire surface has been generally propagated throughout the section. The section has its Xiaodong Commune, and all the communes and brigades have their own advanced dike sections. Every level grasps a point, and from the point, they lead the entire surface. This has all been visibly effective.

## Carry Out Policy; Formulate Systems

During the past few years, we have earnestly carried out the Party's class line, correctly distinguishing and handling the contradictions of two different natures. We have dealt a firm blow to the class enemy's sabotage of dike activities. We have patiently criticized and educated those among the masses of the people who have accidently violated dike maintenance regulations, but we have been strict with those who would not change after repeated education and when the nature of the circumstances has been serious. In so doing, we have embodied the Party's policy and reaped excellent results.

When managing the dikes' trees and distributing their benefits, we have followed the principle of heeding the interests of both the state and the collective. Our policy has been one of "state owned and brigade operated, sharing the benefits." The state's share of the income from lumber is 60 percent. The brigade's is 40 percent. The state's share of the income from fruit trees is 30 percent, and the brigade's is 70 percent. All of the income from tree branches and tops and dike grass belongs to the dike maintenance team. The state pays the going price for the willows used for emergencies.

In order to encourage the masses to catch animals which harm the dikes, we formulated an appropriate method of rewards, offering rational remuneration according to the size of the animals, the extent of the harm, and the difficulty of catching the animals. In recent years, the number of animals which harm the dikes has been markedly reduced due to the great efforts of the masses to catch them.

We also formulated some necessary systems of work. The main ones were:

A management responsibility system for the dike section: The big dike is managed in sections by the relevant communes and brigades, with the participation of people sent by the dike maintenance section. The management of the dangerous portions is sectioned off to work units [ban], and each work unit is divided into groups [zu], in order to make specific people responsible for embankment reinforcement works [baduo luoshi daoren]. This provides a clear division of labor and strict responsibility, bringing into full play the initiative of the communes and brigades, as well as that of the work units and groups.

A system of investigation and appraisal: The commune dike maintenance group is appraised every two weeks, and the dike maintenance section once every month. Once every six months, a joint investigation and appraisal is made by the section and the communes. This investigation and appraisal includes four items: (1) visiting and studying each other; (2) commending good people and good deeds; (3) summing up previous work, affirming its achievements and discovering its deficiencies, while arranging subsequent work and setting tasks, quality criteria and times; and (4) appraising and selecting advanced individuals and units.

A system of files on embankment reinforcement works [baduo]: We have acquired a detailed understanding of each saoba* site built before liberation by visiting with the masses, investigating xian gazeteers and checking monument inscriptions. We have found out the history of the projects that were newly built, built

*A cylindrical bundle, or fascine, of tree branches, twigs, straw and gravel used like a sand bag. — J. E. N.

on a rush basis or rebuilt after liberation. We have discovered and recorded, item by item, the main conditions of existing projects, such as their scale, structure, amount of materials used, stability, diversion properties and flood prevention standards. We have set up a projects file containing this information, so that it is at our fingertips.

We also stipulated: It is prohibited to dig wells or build other structures which endanger the safety of the dike within 50 meters of the inside of the large dike or 100 meters of its outside. It is prohibited to fish by using explosives near the dangerous sections. It is prohibited to gather soil or to cultivate land on the body of the dike or in the shade of the willow trees. Except in flood emergencies, it is prohibited to drive a vehicle on the dike on a rainy day, and caterpillar tractors are strictly prohibited from going on the big dike. It is prohibited to chop down trees at will on the dike. It is prohibited to use any of the dike project's materials reserved for flood prevention on one's own initiative. These stipulations have played a definite role in strengthening the dike management work.

*Reading 10*

# STRENGTHEN THE MANAGEMENT OF MECHANICAL WELLS; DEVELOP THE BENEFITS OF INCREASED OUTPUT

Water Conservancy Bureau,
Pinggu *Xian*, Beijing Municipality*

Pinggu xian is situated in the southern foothills of the Yan Mountains. It is criss-crossed by the mountain range, and there are rolling hills. The Gou and Cuo rivers traverse the entire xian, so it has comparatively rich water resources. Before liberation, however, this place "had drought nine years out of ten, with drought in the spring and flooding in the autumn." The level of agricultural output was very low. During the early period after liberation, the entire xian (with the exception of scattered vegetable fields) had practically no irrigated land, and the output of grain per mou was only about 100 jin.

Under the leadership of the Party, and following Chairman Mao's proletarian revolutionary line, the broad masses of poor and lower-middle peasants of Pinggu xian, with stout hearts and high ambitions, resolved to make a thorough change in the poor, backward appearance of the xian. They developed the spirit of self-reliance and arduous struggle and engaged in water conservancy in a big way. They built a large number of water projects, one after another, linking reservoirs, canals, mechanized wells, and water-pumping stations so that the irrigated area reached 357,000 mou, or 77.5 percent of the xian's total cultivated area. Except in the mountains, all land was basically

---

*Beijing shi Pinggu xian shuili ju, "Jiaqiang jijing guanli, fahui zengchan xiaoyi." From Shuili guanli gongzuo jingyan huibian [Compilation of Experiences in Water Management Work], Beijing, 1973, pp. 134-138.

subject to water control. For four successive years, the output of grain and cotton exceeded the "Program."* In 1971, the xian's output of grain per mou was 588.3 jin, and the output of cotton per mou smashed the 100-jin mark.

The mechanized well has been one of the key items in the water conservancy construction of Pinggu xian. Since 1962, a total of 477 mechanized wells have been dug, irrigating an area of 140,000 mou, 39 percent of the irrigated area of the entire xian. The management policy for the mechanized wells has been to dig each one properly, then manage it properly, and then use it properly. Thus, the mechanized wells of the entire xian have basically been maintained in good working condition. On the average, each mechanized well waters about 300 mou [20 ha.] of land, making effective use of well irrigation. In 1972, in the struggle against drought, the various leadership levels vigorously promoted the management of mechanized wells and the provision of on-field works. As a result, there was a bumper harvest of summer grain in the entire xian. Compared with 1971, the total output increased by 11 million jin, and output per mou increased by 30 percent. Because of the serious drought, the total annual output of the entire xian was lower than that of 1971; however, the total output per mou yields of most of the mechanized-well irrigation districts exceeded the highest level in history. The chief methods adopted [by Pinggu xian] in the management of mechanized wells have been the following:

## Strengthen Education; Elevate Knowledge

The knowledge of the broad masses of Pinggu Xian concerning the importance of strengthening the management of mechanized wells went through a process of practice, knowledge, more practice, and more knowledge. In the beginning, some of the communes and brigades did not have any experience in the use

---

*In this area, the National Agricultural Development Program targets are 400 jin/mou for grain and probably 40 or 60 jin/mou for cotton (the guidelines for cotton, unlike those for grain, are not specified geographically).

of mechanized wells. They only understood "digging" the wells, not "managing" them; after digging a mechanized well, there was someone to use it, but no one to manage it. In addition, the land was uneven, and the canal system was not complete. Even though the number of mechanized wells increased from year to year, the benefits did not manifest themselves. After the xian departments in charge went down into the basic levels and discovered this problem, they and the masses earnestly studied Chairman Mao's great teaching that "water conservance is the lifeline of agriculture." In order to understand it, they raised good management of the mechanized wells to the high level of the struggle between the lines. At the same time, they helped the commune sector set up necessary management systems and trained a group of mechanics, greatly increasing the effectiveness of mechanized-well irrigation. For instance, Tianjing Brigade of Machangying Commune used to be a hilly area: "Tianjing had four big hills; no matter what was planted, it did not grow." After 1963, when two mechanized wells were dug, some of the cadres and commune members opined, "Watering the ground is not like waiting for rain." Their management became lax, and as a result, one well only watered several dozen mou, and the output per mou was only 190 jin. Through study and site visits, the cadres and the masses summed up the lesson of this production brigade with respect to mechanized-well management: Because there was no one to manage the equipment or maintain the cistern and because the canal system was not completed, irrigation was ineffective, and the output of grain was low. This raised their enthusiasm for well management, and they decided that a deputy secretary of the brigade's Party branch should take charge of mechanized-well management. They also provided themselves with full-time well-management personnel and set up a necessary system of rules and regulations, thus guaranteeing the sound utilization of the mechanized wells. In 1971, each of the brigade's four mechanized wells watered an average of more than 600 mou, thus promoting the development of agricultural production. In that year, the output of grain per mou reached 488 jin, an increase of one and a half times over that of 1967.

## Level the Land in a Big Way and Complete the Canal Systems

In the course of practice, the broad masses and cadres came to realize that unless time is spent to level the land, the effectiveness of the mechanized wells cannot be brought into play very well. Acting on this experience during the mass movement to "learn from Dazhai in agriculture," the various levels of Party organization embarked on leveling the land in a big way and completing the canal systems. In keeping with the locality's rolling hills and the great differences in terrain, they adopted the method of first leveling the land into strip checks [qi] and then further leveling and rebuilding them into larger fields each year thereafter. One winter, the xian invested over 3 million labor days in leveling over 80,000 mou and equipping it with ancillary works. In 1963, Nandingfuzhuang Brigade of Machangying Commune dug three mechanized wells. At the very beginning, due to the unevenness of the land, when it was watered, "the ditches were full, but the land had no water," so the development of production was slow. This production brigade absorbed the lesson, and starting in 1965, they have leveled land and built ancillary works every year. Now 1,600 mou of cultivated land have basically been turned into gardenlike fields. A professional water-use crew has also been established so that each mechanized well, which originally watered 10 mou in twenty-four hours, now waters 50 mou, with a maximum of 70 mou. The amount of electricity used and the electricity fees have been reduced in proportion to the increase in effectiveness of irrigation. In 1968, 700 mou was double cropped, and the land was watered three times. In 1971, 1,300 mou was double cropped, and the land was watered five times, the cost being 56 percent cheaper than in 1968. At the same time, the output of grain per mou was 732 jin in 1971, a 36.3 percent increase over 1968.

## Set Up Organized Groups to Put Management in One Line Down to the Base*

In order to accommodate the flourishing development of electrical irrigation, Party organizations and revolutionary committees at all levels in Pinggu xian set up management groups at each level from xian to brigade and gradually strengthened the various elements of the management system. The xian departments of agricultural machinery, water conservancy, and electric power have been mutually coordinated. Together they have assumed responsibility for the construction and inspection of electrical irrigation projects throughout the xian and for training the mechanics. They have also set up management cards for each well. Each commune has one full-time cadre responsible for inspection, management, and maintenance of all its mechanized wells. The brigades have organized management groups, each built around a principal responsible cadre in charge and a core of mechanics. The method of assigning people to designated wells has been adopted. All this has put management in one line down to the base. Thus, on every level there is someone in charge; for every well there is someone to do the managing; and there are means to carry out management. For example, Yuegezhuang Brigade dug three mechanized wells and built five pumping stations, one after another, watering a total of 3,900 mou. Because this brigade did a relatively good job of managing these mechanized wells and pumping stations, its effectiveness was comparatively high. On the average, 47 mou were watered per kilowatt, and the wheat fields were generally watered seven or eight times, so that the output of grain and cotton continually rose. In 1972, the output of summer grains was 493 jin per mou, an increase over 1971 of 183 jin per mou. For the entire year, the output was 900 jin per mou, an increase of 123 jin over 1971. They had three main experiences: First, they carried out line edu-

*Yiguan daodi (一管到底), a word play on "thorough" (一貫到底). – J. E. N.

cation. From the management personnel to the broad masses, everyone took loving care of the facilities, the masses managed the wells, and every household was responsible. Second, the brigade cadres in charge formed a management group specifically responsible for electrical irrigation using the mechanized wells and pumping stations. Third, they had a complete management system which they adhered to. For example, before the flood season, they would inspect the wells and raise the pumps to strictly prevent inundation. Every year before the spring irrigation, they made a major overhaul of the machinery and pumps. After the summer harvest and after the autumn, minor repairs were conducted. They reached the point where they did not go out of the production brigade for minor repairs and they conducted regular maintenance. They also observed the water level at regular intervals to discover problems and quickly handle them so that the mechanized wells and pumping stations were always kept in excellent condition, thereby guaranteeing that the farmland would be irrigated at the right time.

## Overall Planning and Rational Distribution

In developing its well irrigation work, Pinggu xian engaged in overall planning so as to strengthen its unified leadership. It formed an electrical irrigation project planning group composed of the xian water conservancy, electric power, and agricultural machinery departments. One by one, they implemented the electrical irrigation project plans proposed by the communes and the brigades. The xian, commune and brigade levels conferred together and determined the actual placement of the wells in order to achieve overall planning and rational distribution. For example, they regulated the distance between the wells and distributed them evenly. Areas which lacked surface water sources were the first to develop well irrigation, and gradually irrigation districts combining wells and canals were developed so that the irrigated area increased from year to year and the irrigation was increasingly effective year after year.

With the development of agricultural output and continual improvement in the cropping system, the multiple cropping index increased continually. The original plan for distances between wells was thus no longer suitable. In accordance with their many years of practice, they felt that in the Pinggu area the appropriate distance between wells should ordinarily be 250 to 300 meters, with each mechanized well guaranteeing the watering of 250 to 300 mou. Thus, they proceeded to revise the original plan. They reduced the distance between wells, and at the same time they adopted the method of drawing water from different strata, in order to avoid having adjacent wells interfere with one another. The original depth of the wells was generally around 80 meters, but the new supplemental wells had a depth of around 120 meters.

During the great drought of 1972, the groundwater level in Pinggu xian generally sank four to five meters. At the same time as it actively increased the digging of deep wells, this xian also paid attention to the maintenance of old wells, so that abandoned wells were revived, and old wells were renovated. In the struggle against the drought, the vast majority of the mechanized wells in the xian had their engineering works fixed up and their water-lifting equipment refurbished. Of these, over two hundred lower bases [xiazuo] alone were installed, thus solving the contradiction that water could not be drawn because the water level was dropping. Despite the great drought, they were still able to irrigate at the appropriate time. For example, Xujiawu Brigade had four mechanized wells and four wide-mouth wells, controlling a total of more than 2,000 mou. In the great drought of 1972, some of the bases of the well equipment were lowered about six meters, guaranteeing eight to nine general waterings for 1,000 mou of wheat, so that the output per mou reached 515 jin, an increase of more than 130 jin as compared to 1971. The average output per mou for the entire year reached 1,053 jin, nearly double that of 1965.

Pinggu xian has made great strides in the field of mechanized wells and played a distinct role in stimulating agricultural production, but there are still a number of problems, and the untapped potential of the mechanized well equipment is still very great. For example, the position of the outlet pipe for some mechanized wells has been installed too high, and water head loss is considerable, wasting electricity. Some of the land also is not level enough, so that the outlet ponds and canals seep or leak water, and so on. All of this prevents the full benefits of mechanized wells from being brought into play. In addition, in April 1972, the xian's mechanized wells, with 3892 kw. of installed machinery, watered about 36 mou of land per kilowatt. Because the level of the ground water has plummeted in the struggle against drought, they have changed some of the electrical machinery to a larger size so that there has been some reduction in the average amount of land watered for each kilowatt. Thus, the issue of how to select equipment for comparatively large changes in the level of the ground water awaits further study and improvement.

# III Appendix: Regulations

*Reading 11*

# PROVISIONAL MEASURES FOR THE PLANNED USE OF WATER

## Ministry of Agriculture*

**In January 1965, these measures were issued by the Ministry of Agriculture of the People's Republic of China to the provinces, autonomous regions, and municipalities for trial implementation. In response to readers' requests, we are publishing the entire text as a reference for irrigation districts in carrying out planned water use. — Editor.**

### Chapter One: General Principles

Article 1. Planned water use is an advanced method of meeting the needs of planned agricultural production and of scientifically managing the utilization of water in irrigation. All the irrigation districts should actively carry out planned water use in the spirit of adaptation to local conditions, starting from the coarse and moving toward the refined, and gradually improving.

Article 2. Planned water use means to store, divert and allocate water in a planned way and rationally to carry out irrigation in accordance with the laws governing the water requirements of agricultural crops and the conditions of the soil,

*Nongye bu, "Guan'gai jihua yong shui zhanxing banfa." From Nongtian shuili yu shuitu baochi [Farm Water Conservancy and Soil Conservation], May 1965, pp. 16-20.

the water sources, and the project water supply. Its aims are: to utilize water sources fully and develop project benefits; to save water and increase the effective rate of utilization of water, thus reducing irrigation costs; and to promote high and stable agricultural yields in the irrigation districts.

Article 3. To carry out planned water use, one must concretely and properly grasp the six links of tong, suan, pei, guan, ding, and liang. 統, 算, 配, 灌, 定, 量

1. Tong [unification] – The storage, diversion, allocation, irrigation, and drainage of water should have a unified plan.

2. Suan [calculation] – Calculations and rational arrangements should be made with respect to the amounts of water supplied and needed, the periods of water use, irrigation tasks, necessary labor and animal power and so on.

3. Pei [allocation] – The rational assignment of water and water allocation in the irrigation district is handled in a unified and centralized way by professional management organs in accordance with the plans formulated by the irrigation district management committee or conference of representatives and approved by higher-level leadership organs. No other organization or individual is allowed to interfere or give directions at random.

4. Guan [irrigation] – A rational irrigation system, rational irrigating methods, and rational irrigating techniques should be implemented.

5. Ding [fixity] – An individual responsibility system with fixed tasks, quality, and personnel should be carried out.

6. Liang [measurement] – The main canals and water distribution points can control and adjust the amount of water and carry out water measurement.

Article 4. When formulating the water use plans, the management departments of the irrigation district should satisfy the irrigation requirements for agricultural production within the irrigation district. The water-using units of the irrigation district should also consider the conditions of the irrigation water sources and projects in arranging their agricultural production plans. This enables the water use plan to be both active and reliable in promoting agricultural production.

Article 5. In the formulation and execution of the water use plan for the irrigation district, everyone must strengthen the leadership, follow the mass line, and carry out the principle of the three-in-one combination of the leadership, the technical personnel, and the masses benefited so that irrigation work can better serve agricultural production.

## Chapter Two: Classification of Water Use Plans and Procedures for Review

Article 6. The formulation of the water use plan should be made by the irrigation district management organ by collecting [information on] water use requirements by canal system and by crop at scheduled times from the water using units (such as the production brigades, the production teams, or [state] farms). It should consider [this information] and draw up an overall balance in keeping with the supply capacity of the water sources and the project, in coordination with the weather forecasts. After the conference of representatives of the irrigation district or the irrigation management committee has discussed and approved [the plan], it should be reported to the higher-level leadership organs for review and approval.

Article 7. The water use plans of the irrigation districts can generally be divided into two categories.

1. The water use plans of the canal system. These are formulated by the management organs of the canal system. They set the water allocation norms, down to the basic-level management organizations (that is, the main, branch, and sub-branch canal mass management committees or the irrigation management organizations of the people's communes or state farms). The large-scale irrigation districts may formulate plans at different levels. The canal system management organ formulates plans which are given to the various branch management organs (such as the management office or station). Then the branch management organs formulate plans which are given to the basic-level management organizations.

2. The basic-level water use plans. These are formulated by the basic-level management organizations for allocating water to the water-using units. Small-scale irrigation districts may also formulate plans from the canal system management organ directly to the water-using units.

## Chapter Three: Formulation of the Water Use Plans for the Canal System

Article 8. The formulation of water use plans for the canal system should generally include an annual water use plan and quarterly (or periodic [for each irrigation]) water use plans. The annual water use plan outlines irrigation tasks and targets for the entire year, balancing in an overall way the water supplied with that required and serving as a basis for the water use management work of the irrigation district for the entire year. The quarterly (or periodic) water use plan is the plan which concretely formulates the irrigation tasks and targets, water diversion and water allocation for each quarter (or period).

If in one year the irrigation district only uses water in individual quarters or if the number of times that water is used is very small, then it is only necessary to formulate a quarterly water use plan or a periodic water use plan.

Article 9. The annual water use plan of the canal system includes the tasks and requirements (such as the area to be irrigated, the coefficient of effective utilization of the canal system, the irrigating efficiency, and other norms); the irrigation system; and calculations for the balancing of water supply and demand and measures for balancing water amounts.

Article 10. The irrigation system must correspond to the water requirements of the agricultural crops and the conditions of the soil. At the same time, consideration should be given to the expected supply capacity of the water sources and the effective amount of rain, the conditions of the projects, and other measures for agricultural production in the irrigation district. The irrigation systems in saline-alkalized districts should also pay attention to the prevention of salinization or alkalization of the soil. If, in the same irrigation district or for the same crop, the area's conditions are exceptionally different, a different irrigation system should be established for different areas.

In the formulation of the irrigation system, the experiences of the masses in irrigation should be summed up, and the results of research in irrigation experimentation should be utilized in accordance with local conditions.

Article 11. Computations for balancing the amounts of water should be made in accordance with the expected supply capacity of the water sources, the amount of water that the canal headworks can divert, the amount of water that is used for irrigation, and so on. In keeping with the irrigation rotation or the stage (or time period) in the growth of crops, the supply of water should be balanced with its demand, discrepancies in the supply and demand of water which can arise in the irrigation district during various periods should be analyzed, and vigorous measures should be adopted, such as tapping the latent potential of water sources, economizing on water use, and so on.

Considering the flood storage capacity, the useful storage level, the water inflow at different periods, the amount of water for irrigating and the amount of water for other uses and losses, a reservoir irrigation district may draw up calculations balancing water supply and demand and formulate an operations control plan for the reservoir. In medium- and small-scale irrigation districts, when calculations have been made balancing supply and demand, the norms of the amount of water which can be drawn during the various stages may be transmitted to the water-using units at one time or in stages. Knowing how things stand, the water-utilizing units can then arrange their irrigating plans, and promote economy in their use of water.

The expected supply capacity from water sources and the effective amount of rain in an irrigation district may be determined from hydrological and meterological forecasts by using frequency analysis. Irrigation districts which lack data can do their analyses and determinations according to past experience in irrigation water diversion and water use.

Article 12. The quarterly (or periodic) water use plans for a canal system are concretely formulated on the basis of the annual water use plans and in accordance with the verified tasks and requirements of irrigation, the irrigation system and the balance of water supply and demand. Their contents include the tasks and requirements, the irrigation system, the water diversion plan, the water allocation plan, and the measures for executing the plan.

Article 13. The quarterly (or periodic) plans for the diversion of water are formulated in accordance with the supply capacity of the water sources for the corresponding quarter (period), the amount of flow that may be diverted from the canal headworks, the amount of water used for irrigation, and so on. They concretely determine the amount of flow and the time of water diversion from the canal headworks during the irrigation period and serve as the basis for quarterly (periodic) irrigation water diversion.

Article 14. The quarterly (or periodic) water allocation plans for a canal system are formulated in accordance with the water diversion plan, the irrigated area of the various levels of canals, the water requirements of the crops, the capacity of the canals for carrying water, and the effective utilization coefficient of the canal system. They rationally distribute quantities of water to the basic-level management units or water distributing canals.

## Chapter Four: Formulation of the Basic-Level Water Use Plans

Article 15. The basic-level water use plans are formulated in accordance with the water allocation norms of the quarterly (or periodic) water use plans of the irrigation system and the water use demands of the water using units. The principal contents include: the tasks and norms, the water allocation plan, and measures for executing the plan.

Article 16. If, when formulating the basic-level water use plans, the subbranch canal (or branch canal) adopts the method of rotational irrigation by block [zu], the following points should be heeded in demarcating the rotation blocks:

1. The sum of the maximum water carrying capacities of the canals carrying water simultaneously to each of the irrigation rotation blocks should be able to handle the flow apportioned by the next higher level of canal, and at the same time the flow of the various rotation blocks should be as equal as possible.

2. The canals of the rotation blocks should be as close together as possible in order to reduce transmission losses of water and to facilitate the allocation of water.

3. When demarcating the irrigation rotation blocks, it is necessary to consider the difficulty of diverting water in the canals within the rotation blocks, the agricultural activities of the water using units, and labor and animal power conditions. The water use customs of the masses should also be heeded.

The above method can also be used for reference when the water use plan of the canal system adopts rotational irrigation.

Article 17. After the basic-level management committee has discussed and approved it, the basic-level water use plan should be reported to the management departments of the canal system, and the water using units should be notified so that things will be done according to the plan.

## Chapter Five: Implementation of the Water Use Plans

Article 18. After the water use plan has been finalized, the irrigation district's management organization, relying on the Party and state leadership in the area benefited, should actively adopt measures to organize and mobilize the masses to carry it out resolutely. If conditions change while it is being implemented, rational readjustments should promptly be made in the original plan.

Article 19. The water using units should do the following work properly:

1. Ensure that specific people are in charge of guiding the various items of work within the benefited area of the unit, such as water use management and project maintenance.

2. Strengthen the water use organization. The production brigade or production team should establish a watering (water releasing) organization, with the team or canal system as the unit, in which the poor and lower-middle peasant commune members predominate, and it should designate specific persons to water the land. They should set up an organization for [protective] canal maintenance and divide the canal into sections, fixing responsibility all the way down to specific individuals. Moreover, they should rationally solve the problem of labor compensation.

3. Repair and improve field ditches, small-scale structures and irrigation equipment and properly repair projects in the fields. In the dry crop irrigation districts, the work of digging ditches, making strip checks [qi] and leveling land should be done properly. In paddy rice irrigation districts, field ridges and field drainage and irrigation ditches should be kept in good repair. Irrigation tools and lighting equipment should be well prepared.

4. Put the irrigating plan into effect and rationally arrange labor and animal power, determining the order of irrigating shifts and systems for their relief. Furthermore, the irrigation and patrol personnel should be notified of these so they may water the land and maintain the canal on schedule.

5. Strictly observe the water use rules and regulations and divert water for irrigation at the designated places in accordance with the amount of water allocated and the times for irrigating. There should be no fighting over water, theft of water or excessive diversion of water. Irrigation should be carried on day and night, and there should be no unnecessary stoppage or release of water. Ensure responsibility for matters within each canal section so that no loss of water through breaks in the canals can occur.

6. Promote rational irrigating methods and improve and elevate irrigating techniques.

7. Closely integrate irrigating with other technical measures for agricultural cultivation. In dry crop areas, these include preparing the soil at the appropriate times, cultivating, and

harrowing to retain soil moisture. In the rice paddy areas, they include plowing and raking at the appropriate times and draining and drying the fields.

Article 20. Basic-level management organizations should do the following work properly:

1. Help the production brigades and production teams establish sound watering and canal maintenance organizations and formulate a water use system [of rules and regulations] or water use pacts.

2. Organize the water using units to repair the canal structures properly, safeguard the integrity of the sluice gates and opening and closing machinery, paint and clean at regular intervals, and ensure mobility in opening and closing.

3. Conscientiously implement the water use plan of the canal system, concretely formulate periodic water use plans, and properly carry out the water allocation work within the management sphere.

4. Regularly inspect the quality of watering by each water using unit, the amount of water diverted, and the extent of completion of the irrigation tasks and promptly make reports of these to the management organ of the canal system.

5. Implement the directives and resolutions of the management organ and transmit the opinions and demands of the masses to the local Party and state leadership and to the irrigation district management organ.

Article 21. The management organ of the canal system should do the following work:

1. In accordance with the spirit of "being both worker and peasant," establish and strengthen the branch management organs, water allocation organizations, and basic-level management organizations.

2. Strengthen the various water use rules and regulations, propagate the significance, contents and aims of the water use plans, and teach the water using units to observe the rules and regulations.

3. Study and discuss the water use plans and concrete measures to implement them. Organize the basic-level manage-

ment units and water using units to carry them out.

4. Before and after each irrigation, inspect and repair the conveyance channels, the various kinds of structures, the mechanical and electrical equipment, the communications equipment, and so on. Before releasing water, large-scale irrigation districts should also release some water to test the canals (or machinery).

5. Conduct short-term irrigation training classes, continually raising the political and professional level of the management and irrigating personnel.

6. In the process of carrying out the water use plans, water allocation personnel of all levels should do a good job of allocation. If they encounter special conditions and change the plans, they should immediately notify the basic-level management organizations and the water using units.

7. At regular intervals, report to the local Party and state leadership on the situation, informing them of problems, presenting opinions, and seeking the support of leaders at all levels.

8. Strengthen the ties with the people's communes, the production brigades and the production teams in order to understand production arrangements. This allows the close integration of water use with agricultural production.

9. Management cadres at all levels should go down into the basic levels, investigate and study at selected spots, participate in the practice of labor and promptly sum up and promote mature and advanced experiences in irrigation water use work.

10. Strengthen ideological and political work and carry out class and socialist education among the staff and workers, elevating their consciousness. Carry out competitions and fire up enthusiasm for labor among the management and irrigating personnel, so that a good job is done in irrigation work.

11. In areas subject to flooding and salinization, attention should be paid to the elimination of flooding and control of salinization. Attention should be paid to maintenance of the drainage projects.

Article 22. Water allocation.

The water allocation organizations in the irrigation districts should generally adhere to the following principles and systems:

1. Principles of water allocation.

(1) Under normal conditions, water diversion and water allocation should be in accordance with an approved plan; this cannot be changed at will.

(2) Irrigation districts with many kinds of water sources should unify the disposition of water sources, the allocation of water and the projects utilized.

(3) When water sources are insufficient and rotational irrigation is carried out, priorities must be established: drinking water for people and animals; areas of severe drought; areas in which the economic benefits of irrigation are comparatively high, and areas that have been benefited for a long time.

(4) For projects whose main purpose is irrigation, other uses of water should not affect the use of water for farm irrigation. During nonirrigation periods and when water sources are not abundant, water should not be released solely for the generation of electricity, processing, or fishing.

2. The system [of rules and regulations] for allocation work.

(1) Before water is released, control and water-measuring equipment must be meticulously inspected and repaired and data collected pertinent to water allocation (such as a layout of the canal system and the main structures; curves showing the relationship between water level and volume of flow; the water diversion plan; and the water allocation plan).

(2) During the period of water release, pay attention to understanding the weather forecasts, the soil moisture conditions in the irrigation district, the status of water sources, the water requirements of crops, and the conditions of water diversion and water use by the basic-level management organizations and water using units.

(3) If special conditions are encountered in the process of allocating water, promptly notify the canal system management

departments so they may take action on the matter.

(4) During water release periods, the water allocation personnel must take turns on day and night shifts and fill out a detailed daily work record.

(5) Linkages between the upper and lower levels must be strengthened by announcing at fixed intervals the conditions of water sources, water diversion, and irrigation water use so that the work of the leadership at all levels and the basic-level management units can be guided by their prompt comprehension of the prevailing conditions.

Article 23. Water measurement.

An irrigation district should measure water in a planned manner at the canal headworks, the water allocation points, the water distribution points, and specially designated canal sections or land sections. Efforts should be made to make the water measurement methods simple, convenient, and easy, gradually raising the degree of precision. Also, insofar as possible, the existing hydraulic structures should be used for water measurement.

Article 24. Changes in the water use plans.

If conditions change during the period of irrigation but their effect is not great, temporary readjustments may be made in carrying out the plan. When any of the following conditions with greater effects occur, the water use plans should be changed:

1. Changes in the irrigation water sources, electrical sources, or irrigation tasks;
2. Comparatively great changes in the weather;
3. Breakdowns in the project or equipment.

Changes in the plans may be made by adopting these measures in accordance with concrete conditions:

1. Advancement or postponement of the dates of irrigation.
2. Readjustments in irrigating quotas.
3. Increases or decreases in the number of irrigations.
4. Stopping water diversion or extending the period of diversion.
5. Readjustments in the area irrigated.

6. Centralization of water use, with rotational irrigation by blocks.

Changes in the plans should promptly be reported to the higher-level leadership organ and made known to the basic-level management organizations, the water using units, and all levels of water allocation personnel.

Article 25. Irrigating methods and techniques.

1. Irrigating methods: Dry crop irrigation districts should use furrow irrigation for wide-row crops and adopt border-strip irrigation for densely planted crops. Paddy rice irrigation districts should carry out rational irrigation and drainage. The irrigation district management organ should duly sum up irrigation methods and experiences which yield bumper harvests and popularize them in accordance with local conditions.

2. Irrigating techniques:

(1) In dry crop irrigation districts, maintain uniform moisture of the soil. In paddy rice irrigation districts, maintain suitable basin irrigation water levels and pay attention to draining and sun-drying the fields.

(2) Irrigate according to quota to prevent water losses in the fields. Make every effort to avoid plot-to-plot irrigation. In dry crop irrigation districts, make every effort to reduce deep-stratum seepage and control the rise of the water table.

(3) With the precondition of ensuring its quality, make efforts to raise the effectiveness of irrigating.

(4) Irrigating should be closely integrated with such agricultural measures as leveling the fields, applying fertilizer, and cultivating.

Article 26. Water storage and conservation.

With the precondition of ensuring the security of the projects, reservoir and pond irrigation districts should pay attention to storing while using, and raise the coefficient of restorage. At the end of the flood season, the opportunity to increase water storage should be seized. Ponds and reservoirs with small rainfall catchment areas may adopt methods such as digging water diversion ditches to expand the area of rainfall catchment and increase the water inflow.

To strengthen the conservation of water supplies and increase the ability to resist drought, rice fields, winter paddies, and fields storing water [tunshui tian] must be closely coordinated with agricultural cultivation measures, intensively cultivated and carefully fertilized; and field ridges must be repaired and breaks in the fields stopped up.

Article 27. Every irrigation district should actively develop all kinds of observation work, including such things as the water level, the volume of flow, and the sand content of irrigation water sources; the runoff coefficient of the upper reaches of reservoirs in irrigation districts having reservoirs; the canal water carrying capacities, the time of flow, and losses in transporting water; the structures and volume of flow coefficient of water measurement equipment; changes in ground water, soil moisture, and soil salinization; and irrigating quotas and necessary meterological conditions.

Article 28. At the end of the irrigation season, the irrigation district management organs should sum up experiences in water use work, and analyze and study the conditions and results of carrying out the water use plans and their results. They should also report [this] to the higher-level leadership departments.

## Chapter Six: Supplemental Regulations

Article 29. The water conservancy departments of the various provinces, autonomous regions, and directly administered municipalities, may also act in accordance with the spirit of these measures and, in conjunction with the concrete conditions of their localities, formulate measures for carrying out planned irrigation water use in the provinces, autonomous regions, and directly administered municipalities.

Article 30. These measures are effective from the day of promulgation.

(Ministry of Agriculture, the People's Republic of China. Promulgated on January 18, 1965)

*Reading 12*

# NOTIFICATION ON THE "REPORT OF A FEW OPINIONS REGARDING THE COLLECTION AND USE OF WATER FEES IN IRRIGATION DISTRICTS," APPROVED BY THE STATE COUNCIL AND RETURNED TO THE MINISTRY OF WATER CONSERVANCY*

**January 25, 1958**

The State Council agrees with the Ministry of Water Conservancy regarding its "Report of a Few Opinions Regarding the Collection [zhengshou] and Use of Water Fees in Irrigation Districts." We are now returning it to you. Please act in accordance with the opinions mentioned in the report.

## Report of a Few Opinions Regarding the Collection and Use of Water Fees in Irrigation Districts

(December 27, 1957)

China now has 520 million mou of irrigated land. Water fees are the main method of financing the expenditures for such things as the annual repair, maintenance and management expenses of the state-operated irrigation districts and the comparatively large irrigation districts which are jointly operated

*"Guowu yuan pizhuan shuili bu guanyu guanqu shuifei zhengshou he shiyong de jidian yijian de baogao de tongzhi." From Zhonghua renmin gongheguo fagui huibian [Collection of Laws and Regulations of the People's Republic of China], 1958, pp. 377-379.

by cooperatives. During the past two years, water fee collection conditions have been comparatively poor. In general, it has not been possible for collection plans to be completely fulfilled, and this has affected project upkeep and maintenance and the development of irrigation management work. The main reasons for the inability to collect water fees are: In some places the local leading cadres do not clearly recognize that the irrigation water fees are part of agricultural production costs. Thus, they do not sufficiently emphasize and support the work of water fee collection. Another reason is that some places have suffered reduced production because of natural disasters. In order realistically and effectively to carry out irrigation district management and maintenance, lengthen the lifetimes of the projects, continually improve and expand the projects, and expand the benefits of irrigation, we must strengthen water fee collection work. This ministry has now formulated a few opinions regarding the collection and use of water fees in the irrigation districts. We are submitting these to you for examination and approval and for transmittal to the various provinces, autonomous regions and directly administered municipalities for them to put into effect.

1. The water-using units of the state-operated irrigation districts and the comparatively large irrigation districts which are jointly operated by [two or more] agricultural cooperatives should all pay water fees. The agricultural cooperatives of the irrigation districts and other registered water users (units such as farms, factories, mines, and in transport) should incorporate the water fees that they should pay into their expenditure plans for each year's productive investment. When making their quarterly budget appropriations, the agricultural cooperatives should also incorporate the water fees as items to be deducted so that they can be paid on schedule. The various levels of local Party and state leadership organizations should value and support the collection of water fees.

2. The standards for water fee collection are determined on the basis of expenditures for project upkeep and maintenance and management costs and also in keeping with production increases

in the irrigation districts and the capacity of the masses for bearing the burden. Funds may be accumulated in suitable amounts and used for the improvement and expansion of the projects. The amounts to be collected may be worked out by the provinces, the autonomous regions, and the directly administered municipalities themselves.

3. Irrigation districts operated singly or jointly by agricultural cooperatives should themselves determine in accordance with the customs and concrete conditions of their localities whether their operating and management expenses should be raised through the collection of water fees or through other methods.

4. The management expenses of irrigation districts which have recently become operational and which during the first year do not have income from water fees should be incorporated into the budget for project construction. On state-operated projects, those [management expenses] which have not been incorporated into the [construction] budgets can be met temporarily by local water control expenses. The burden should be borne by the cooperatives benefited for projects operated singly or jointly by cooperatives.

5. The utilization of water fees should be done in accordance with the principle that water should support water. [These] designated funds should be used for designated purposes. They should not be treated as local financial income; nor should they be transferred for use as expenditures on nonwater activities.

6. Efforts should be made to be thrifty in water fee expenses and to prevent waste. The local leadership departments should regularly supervise the receipt and expenditure of water fees.

7. As long as it does not affect their normal management work, the management organizations of the irrigation districts may use all the irrigation district's beneficial conditions and raise fish, plant vegetables, cultivate cash crop trees, and so on. Irrigation districts which have mechanized pumping may also carry on sideline production such as rice milling and processing to augment their incomes and reduce the water fee burden borne by the masses.

8. The concrete measures for water fee collection, utilization and exemption should be determined and implemented by the various provinces, autonomous regions, and directly administered municipalities themselves.

*Reading 13*

# REGULATIONS CONCERNING WATER PROJECT MANAGEMENT IN ZHEJIANG PROVINCE (TRIAL DRAFT)*

May 1972

Since the founding of the nation, the province has constructed a large number of water projects under the guidance of Chairman Mao's revolutionary line. This is an important material basis for achieving the goal of "having water when droughts occur, and draining water when flooding occurs." Effectively strengthening management work is an important measure for guaranteeing the security of the projects and the lives and property of the people, for fully developing benefits, and for better serving agriculture, industry and transportation. The following management regulations were formulated for this reason.

Article 1. The Party organizations and revolutionary committees at every level must strengthen their leadership over water management work. The functional organizations of the prefectural, municipal and xian water departments should correspond to one another, and the departments should provide full-time personnel to be in charge of water management work. They should prevent and correct erroneous tendencies such as emphasizing construction while neglecting management and emphasizing projects while neglecting their effectiveness. They should earnestly grasp the ideological and organizational

*"Zhejiang sheng shuili gongcheng guanli tiaoli (shixing caoan)." From Shuili guanli [Water Management], Shanghai, 1975, pp. 36-39.

growth of the water management ranks and properly manage and use water projects to implement the policy of building a project, then outfitting it, managing it properly, and making it yield benefits.

Article 2. Set up and strengthen management organizations and establish a clear management system. There must be people to manage both large and small water projects. The larger water projects should set up and strengthen specialized management organizations.

The state owns water projects undertaken by the state. Water projects undertaken by the collectives are owned by the collectives. The ownership of those projects which are undertaken with both state and collective investment should be based on the principles of the contributions to unity, to the development of production, to the consolidation of the collective economy, and to the management and maintenance of the projects. The xian and the local communes and brigades (or teams) should negotiate how this is to be handled.

Regardless of whether a water project is undertaken by the state or the collectives, or jointly by the state and the collectives, if it benefits or affects a single brigade, commune, xian, or prefecture, that brigade, commune, xian, or prefecture is responsible for organizing its management. If the area benefited or affected involves two or more brigades, communes, xian, or prefectures, then in principle, the next higher level should be responsible for organizing the management, or else that level should commission the unit primarily benefited to be responsible for organizing management. A water project which simultaneously has many kinds of benefits, such as flood prevention, irrigation, electricity generation, and fisheries, should carry out unified management. The management work of all the water projects should be the specific responsibility of the departments at all levels which are responsible for water control.

Article 3. We must rely on the masses and combine mass management and professional management. For relatively large water projects in which the benefited area is two or more production brigades, management organizations (such as management committees or poor and lower-middle peasant water management conferences of representatives) should be set up and strengthened to supervise and coordinate the work of specialized management organizations and to discuss and determine the various kinds of problems in water project management.

Article 4. The main tasks of the management organs are: to study and carry out Chairman Mao's directives on water conservancy construction and the Party's policies; to build up the management organ in a revolutionary way and do mass management work well; to guarantee the working condition of the equipment and the security of the projects; to fully develop the benefits of the projects and make every effort to expand them; to actively promote comprehensive utilization; to carry out scientific experimentation; to sum up and promote advanced experiences; and to continually elevate the level of management work.

Article 5. In accordance with the principle of using the cream of the crop, professional management personnel should be provided or reinforced. No matter whether they are management personnel of state or collective projects, there should be relative stability; they should not be transferred to other duties at will.

The management personnel should be politically reliable, have a strong sense of responsibility, be closely linked with the masses, be knowledgeable about agricultural production, and be enthusiastic about water conservancy activity.

The leaders at every level must show concern for the politics and livelihood of management personnel. The labor compensation and food rations of full- or part-time commune and brigade management personnel should be equivalent to the income of cadres of the same grade or to that of commune members of the same grade of labor power in the local communes and brigades. The kinds of pay and conditions they receive should be comparable to that of workers at corresponding levels in agricultural enterprises.

Article 6. Whether large or small, water projects must

mobilize the masses for discussion and set up and strengthen both the various rules and regulations for water management and mass pacts for maintenance. These should be effectively implemented.

Maintenance systems must be set up for water projects and equipment in order to carry out regular inspections, upkeep, and maintenance at fixed intervals. Inspections before the flood season should be properly and effectively stressed to resolutely eliminate hidden troubles in dangerous sections. Earth, stone and other materials reserved for use in flood prevention and emergencies may not be removed at will.

On the dams, dikes and canals, there is to be no willful cultivation, making of breaches, grazing, burials, and so forth. It is strictly forbidden to carry out activities which impede security and normal operations in the vicinity of any kind of hydraulic structures. The construction of projects on the embankments, waterways, reservoirs, and flood-detention basins requires the prior agreement of the departments in charge of water control. This must also be reported to the higher-level revolutionary committees for approval before [such projects] are carried out.

The operations of water facilities, such as reservoirs, culverts and gates, and mechanized and electrical drainage and irrigation stations, should be strictly and systematically controlled. A responsibility system and a system of duty shifts should be set up. To guarantee the security of the projects, nonmanagement personnel should not be allowed to impose their will on operations.

The water projects which are mainly for irrigation should clearly foster the ideal of serving agricultural production and rely on the masses to level the land, properly undertake ancillary works, establish systems of rational water allocation and rational irrigation, strive to expand the area under irrigation, and promote high and stable agricultural yields.

Water projects, especially reservoir projects, should improve project and hydrological observations and, at the proper times, they should record and arrange data on the performance [yunxing] of the project equipment and on observations and set up project management files.

A sound financial accounting system is necessary. The responsible departments, the financial and economic departments, and water management organizations should strengthen their supervision over the management and utilization of the water fees and other economic benefits. The depreciation expenses on the various kinds of equipment may not be transferred to other uses.

Violators of the water management system or those who endanger the security of the projects should be criticized and educated or punished in accordance with the seriousness of the case.

Article 7. All water using (beneficiary) units should pay water fees to the water management organizations. Only small fees may be collected from boats for passage through navigation locks or field embankments.

In accordance with the principle of "rational burden, regulating outlay according to income, and having a slight accumulation [of funds]," the mass water management organizations should discuss and draw up standards and methods for collecting water fees. This should also be submitted to the responsible departments for approval and put into effect. The financial departments may be requested to collect water fees on behalf of the larger irrigation districts.

The water fees are funds collected and spent by a given unit. They are used for project maintenance and ancillary works, for the management personnel expenses, for the installed observation equipment, and so on. The payments may be carried forward in successive years for continuing use. They may not be used for nonwater expenses or as local financial income.

Article 8. Under the preconditions of holding to a socialist orientation, guaranteeing project security, fully developing project benefits, and serving agricultural production, any water projects which may be used comprehensively should fully tap the latent potential of water and soil resources surrounding the project and of project facilities and should actively promote comprehensive utilization through the development of multiple operations such as fisheries, processing with water power, electric power generation, and agricultural sideline production. Irrigation, electric power, fisheries, and so on should be secondary to flood prevention in water projects which are mainly for flood prevention. Electric power, fisheries, navigation, processing with water power, and so on should be secondary to irrigation in water projects which are mainly for irrigation.

In order to prevent losses stemming from erosion, the banks of the dikes, ponds, and canals, the area near the gates and embankments, and the environs of the reservoirs should all rely on the masses to devote major efforts to plant trees and spread greenery, strictly prohibiting the felling of trees for private use.

Under the precondition of guaranteeing agricultural production, comprehensive utilization of water projects requires setting up a unified management organization, carrying out a unified plan, unifying management, and unifying administration. The income from comprehensive utilization should be used for project maintenance, equipment maintenance, ancillary works on the projects and for expanded reproduction [investment]. Appropriate deductions may be made from the income of the state-owned water projects that have comparatively great benefits by the department in charge of water control in the local prefecture, municipality, or xian and used to make overall readjustments for developing water control in the prefecture, municipality, or xian.

Article 9. Strengthen security and defense work. We must raise our revolutionary vigilance, overcome slackening of our guard, and strengthen the concept of preparing for war. The important water projects must be defended by militia or regular troops and must deal resolute blows to the sabotage activities of class enemies.

# About the Editor

James E. Nickum received his B.A. from the University of Kansas and his Ph.D. in economics from the University of California, Berkeley. He is currently a Research Associate at the Center for Chinese Studies, University of California, Berkeley, and a consultant on China's water problems to the World Bank and the United Nations University.

Dr. Nickum is the author of Hydraulic Engineering and Water Resources in the People's Republic of China (1977) and other works on China's water resources. In 1980 he participated in a symposium and field study on the environmental effects of long distance water transfer from the Chang Jiang [Yangtze River], jointly held by the United Nations University and the Institute of Geography of the Chinese Academy of Sciences. He is co-editor of the volume of symposium papers to be published soon in both Chinese and English.